"Davis and Prosmushkin are ... fering simple, easy-to-apply tools for anyone looking to communicate more effectively, create immediate change in themselves, and help others to transform their lives personally and professionally. This is a fascinating journey into the science behind it all, revealing what is often the domain of psychotherapy and coaching, demystifying NLP for a new generation."
—John Kilcullen, creator of the international bestselling For Dummies series

"A transformative guide that brings the principles of NLP into a clear, actionable format, empowering readers to create meaningful changes in their lives. . . . Through real-life examples and scientifically backed insights, this book offers a roadmap for anyone looking to unlock potential, improve relationships, and navigate personal challenges. If you're ready to discover what truly moves the needle, this book is your essential companion on the journey to change."
—Dr. Bradley Nelson, bestselling author of *The Emotion Code*

"It has been fifty years since neurolinguistic programming got its name and became a unique discipline. It is rewarding to know that, after all this time, NLP is still able to provide, as [the] authors assert, *The Difference That Makes The Difference*. . . . This book is a great introduction to NLP for anyone who is interested in exploring how to create positive change in themselves and others."
—Robert Dilts, author and NLP leader

"A gem of a book that will enable you to help others with problems they are having, from poor relationships to career stagnation, [and] help you with issues in your own life, from lack of motivation to abrasiveness in the workplace. This book is a keeper."
—Srikumar Rao, TED speaker, author, and executive coach

THE
DIFFERENCE
THAT
MAKES
THE
DIFFERENCE

NLP AND THE SCIENCE OF
POSITIVE CHANGE

JOSH DAVIS, PhD &
GREG PROSMUSHKIN

ST. MARTIN'S
ESSENTIALS
NEW YORK

Josh dedicates this book to Daniela—you know why.
And to my children, Rafa, Sofia, and Leo—
in case you're ever in need of some wisdom, look in here. I love you.

Greg dedicates this book to Irina, Celia, Zakery, and Victoria—because
without you, none of this would mean as much. You are everything.

First published in the United States by St. Martin's Essentials,
an imprint of St. Martin's Publishing Group

THE DIFFERENCE THAT MAKES THE DIFFERENCE. Copyright © 2025 by Josh Davis and Greg Prosmushkin. All rights reserved. Printed in the United States of America. For information, address St. Martin's Publishing Group, 120 Broadway, New York, NY 10271.

www.stmartins.com

Designed by Steven Seighman

The Library of Congress Cataloging-in-Publication Data is available upon request.

ISBN 978-1-250-34908-8 (trade paperback)
ISBN 978-1-250-34909-5 (ebook)

Our books may be purchased in bulk for promotional, educational, or business use. Please contact your local bookseller or the Macmillan Corporate and Premium Sales Department at 1-800-221-7945, extension 5442, or by email at MacmillanSpecialMarkets@macmillan.com.

First Edition: 2025

10 9 8 7 6 5 4 3 2 1

CONTENTS

SECTION 3. How to Change Someone's Mind (Yours or Theirs)

INTRODUCTION

Change is hard . . . except when it isn't. To be fair, we've probably all had experiences where we've wanted to make a change for a long time and haven't succeeded. Some people can spend years wanting to improve their relationships with their kids, for instance. Others may want to up their game at work so they can move to the next level of income or responsibility, but make little headway. Many more find that, try as they might, their physical fitness never really changes. For these and other changes we want, people may put in tremendous effort, investment, and energy, and still find few results. In that sense, it really is often hard to change. However, most people have probably also had moments where something changed one day, irrevocably, and for the better. It may have been due to a shift in thinking, a life event that gave them perspective, a conversation, or landing on a new strategy. For example, suddenly, after talking to the right friend about it, they came to understand their kid's needs better and that led to a breakthrough in how to connect. Often people have tried many ways to make the change they seek. But it ultimately happens when they find the difference that makes the difference. It's about finding the most useful ways of thinking, feeling, and behaving—the right *who, what, when, where, why,* or *how.* Once we find this difference, change can be instantaneous. Finding that difference, and doing so quickly, is what NLP is especially useful for.

NLP stands for neurolinguistic programming. At the heart of NLP is a process for understanding what makes people tick—yourself and others. When we understand how we and others think, feel, and act in key situations, we have the raw material with which to make change happen, often quickly and profoundly.

This is probably why Tony Robbins said in his book *Unlimited Power*, "The most powerful tools that I know of [. . .] come from a technology known as neurolinguistic programming."

More than forty years in the making and supported by research, these lessons are nonetheless often new to people both in their business and personal lives. This is because the lessons can be very technical, and they come from a field that few people have had reason to look to. They come from a field whose practitioners don't just think about change in the abstract, but practice it in their professional lives all day every day, and across an extraordinary range of contexts and audiences. NLP was created by studying the methods used by renowned and widely admired psychotherapists who were extraordinary at helping people change quickly and in lasting ways. Many of the principles and concepts that these giants of psychotherapy followed have been researched and published in academic journals, and are often referred to as parts of evidence-backed therapies like CBT, DBT, ACT, or family therapy.

This book demystifies those teachings, shows how neuroscience and psychology research support them, and provides simple steps to apply these teachings in your professional and personal life.

These teachings include understanding how to:

- Read the situation and the people involved.
- Help people change their limiting beliefs.
- Build rapport and establish trust quickly.
- Choose your emotional state and your state of mind.
- Let go of old triggers and help others do the same.
- Understand what uniquely drives each person you interact with.
- Help people shift their perspective.
- Flexibly handle any question or point of resistance that comes your way.

- Speak to people in a way they can truly hear you.
- Get others to want to listen to you, and want you to influence them.
- Win over skeptics.
- Build self-confidence.
- Know and communicate your value.
- Own the narrative.
- Earn the right to be heard.

In the process of learning these skills, people also learn how to change themselves. They stop being the ones wishing their lives could be different, and start being the ones who actually took charge of their lives. And they learn to model excellence—if others can do it, so can they.

To illustrate, here's one of the NLP tools for building rapport and trust quickly. Imagine trying to reason with someone who is agitated, angry, or upset, and it's going nowhere. When someone is in a state like that, our first response is often to go to the total opposite state. In measured, calm tones, with steady, slow gestures, and while standing fairly still, we say slowly, "Calm down. You've got to calm down." Occasionally that works. But often the upset person only gets more upset and tries to prove why they should be upset or deserve to be upset. It has the opposite effect.

In those instances, it turns out to be better to first validate their reality. Meet them where they are, and join them. This lets them know you understand, you are on their side, you understand how they see the world, you can be trusted. Instead of immediately going calm and measured, go in the other direction—with some energy and movement, and emotion in your tone of voice, you can say, "That's messed up! It makes sense that you're upset!" For many people that is counterintuitive at first, until you see how it works. When you do this, you've started to strengthen rapport and are beginning to earn the right to lead them out of that state to a calmer one. Then you can gradually calm your voice and body posture, and say, "Alright, let's see if we can figure out what to do here. Let's take a second and calm down." Many people are ready to start getting calm at this point, and do not feel the need to prove they deserve to be upset anymore. The meaning of the communication is largely unconscious, but it is felt, and that's what the upset person needs in order to connect. This tool is called pacing and leading—first go at their pace, walk with them on the path they are on, then lead them to a more useful place. We'll explain more about why this tool works, the science to support it, and how to use it well in chapter 21.

This is only one of dozens of tools found in this book that can help you find the difference that makes the difference. We'll also help you take on eight foundational beliefs identified by NLP that enable people to use these tools most effectively, go beyond their former limits, and help others do the same.

How This Book Came About

The lessons from NLP have been inaccessible for many people for a long time. Because NLP was started by modeling the techniques of certain skilled psychotherapists, NLP has often been taught as a workshop for psychotherapists. In more recent times, it has also frequently been taught as a workshop for executive or life coaches. For these audiences, it is aimed at helping people master the one-on-one context of therapy or coaching devoted to intense individual change work. It commonly has been the case that someone studying NLP who is not a psychotherapist or coach has had to do their own work to figure out how the learning applies to the challenges they face. For those who understand the potential, it has been worth it. But it has kept far too many people from discovering what is here for them.

Greg was one of those people taking NLP classes who was not a psychotherapist or coach. As a result of applying what he learned, he made breakthroughs in his work as a trial lawyer, and stepped into his own as an entrepreneur. Both are contexts where his ability to communicate, influence, and help others change their thoughts, feelings, and behaviors were incredibly valuable. But he also saw that his colleagues and coworkers were missing out and wanted to do something about it.

One afternoon, years after Greg had first studied NLP, Josh was teaching his course on public speaking, which draws a great deal on NLP. Greg showed up to take it. Greg's been a trial lawyer for thirty years, which means he has thirty years' experience communicating and influencing people for a living. But even though he was already a pro at public speaking, he wanted to see if he could learn more—an attitude he was able to truly embrace through NLP. While he was happy to find some things that were new and useful, what also caught his attention was the way it was being taught. Simple, powerful, and immediately useful for each person, no matter what kind of work they did. Greg had been waiting for such an opportunity.

At a breakout, while Greg and Josh were chatting, Josh mentioned that he was searching for a new venture. Greg, using his NLP skills, took a moment to really understand Josh's motivations. He spotted the way Josh spoke about his love of the craft of teaching, for example. Greg paused. "NLP for lawyers, NLP for managers, NLP for educators . . . NLP for your specific needs," he said. As wonderful as NLP was, there was a gap in how it was taught that was keeping many people from accessing it. The idea was simple—take that extra step to translate NLP into something that people can easily apply to their work. By the end of the first conversation, they both realized this was for all people whose work depends on communicating, influencing, or helping people change. It would benefit everyone, from a homemaker to a Fortune 500 CEO. But that extra step of translating NLP into something easy to apply was missing.

Soon, it became clear this was the right partnership for an idea that would fill an important need in a way quite unlike anything else could.

Josh has been a trainer at one of the premier schools of NLP, the NLP Center of New York, for over a decade, and holds a PhD from Columbia University, where he studied psychology and neuroscience. Josh grew up around NLP, too—you might think of him as an NLP native. His parents, who ran the Family Therapy Institute of Alexandria for forty years, were some of the early students of NLP's founders, John Grinder and Richard Bandler. His parents made NLP central to a highly successful practice, and led one of the first NLP training centers. Josh is also an educator—from inner-city public schools to the Ivy League, to top business schools, and for leadership development inside some of the world's largest and most influential organizations. One of his greatest loves in life is to work out how best to teach an idea.

Greg is a sought-after trial lawyer and a serial entrepreneur with a rags-to-riches story, who has successfully exited multiple seven- and eight-figure businesses. He has long been a student of NLP. Greg understands the specific challenges facing the NLP student who is not a psychotherapist or coach. He's passionate about getting those around him to thrive, so he loves finding ways to put the lessons of NLP to work.

Josh will introduce the concepts. Greg will share practical applications of this powerful technology through proven real-life examples to which everyone should be able to relate. And both Josh and Greg will speak to and offer examples of how NLP has been a major source of their own success.

The Beginnings of NLP

A little bit of a deeper dive into NLP's history helps explain why it is so distinct and powerful. It began in the mid-1970s when linguist John Grinder joined forces with Richard Bandler, while at UC Santa Cruz. They sought to find the answer to why certain professionals, specifically psychotherapists, were achieving much better results than their peers. These results were quicker and more reliable. Sometimes they achieved desired outcomes even within a single session that would take others much longer.

The innovators that NLP's founders studied included Milton Erickson, one of the principal developers of hypnotherapy in the United States; Virginia Satir, often considered the mother of family therapy; as well as the Gestalt therapist Fritz Perls. Within psychotherapy these are the names of historical giants in the field.

Part of Grinder and Bandler's approach was to observe and unpack the language patterns used by the therapists they studied, as well as the language patterns from patients that those great therapists clued into. This expanded to nonverbal communication patterns, too. They also studied other great influencers and thinkers, such as Gregory Bateson,[1] to understand how people work in a system of other people.

When the developers of NLP set out to teach what they had learned, some of the greats they had studied recognized the breakthroughs NLP had achieved. Milton Erickson reviewed their work and said, "[Bandler and Grinder give] a much better explanation of how I work than I, myself, can give." He added, "I learned a great deal about the things that I've done without knowing about them."[2] Family therapy pioneer Virginia Satir described Grinder and Bandler's work as having identified what it was about an interaction between people that enables change to happen. She said, "Now the knowledge of the process of change is considerably advanced."[3] What the founders of NLP had done was to make it much easier to know what was important to focus on and what steps to take to help someone change their thoughts, feelings, or behaviors.

Ultimately, Grinder, Bandler, and their colleagues, such as Robert Dilts, Judith DeLozier, and other early developers of these tools, organized their findings into a set of powerful teachings and methods for teaching that can be applied to many contexts.

Over the years, other motivated students beyond those involved in psychotherapy have discovered NLP and found it to be a game changer— lawyers, salespeople, athletic coaches, managers, leaders, entrepreneurs, teachers, doctors, artists, designers, parents, and so on—anyone who needs to communicate or drive change. These people have often leveraged what they learned to stand out in their fields. However, it has remained limited to a group motivated enough to get past some of the technical aspects. For example, NLP uses language like identifying modal operators, stepping into the meta position, and shifting submodalities.

While NLP continues to thrive, it has remained among the secrets of success for a privileged few beyond the confines of psychotherapy and coaching. With this book, we aim to greatly expand what people from all walks of life and professions can accomplish, by making the lessons of NLP more accessible.

To help achieve this aim, we draw the links between the tools of NLP and how you can apply them in your particular line of work or personal life. We also connect the concepts and tools of NLP to the science behind them. There's a lot of advice out there. We believe that when science supports advice, it helps you know whether to trust it, and whether it's worth investing your time and effort in following it.

A Few Concerns

Everything has its critics. If you go online and google anything, you'll find people with strong opinions saying it's great or it's terrible. How can you know what to believe?

We think a good way to answer that question is to honor the concerns that are out there and try to address them. Here are a few concerns that may be holding some of our readers back and could limit them from getting the most from this book.

The first concern: Some people picking this book up may have come across critiques of NLP, calling it a pseudoscience, for example. That's a serious statement to make and deserves to be considered. While we disagree with that statement, there is a positive intention behind it that we can support. That positive intention is to look for scientific support for claims. We agree with critics who believe that when something from NLP runs counter to research, it should be adapted to fit with research, or dropped, if appropriate. We have also noticed that such critiques of NLP usually seem to focus on one tool, in particular, which pertains to eye movements. There are some legitimate criticisms of that tool—we discuss the tool and those criticisms in further detail in chapter 17. There's one other concept that we think should be adapted based on research too—we discuss that in chapter 20. That concept is a little bit like the popular theory of learning styles—e.g., being a visual learner versus someone who does better with hearing an idea. As you'll see, those two tools make up only a tiny fraction of what NLP teaches. We believe that most of what NLP teaches seems to align with scientific research. We draw those links throughout this book.

A second concern for some people is that someone might use the tools of NLP to manipulate someone else in a negative way. This concern actually is based on a belief that the tools are very effective, just the opposite of the first concern. We believe it is important to teach any tools for influence and change—NLP or otherwise—in an ethical way. Anything powerful can be used for good or for bad. This concern is not unique to NLP. It is relevant for all teachings that have to do with influence and change. We hope you will agree that the ways in which we teach these tools, offer examples, and help people apply them in this book are done in a positive way—in service of helping lift all people up. The community we seek to serve are those who plan to use these and any tools of influence and change ethically. In addition, we believe that trying to manipulate someone to do something they don't want to do doesn't even really work—it erodes trust and limits your long-term ability to influence and lead change. In fact, we would go so far as to say that you can't really change anyone's mind or behavior in a meaningful and lasting way unless it is something they want and that works for them.

The third concern has to do with why we should study NLP as opposed to other teachings about influence and change. For example, if NLP contains a collection of concepts and tools similar to an assortment of what might be found in CBT, family therapy, or Gestalt therapy, then why not study those systems directly? We think the most useful answer is that NLP is more than a collection of tools and concepts—it includes two things that enable the people who learn it to be extraordinarily effective at using what they learn. The first is that NLP teaches the attitude that enables someone to be most successful with those tools and concepts. We teach that attitude in section 1 of this book, "The Right Mindset: Eight Beliefs That Will Make You Limitless." The second thing unique to NLP is that the method that was used to discover these tools and concepts is part of the teaching—it is a process NLP calls modeling and we introduce it more fully in chapter 2. In this way, NLP allows people to keep learning from others beyond the initial set of tools taught—setting people up to model excellence wherever they encounter it. We also just think it is a particularly wonderful set of tools and concepts.

On a related note, because these tools do largely come from studying how great psychotherapists communicated and helped people change, some people may be tempted to think they are learning to do therapy. They are not. That would be an incorrect reading of this book. States and countries have licensing boards, or an equivalent, for therapists that make it clear what is required for such work. Instead, our goal is to share principles to apply to the everyday kinds of work and life challenges that we all face. The teachings we offer in this book are not intended to equip you to help someone with an issue requiring a licensed therapist.

If you are someone who has any reservations about NLP, and yet remains curious whether there could be something in this book for you, we have a request. Until you finish reading this book, act as if you are open to what there is to learn. Once you have finished, and you have a deeper understanding of what we have to offer, how it can be used ethically, and how it is supported, or not, by research, you are free to go back to any beliefs you may have had about NLP.

How to Read This Book

The simplest answer is any way that feels right.

We know that a large number of our readers think of books as something you either listen to (e.g., while jogging or driving), or read when you have some time (e.g., on the subway, when lying in bed, or while waiting for an appointment). You love nonfiction and self-help, but you're not looking for a workbook. Your job is to receive the messages in the book. You'll take in the lessons by osmosis—as the advice, lessons, evidence, stories, and so on lead you to see connections to your own needs. At times, when something seems especially relevant, you're likely to thoughtfully reflect in your mind on how it applies to something specific you're working on. You might even pause from time to time to capture an insight in your notes somewhere. If that's you, this book was designed for you. Reading or listening to it will open many new doors for how to quickly understand people and help them change. You'll be very happy you read it.

We also know that a substantial number of you want to accelerate your skill growth, and want to be more active in applying what you learn. You want to maximize what you get out of this book. You want the opportunity to interact with the book as you go, like in a conversation. You want to change how you operate in deep and lasting ways, and want to start doing so now. You're in the right place. This book was also deliberately designed for you. Throughout the book, we've provided questions for all readers to reflect on. We invite you to pause and write down the answers to each of these questions as you go. It will help you capture each lesson and apply it to your own individual challenges and needs. For those who are looking to read in this way, it is a wonderful and powerful road to take. If you like to write directly in your books, you can either write on the pages, or there's also a collection in the appendix of all the question prompts in the book, organized by chapter, with a good amount of space to write after each.

No matter which of these ways you choose to read this book, welcome, and we're happy you're here. This book is intended for you, and we look forward to taking this journey with you. It's going to be an awesome ride.

The Journey You'll Go On

First, we'll help you set some goals for this book in chapter 1, and specifically, we'll use NLP to help you set them in ways that can greatly increase your odds of success.

Then the book is divided into three sections:

- In section 1 (chapters 2–9), you'll learn the best mindset for being a great communicator and change agent.
- In section 2 (chapters 10–19), you'll learn tools to quickly understand someone.
- In section 3 (chapters 20–28), you'll learn how to change someone's mind (yours or theirs).

Each section builds on the last so your capabilities will be multiplied if you go in order, but each section can stand alone, and provide a lot of value, if you're eager to jump ahead.

At the end, you'll find a conclusion with a summary of all the tools and concepts in this book, along with reminders about what to use them for, and how to use them. And you'll find an appendix, where you have space to write down your thoughts in response to the various thought experiments and questions we offer in the book.

Every time we reference scientific evidence in the book, we've included the specific articles we're talking about. You'll find this information in the notes for each chapter. We want everyone to be able to access the research—we believe this will help NLP endure and increase in its influence. You won't just have to take our word for it when we make claims. And you can actually cite the sources if you go out and try to share some of the messages of the book with others.

1

DO YOU KNOW WHERE YOU'RE GOING?

P art of being human is that we have goals that we really want. And one of the great frustrations in life is how many of these goals just hang around—we just keep not getting there. We might take action and then after a while give up, or we might never even really get started. We can have the best of intentions, but time or distractions or something always seems to get in the way.

Maybe the goal is to work for yourself. A lot of people think they'd be so much happier that way. From time to time they get excited about taking that leap, but it seems so unrealistic, and they never really do anything about it. Or maybe the goal has to do with health. Some people are unhappy with their weight and their energy for years. They've paid for expensive gym memberships and read about the latest diets, but nothing seems to stick. Within a few months, they're back to their old habits and it feels harder than ever to make progress. Or maybe the goal is about a relationship. Many people struggle in their relationships—either personal or at work. They try, they really do, but it all feels kind of pointless as the same patterns just play out again and again.

Anyone reading this book probably has some way in which they'd like to change themself or their situation, or get others to change. We have good news—NLP is a treasure trove like no other for making change happen.

It will help to have a goal in mind while you read this book. That way, in your mind, you can try on what we're sharing and see how it fits for your goal. So take a moment and pick something you'd like to change or improve at.

We know that some people like to skip the intro stuff at the beginning of a book. In case you're joining us in chapter 1, welcome! Since this is the first time we're inviting you to pause and reflect on your own situation, here are some quick guidelines for those who just joined us about the reflection questions in the book. If you're someone who wants to listen to this book, while exercising or driving, for example, or read without a pen in hand, then just quietly reflect for a moment about the questions. You might even choose to pause for a minute to think and then begin again when you're ready. If you're someone who likes to write in your books, go ahead and write on the page in the printed version. If you prefer, there's a journal in the appendix (or to download for free at www.nlpdifference.com) that has every reflection question in this book, and plenty of space to write after each one. You'll find another tool for applying the learning in the appendix, too, if that's the kind of thing you're looking for. Any of these ways of reading and engaging with the questions are great ways to get meaningful value out of this book, depending on how you like to learn.

So now . . . your goal: What's something you'd like to change or improve?

We've invited you to choose a goal. But we're not going to stop at just having that goal in mind. We're going to help you state that goal in a way that greatly increases the odds of success.

When people set goals they often doom themselves from the start. This is true whether the goal is a big one like opening a restaurant, or a small one like persuading someone to consider your point of view in a conversation.

Here are some common goals that are often doomed from the start:

"I want to get in shape."
"I don't want to be anxious and worried anymore."

"I want to have more influence."
"I don't want to work for someone else anymore."
"I need to change the culture on my team at work."
"I have to get my kids to be more respectful."
"I want to be rich."

These are all perfectly reasonable things to want. Without knowing what to look for, it's hard to know what's wrong with them. What these goals all share is that they are not what would be called well-formed outcomes in NLP.

Below is another goal that has the same problems where it's a little easier to spot the issues. Let's say you tell your family you want to go on vacation. Then your partner says, "Get in the car, let's start driving." Some questions should arise . . . Where to? What will it cost? For how long? What will happen if you don't show up to work for who-knows-how-many-days? What will you do with the kids?

Many people would not end up getting in the car at that point. If you're like most people, you're more likely to take a vacation if you know where you're going and when, and can make sure it will not cause other problems, like getting fired from your job, or the kids' grades suffering.

All those things create resistance. And when there's too much resistance, we don't move forward. Essentially, it would hurt too much to take the vacation. Just continuing to work without a vacation would be less painful.

One morning Josh was out for a bike ride. His then four-year-old son was in the kid seat on the back. They were headed to preschool. "Can you go faster, Daddy?"

"Ugh," Josh groaned. "I want to, but it just feels so hard this morning." Josh was trying to move his legs, but they felt heavy and the ride seemed to him like it would never end. After dropping his son at school he heard a noise as he pushed his bike along the sidewalk. The brakes had been rubbing on the wheel the whole time.

Anyone who has tried to ride a bike with the brakes rubbing on the wheel or drive with the emergency brake on will know the feeling. We often find that we want to move forward but something is holding us back, making every step forward feel like walking against a hard wind.

To see whether the brakes are rubbing against your goal, answer these five questions:

As you've stated your goal . . .

1. Is it focused on what you want instead of on what you don't want?
2. Will getting your goal cause you other problems?
3. Is it within your control?
4. Can you clearly define success?
5. When and where, specifically, do you want it?

Some of these will be familiar to any successful person. We find that even when someone consciously knows they should check for these, when they actually do check, often at least one is causing resistance. To see how this happens, here are some examples.

QUESTION 1
Is it focused on what you want instead of on what you don't want?

Ever since he was a teenager, Greg struggled with being overweight. Initially he didn't like how he looked and felt. He told himself, "I don't want to be fat anymore." It was clear what he didn't want. But not so clear yet was what he did want, which was a setup for failure.

Not all motivation is the same. Being motivated by what you don't want can lead to outcomes different from being motivated by what you do want. Broadly speaking, we can distinguish between two motivational systems in the brain.[1] The Away system (motivated by what you don't want) can get the fight-or-flight response going. It can be quick, powerful, and the emotions involved are things like anxiety or fear—stuff that makes you agitated in one way or another, and you're seeking relief. It can motivate you to make a change, but *what* change? To get to a specific goal, we recommend tapping into the Towards motivational system (motivated by what you do want). It is not always as intense, but it is always in the direction of some destination.

The emotions include feelings like excitement and desire. If you fall short when you're focused on what you're moving toward, you might feel sad or dejected, but not anxious or agitated. Both systems motivate, but differently, so they are not always interchangeable.[2] They include different brain systems, different bodily reactions, different emotions, different concerns, different focus, and often different consequences. For goals, we suggest you focus on either the Towards system or leverage both systems.

It was not enough for Greg to say, "I don't want to be fat." That was a powerful motivator, but it only served as a wakeup call, because he had nowhere to go with it. He needed to define what he was moving toward. Eventually he created the answer: "I want to be 215 pounds, with a body mass index [BMI] of 20, and 15 percent body fat." With that, he had something to move toward, and could get excited as he found ways to make measurable progress.

Is your goal, as you have it in your mind, focused on a negative thing you are moving away from or a positive thing you are moving toward?

If it is focused on what you're moving away from, what is the positive thing you're moving toward?

QUESTION 2
Will getting your goal cause you other problems?

This question is often a game-changer for people.

Josh was coaching a woman who we'll call Andy, who told Josh in so many words, "I want to be rich . . . I'm tired of struggling with finances. Something has to change." Josh asked Andy, "Will getting your goal—being rich—cause you other problems?" At first, Andy just looked at Josh like he was crazy. How could being rich cause a problem? Why would you not want to be rich? But after thinking it over, her answer was, "Yes, it would cause some problems."

The only ways she could come up with to be rich involved working at jobs that would have taken her away from her kids too much while they were young. Also, she would have had to do a lot of self-promotion and sales. "I don't want to be that person," she said. And Andy then realized that was why her goal had been a nonstarter for years.

In NLP, this question helps you do something called the ecology check, borrowed from the science of ecology.[3] Remember learning about ecosystems in school? The frogs eat the mosquitoes, the birds eat the frogs, the foxes eat the birds . . . (a few more steps) . . . and the mosquitoes feed on the animals, and it all repeats. It's a balanced system. If you change any part of the system, it has effects everywhere else. Add some runoff from nearby power plants into the water, and suddenly the frog population shrinks. Then mosquitoes get out of control, and a bunch of other problems follow.

This happens in human systems too. Research in family therapy shows it.[4] A woman in her forties has a history of alcoholism. It is slowly wrecking her work and family life. She very much wants to stop drinking and has tried before. Her family supports this. They all really want it, in the sense that they strongly wish it to be the case. But the ecosystem is pushing back. It turns out that the family only connects on an emotional level when Mom is drinking. Take the drinking out and you take out the emotional connection. They all still crave emotional connection. The pressures will build and she will start drinking again. To stop her drinking, the family will need to learn new ways to connect emotionally without alcohol. It will be a new balanced ecosystem, a healthier one.

It doesn't work to just change one piece of an ecosystem. You need to find a new balance that works for the whole system. No matter how much Andy wanted to be rich, if it caused her other problems that were not acceptable to her, then she just wouldn't make progress.

Often people think that what matters is how much you want a goal. Not true. You can want something passionately and for your whole life and never take the steps to get there. Instead of thinking about how strongly you desire a goal, we invite you to think about how *fully* you want a goal. If some part of you doesn't want the goal, you'll resist your own progress.

For Andy to make progress, she would have to solve three problems together: (1) find a way to make the money she wanted; (2) find a way to have a relationship with her kids while they're young that she feels good about; and (3) find a way to be the kind of person she wanted to be while marketing herself. The system would push back if she didn't address all three.

As another example, let's come back to Greg. He really wanted to lose weight, look better, and get healthy. This lasted well into adulthood. But his attempts at losing weight led to unanticipated and unacceptable outcomes. There were fewer nights out with friends eating comfort foods with beer. He had to give up leisure time in exchange for calorie-burning activities. He was not okay with losing these things.

For Greg, he needed to find a different way to have nights out with friends. And he needed to find calorie-burning activities that fit with his leisure time. Ultimately, this ended up including making some new friends with different interests, and taking on forms of exercise that were fun and social. And, once he got close to his goal of reaching 215 pounds, he decided that losing the last five pounds required more sacrifice than he was willing to give. It required a lifestyle change he felt was too drastic, and for which he would need to alter his core identity in some ways, which he was not willing to do. So, he decided to change his goal to conform with his desired reality. He still opted for a healthy lifestyle, but without wholly depriving himself of certain things that he loved and enjoyed. To this day, he is still a happy 220 pounds with 17 percent body fat.

As in Greg's case, we may find that our initial destination may be nothing more than a zone at which we want to arrive. As we near the goal, we may realize that we want or need the goal to be a little different, or a lot different. In reaching outcomes, it is important to pay attention to the results that we are achieving, while understanding that sometimes the bull's-eye is no longer or never was the target.

To help you think about your situation, here are a few more examples of goals you might have and the kinds of problems that could arise if you worked at or achieved your goal.

GOAL: *"I don't want to be anxious and worried anymore."*
PROBLEM: *"I'm concerned that if I wasn't worried, I'd be careless. I might let my guard down and do something embarrassing."*
GOAL: *"I want to have more influence."*
PROBLEM: *"I'm not prepared for all the attention and responsibility if I succeed."*
GOAL: *"I don't want to work for someone else anymore."*

PROBLEM: *"If I try to work for myself I might fail, and then I'd have to admit that I don't have what it takes. As long as I stay here, I never have to face that fear."*

GOAL: *"I need to change the culture on my team at work."*

PROBLEM: *"It would take a lot of work and might go nowhere. Meanwhile, I have a huge amount of work that has to get done to satisfy our clients. I can't jeopardize our ability to deliver to try to make this culture change happen."*

GOAL: *"I have to get my kids to be more respectful."*

PROBLEM: *"I've heard I need to be empathetic and listen to them. But that would feel like coddling them, and I'm not okay with that given their behavior lately."*

As you think about your goal, will the work you put in toward it cause other problems?

Here's another way to think about the problems that may arise: If you get your desired outcome, what will happen next? Are you okay with that?

QUESTION 3
Is it within your control?

Let's take a look at the vacation idea. You may think that taking a vacation is within your control and so, feeling that you work too much, berate yourself for not making it happen. But if your partner has to get permission to be off work, and the kids would need special permission to do remote schoolwork, those things are not in your control. If you have to find a destination that satisfies other people's sense of fun, it is not entirely within your control. If you don't have the resources to pay for it yet, then it is not entirely within your control.

People who succeed at their goals don't get too attached to things that are not in their control. Instead they focus on what is within their control that will move them in the right direction. It is within your control to research good vacation options. It is within your control to think about how to get your partner and kids interested. It is within your control to call the school about remote work. It is within your control to figure out your budget. If you focus on those outcomes you're much more likely to end up taking a vacation, aren't you?

You might think there's no need for research on this point. It may seem obvious that a goal that is within your control is more attainable than one that is not. However, there is some relevant research, and it adds nuance about how to look for goals that are within your control. For instance, one study looked at how well people learned to throw darts who were new to the game. Those who just set goals about getting a great score did not do so well. Not knowing how to throw darts, it was not really in their control to get a great score. Those who set process goals, e.g., a goal to focus on specific movements when they threw and to think about how to make adjustments the next time, did better. Those process goals regarding how to focus and think are the kinds of things that are more within our control than getting a good score. And an interesting thing happened. Once they started to get better, if they then set goals about getting a great score (once it must have been more in their control to influence the score) then they did even better.[5]

Outside of a game of darts, that shift in how to set goals might look like this. A salesperson who is focused on making the sale (not in her control) often does worse than the one who is focused on understanding the needs of the customer (in her control). An author who is focused on publishing a bestseller (not in his control) will probably do worse than an author who is focused on writing a book that is easy and fun to read and addresses a current need (in his control).

Is your goal entirely within your control?

What is within your control that would move you in the right direction?

If you're not sure how to find an outcome in your control, set a learning goal. Those are always within your control. Let's say your goal is to influence someone. That's not entirely in your control. But learning how to influence that person is very much within your control. Research shows that, in many contexts, people who set learning goals tend to outperform people who just try to achieve their goal.[6]

What is a learning goal that would move you in the right direction?

When you think about what is within your control, you also have an easier time answering the fourth question. . . .

QUESTION 4
Can you clearly define success?

Remember Andy who told Josh, "I want to be rich . . . I'm tired of struggling with finances. Something has to change." Andy only had a vague sense of what it meant to be rich. That was a recipe for disappointment.

For example, she had recently moved to a bigger house. She was feeling like she'd made it. Within a month, she went to a birthday party for one of her son's friends at a more expensive house. Suddenly she felt like she was failing. Moving again anytime soon was not a realistic option or one she even wanted. Her wealth and income had not changed. But she was stuck—once again—not feeling rich.

The brain has systems for letting you know whether you're meeting expectations, exceeding them, or failing. Probably the most well-known is called the dopamine system or the reward system. However, it's not just there to give you rewards—to make you feel good. Scientists have shown it's really responding to something called prediction error.[7] Essentially—it responds when your prediction about a reward in the future was not right. If you did better than you predicted, you have a surge in dopamine. It is a very rewarding feeling, and the brain gears up to get you to do whatever got you there again. If you did worse than predicted, you have a decrease, and you tend to feel deflated.

Imagine there's someone you're interested in romantically. You think the moment is right, and move in to give them a kiss. You're not sure how they will respond. After your stomach has time for several loops, they respond in kind. You've exceeded your expectations (remember—you weren't sure), and it feels wonderful. On the other hand, if they pause and tell you they just want to be friends, it feels much worse. Those are the feelings we're talking about.

One of the founders of NLP put it this way: "Disappointment takes adequate planning." You can't be disappointed unless you expected something different. Whenever you find yourself disappointed, it means you had something else in mind. Often, with our goals, we haven't consciously figured out what we really have in mind in terms of success. But unconsciously, we always have something in mind. Unconsciously, Andy was thinking of being rich as meaning that she would have more than the other families at her son's school. Consciously, she didn't care about that. But unchecked, she was reacting as though that's what mattered.

You have the power to take control over how you will evaluate success. Your dopamine system will be evaluating it anyway—that's not a choice. But you can make that system work for you.

So Andy got much more specific about what being rich meant for her. It meant having or making enough money so that she could choose a location she liked to live, pay for college, drive a fun car, take vacations a few times a year, and build toward a retirement in which she didn't have to change her standard of living.

With this definition, she would very clearly know whether she had achieved it. It also changed the goal from an all-or-nothing thing—being rich versus not being rich—to something with many shades of gray. Andy began to evaluate herself based on that definition. She was no longer at the mercy of some wildly all-or-nothing sense of having failed or succeeded just based on a birthday party.

With your goal, do you have a clear idea of what success would look like? Could you clearly know whether you have achieved it?

You get to decide what counts as success or failure (or anywhere in between). Take that power back for yourself.

What would success look like? What would have to be the case for you to clearly know that you have achieved it?

QUESTION 5
When and where, specifically, do you want it?

For some goals, like Greg's weight loss goal, it sounds at first like a silly question. Of course Greg wants to be healthy and fit all the time.

But for many goals, this can be a make-or-break question. For example, is your goal about being more assertive? Do you really want to be assertive in all contexts? What about when you need to be a good listener? Even Andy's goal of being rich might sound at first like something she'd obviously want all the time. But as she reflected on it, she realized she had a real problem with coming across as that out-of-touch rich person with some of her friends from high school. There were contexts where being rich was not what she wanted. It was another source of resistance.

Define the context in which you want your outcome, and you'll help remove that resistance.

Psychological research shows that it is surprisingly effective and reliable to specify the precise context when you set a goal. For example, Greg might specify, "When I go out with friends, I won't order fries or desserts, and I will decide in advance how many beers to have." It helps you overcome resistance from past habits or competing goals. Specifically, identify the time, place, people, setting, and so forth when you want to behave differently. Doing so has been shown to help people achieve goals ranging from health exams to personal development to work and more.[8]

What is the context when you want your outcome? Specify when and where you'll behave differently than you used to, and specify how you'll behave differently.

The Well-Formed Outcome

With the answers to these five questions, we're now in a position to create well-formed outcomes. For example, putting it all together, Andy replaced her initial goal of "I want to be rich" with a well-formed outcome:

- "I want to have the money to pay for college, live in a nice house, drive a fun car, take some nice vacations, and retire well."
- "I want to make this money in a way that won't take me away from the kids too much while they are young."
- "I want to find a line of work where I can feel good about

marketing myself and where I feel I can still be myself with my high school friends."

Greg replaced his initial goal of "I don't want to be fat" with a well-formed outcome:

- "I want to be 215 pounds, with a BMI of 20, and 15 percent body fat." (Later changed to 220 pounds and 17 percent body fat.)
- "I want to get there by changing my diet in a way that still lets me go out at night with friends, and finding ways to exercise that are social and fun."

Andy and Greg have now both reached these outcomes and sustained them for a long time.

What is your well-formed outcome? Remember the criteria:

As you've stated your goal . . .

1. Is it focused on what you want, instead of on what you don't want?
2. Will getting your goal cause you other problems?
3. Is it within your control?
4. Can you clearly define success?
5. When and where, specifically, do you want it?[9]

If you've reflected on the prompts throughout the chapter, you might want to go back and review your answers. Or, having done the thinking along the way, you might simply be in a better spot to create a well-formed outcome now.

What is your well-formed outcome?

This chapter has been about setting yourself up for success at the beginning of your journey. What remains in this book is a series of concepts and tools to use along your journey toward your goals. These concepts and tools are for changing yourself, understanding others, and influencing others to change.

THE RIGHT MINDSET

Eight Beliefs That Will Make You Limitless

In this section, you'll learn how to embody the right mindset for being a master communicator and change agent.

When the founders of NLP studied people who did great change work, they recognized that there were certain beliefs that were extremely useful. They are beliefs to have as bedrock support in all that you do, and they are wonderful ways to approach life. Josh has even made them into formal principles by which he runs his company. While these beliefs would be worthwhile for their own sake, we also present these to you because taking them on provides a foundation for being extraordinarily capable at applying every NLP tool you will learn in this book. In NLP, we refer to these beliefs as the NLP presuppositions, because we invite you to presuppose they are always true.

2

HOW WE EXPERIENCE THE WORLD
IS NOT THE SAME AS REALITY

Here's the big central idea in NLP. People don't react to reality—they react to their experience of reality. Those two things are not the same. So, if you want to understand someone or help them change, rather than trying to understand reality, you should try to understand how they experience reality. Doing so reveals how people get stuck and opens wide the possibilities for change. Once you learn how someone experiences the world, it becomes clear what to try changing in order to help them. You are then in a position to find the difference that makes the difference for them.

This same approach applies also to changing our own thoughts, feelings, and behaviors. When it comes to ourselves, we have a tendency to think we see the world as it actually is. But the same is as true for us as it is for anyone else.

When a person experiences something their brain does not create a perfect replica of that thing in their mind. If Josh is out for a jog and a dog starts charging and barking from a house he's passing, he doesn't capture all the nuances of color in the dog's hair, or how long the tail is. He notices how big it is and how fast it's moving, and whether there is a fence. He might get a rough sense of whether it appears friendly or not, too, if he gets a chance to look right at it. Instead of capturing all the information, people pick up on what's useful or relevant. That's just a fraction of what's out there. What's useful or relevant is that stuff that will help the person get through the situation they're in. This may help explain why neuro-scientists have found that despite the enormous processing power of the human brain, it only processes a very limited portion of the information it encounters.[1]

Rather than capturing all the information out there, how we expect the world to be has a big influence on what we experience. For example, if you were at home and you heard someone call your name, you'd likely think it was a family member. But if you were traveling and, while walking down the street, heard someone call your name, you'd likely think it was not a family member. A good deal of evidence over the years has shown in various contexts that what we experience or remember from a situa-tion depends on what we expect.[2] One well-known study, for instance, had participants write down their impressions of a person they had read about. Someone the participants met in the study, who they were told knew the person they were writing about, would read those impressions. Before writing, one group of participants was told that the person they met liked this person. The other group was told that the person they met disliked this person. Those who had heard this person was liked ended up with more positive attitudes about them than those who heard this per-son was disliked—and this effect increased over the couple of weeks that followed.[3]

Our expectations are based on many things. Just to name a few, they include what is likely, what we've recently thought about or perceived, what we're trying to accomplish, and what we think is important. There are many ways in which the mind influences how we experience the world.

It's actually quite normal for our experience of a situation to be a little inaccurate—with things deleted or distorted. But our experiences tend to be inaccurate in ways that serve us, or reinforce our expectations. If you've ever watched sports, you'll know that the referee will sometimes make a call but the fans from each team see it totally differently. Imagine it's the World Cup. Two players from opposing teams are charging at the ball. They arrive at the same moment and collide with each other. One player falls to the ground hurt and in pain. The other player manages to stay standing and unhurt. The referee runs in and holds up a red card to throw the standing player out of the game. The fans of the hurt player erupt in cheers—justice has been done. It was clearly an act of malice when the other player threw their man to the ground. The fans of the player ejected from the game erupt in anger—how could the referee be so bad at his job and ruin the game based on this? It was obviously a good faith attempt to go for the ball! Incidental contact is part of the game! At the stadium, the replay shows again and again on the jumbotron. Each time, both sides convince themselves only more so of what they believe. The evidence is right there caught on video, after all. Yet both sides see different evidence on that video—different behaviors, feelings, thoughts, intentions.

Research shows that even the experience of basic features of the world can actually be influenced by our goals and abilities, affecting factors as fundamental as perceived size, distance, and speed of an object.[4] For example, the amount of energy you think it will take you to walk somewhere can influence how far away it seems to you.

Speech perception is another good example. You may have noticed that artificial speech recognition still has a long way to go. Anyone who has tried to call customer service knows that even if you start out friendly and ready to talk, by the time you get through the horrendous automated phone system that gets everything you say—and then yell—wrong, you are ready to tear the head off the poor person who finally answers. This is despite huge investments in speech perception from Bell Labs, Apple, and others since the early 1950s. To be fair, we can now speak to ask our phones to look up information that is stored in them, or to play music from an existing list. There are plenty of errors and limitations still, but Siri and Alexa are good enough to be handy for some things. Ultimately, what makes it so hard to create artificial speech perception approaching what humans can do, however, is that the auditory signal doesn't have all the information you need.

A person needs to bring to the table a lot of knowledge. Knowledge about syntax (e.g., which types of words and phrases go where in a sentence), accents, manners of speech, the rules for how phonemes sound in different parts of a word, what different intonations mean (e.g., sincerity versus sarcasm), what's appropriate for the context, and so on. We must predict what's coming on so many levels to make sense of even one sentence. For example, research has shown that people who have degeneration in certain parts of the prefrontal cortex of the brain critical for prediction, but whose auditory perception areas are perfectly fine, really struggle to understand speech.[5] The authors of that research explain that just about every conversation for people with this condition can be hard for them to understand. It might be like when we're on a noisy, crowded train station platform trying to hear the announcement while the train is rushing in.

What's true for basic experiences of size, distance, speed, and speech is true but with even more ambiguity when we perceive a whole situation or the personality of other people. Have you ever had a situation where people make totally different meanings out of the same thing? Two people walk out of a meeting. One says to the other, "That was a disaster. Did you see the way he laughed when I messed up? I just wanted to crawl away and die after that." The other says, "I thought it went great. After he laughed, he really loosened up. I think that's when you won him over. It humanized you."

The facts are simply that the presenter made an error and the listener laughed. Everything else happened in their minds—they perceived two totally different events. There is an old saying that beauty is in the eye of the beholder. Actually, it's not just beauty—just about everything is in the eye of the beholder.

The larger point here is that what we experience is not reality, it is instead a version of reality that serves our needs and is heavily influenced by what is going on in our minds.

NLP uses a metaphor for describing how someone experiences the world that can be helpful—we talk about discovering someone's mental model. Like with an architectural model, a model train set, or a model of a fantasy world in the video game *Minecraft*, after you create the model there are certain ways you can move, certain places you can and can't go, certain rules about what is possible and what is not. The model helps you think about the real world, but it is not the real world. Necessarily, a lot is missing, unknown, or the model could be built in different ways. In a mental model, the components of the model are not train tracks (like the model train set), or cardboard buildings (like the architectural model), or 3-D-looking blocks in a game (like in *Minecraft*), but they dictate how we can move through life and what is possible.

As a result, our mental models of the world guide every major decision in our lives—spouses, friends, careers, and more. They guide our decisions whether we know it or not. That, in turn, has a big impact directly or indirectly on where we are emotionally, physically, and financially in life. So the mental models we build have a huge effect on our success and well-being. However, sometimes our mental models hold us back—they can be outdated, limiting, or simply wrong.

Think about your goal from the previous chapter. Is there a part of your goal or a step that you are resisting or avoiding for any reason? If not, think of something else in your life that you are resisting or avoiding, and have that in mind for the next few questions.

Your mental model about that thing you're resisting or avoiding could be valuable to take a look at. You can answer these questions to start to get a sense of that mental model:

What's the environment like when you try to do that thing you're resisting, and how does that affect you? For example, "It's always after work, and the kids have constant needs, so I'm tired and can't focus."

How do you behave when you think about or try to do that thing you're resisting? For example, "I procrastinate by going on social media. I need to be more disciplined."

What abilities do you lack pertaining to that thing you're resisting? For example, "I have no patience."

How does it serve you to resist doing that thing you're resisting? For example, "I won't have to face my fears of inadequacy."

What do you think of yourself when you resist doing that thing? For example, "I'm a failure. I'm a waste of space."

What's your place in the world, or value to others, when you resist doing that thing? For example, "I'm nobody special, fairly insignificant."

Your answers to these questions reveal aspects of your mental model pertaining to that thing you've been resisting. Some people will look at their answers and say, "Wow, is it any wonder I've been resisting it!?" Regardless of your reaction, as you reflect on where your mind went with these questions, do you see any opportunities to make a change?

Perhaps a change to your environment, behavior, capabilities, beliefs, identity, or larger purpose beyond yourself would help.[6] Each of the questions we asked got at one of these.

Now, let's turn it around. Pick something about your goal from the last chapter that you are wholly embracing already and taking steps toward. If there is nothing yet, choose something else in your life that you are wholly embracing already and taking steps toward for these questions.

We're going to compare the mental model from each of the two cases to look for useful differences.

What's the environment like when you try to do that thing you're wholly embracing, and how does that affect you? For example, "It's during the day, when I am fresh mentally and don't have distractions, so I can focus."

How do you behave when you think about or try to do that thing you're wholly embracing? For example, "I take a deep breath and smile, and gather all the materials I need."

What useful abilities do you have pertaining to that thing you're wholly embracing? For example, "I'm very good at getting to the heart of what's important."

How does it serve you to wholly embrace that thing you're wholly embracing? For example, "It gives me an outlet for creativity and makes me feel productive."

What do you think of yourself when you embrace doing that thing? For example, "I'm a Jedi."

What's your place in the world, or value to others, when you embrace doing that thing? For example, "People are inspired by how I work, and thankful for what I can do."

Is there anything different in the two cases—the one where you resist something, and the one where you embrace something?

Is there anything you'd like to borrow from the one where you embrace something and use it to enhance or expand your mental model for the one where you've been resisting something? Building on the examples we offered, you could change how your environment affects you; take a deep breath and smile; make use of your ability to get to the heart of the matter; use the goal as an outlet for creativity; use the goal to expand your Jedi self-image; consider how others will thank you for working on this goal.

Consider the case of a person who wants to leave their steady job and start their own business. However, they dread networking, and that is holding them back. The components of a mental model that would limit someone from networking and starting on their own could be thoughts and feelings like this:

- "People who sell themselves are slimy."
- "If you try to network, people will think you are fake or desperate."
- "I'm a terrible father if I don't have a consistent income, and I can't be sure I'll make money this way."
- "I can't disappoint my parents. They would never do something this risky."
- "I don't have what it takes. Everyone will see that and look at me with pity."
- "What I'm good at is the technical work. Networking is a necessary evil."

The components of a mental model that enables networking and starting out on your own could include thoughts and feelings like these:

- "People who sell themselves well understand that they really have something important to offer."
- "If you try to network, you will learn how to form meaningful connections with people and might meet people you like."
- "I'm a terrible father if I don't show my kids that people can stand up to their fears and learn to do something that at first seems hard."
- "I can't disappoint my parents. They would be disappointed if I kept my mediocre job and never tried to build for a better future."
- "I don't have what it takes yet. But on some level everyone is just winging it."
- "What I'm good at is the technical work. Now I'd like to add to my skills, and begin learning how to network."

These are just a few examples of the stuff of mental models. They can include beliefs (e.g., "People who sell themselves are slimy"), feelings (e.g., feeling like I'm disappointing my parents), identities (e.g., "I'm a terrible father"), and capabilities (e.g., good at the technical work). Mental models can also include images in the mind's eye—a person might have an image in their mind of a person rolling their eyes when they think, "People will look at me with pity." They can include things we hear in our mind's ear, such as "I don't have what it takes." They can include sensations—e.g., a yucky feeling in your stomach. In short, they include the things that make up our experience of a situation.

What's more, you don't have to be consciously aware of what makes up your mental model for it to affect you. In fact, the mental model is often invisible. It's the background. You think you're experiencing reality, not reality through the filter of your mental model. It can be eye-opening to become aware of what makes up your or someone else's mental model of a situation.

Here's another example. You and your friend get together for coffee, and when you see her, you can tell something's wrong. She looks sad and appears distracted. Then she tells you—she's getting divorced. It turns out it's taking a toll on her work, too, and she's not getting to anything she has to get to.

That's a perfectly reasonable series of events. Getting divorced is causing her to feel and behave this way.

Actually, however, that's not true—getting divorced does not cause her to feel and behave this way . . . unless she does something, too. She has to make meaning out of that event. The meaning depends on her mental model.

In your friend's case, getting divorced means something terrible. As the conversation over coffee progresses, she shares how she can't imagine anyone would want her now, and that she is too old to start over. She fears dying alone, and worries she will live a life of loneliness. We've probably all seen—or been in—a situation in which the end of a relationship has brought on such thoughts. If that were her mental model, how could she not feel so awful?

For a different person, the meaning could be quite different, however.

Suppose you have a different friend who feels she is trapped in a relationship and can't imagine a way out. Then one day you meet for coffee, and she tells you her partner asked for a divorce. She's smiling while she shares the news. She says she's been feeling free like she hasn't in years, like a weight has been lifted. She's letting herself dream about possibilities for a better future she had not allowed herself to consider before. She has energy, and she's started taking classes and spending time with friends. It's a new beginning for her.

Same event—getting divorced. Totally different meanings they made of it, which led to totally different thoughts, feelings, and behaviors.

Perhaps the most researched form of therapy, cognitive therapy, is predicated on this idea. We don't react to situations. We react to the meaning we make about situations. We can't always change the situation, but we can always change how we think about it. Cognitive therapy, in large part, is the practice of first identifying the thoughts that bring about unwanted emotions or limiting behaviors, and then changing those thoughts to something more accurate and useful. The new more accurate or useful thoughts bring about more desirable emotions, and free us to take appropriate action. The impact of changing these thoughts has been extraordinary both in terms of the benefits it brings people emotionally and behaviorally, as well as the wide range of people and types of difficulties it is useful for.[7]

In NLP, we aim to discover these kinds of thoughts. We also do more. When we aim to discover someone's mental model, we are looking for thoughts—as in cognitive therapy—as well as feelings, beliefs, capabilities, a sense of identity, values, and other aspects of someone's subjective experience. Throughout the book, we'll show how shifts to various components of someone's mental model can be the difference that makes the difference, along with the science behind these ideas.

Most limitations are not real apart from our mental models of the world. As we'll see in the coming chapters, most people have many more options than they ever imagined once they expand and enrich their mental models.[8]

At this point, we invite you to presuppose, in every situation you find yourself in, that how someone perceives the world is not the same as reality.

Instead, they are operating from a mental model, a model that is probably impoverished compared to reality, perhaps even inaccurate. Presume you don't know what someone's mental model is pertaining to the situation they find themself in. Presume you don't know everything about your own mental model regarding your own situation. Make it your mission and your deep interest to find out more. The more you understand about the mental model, the easier change becomes.

You will learn not only how to discover the present mental model, but also how to help someone—yourself or others—enrich and enhance that model. Think of it like adding to a model train set new turns, signs, bridges, stations, towns, people, mountains, forests, and so on. It creates new options where previously there were few. Often the new options are better—such as being more scenic, more fun, or faster.

The foundational beliefs in the first section of the book, and the specific tools that follow in the other sections, will all serve to help you quickly be able to understand someone's mental model—yours or someone else's—and know how to experiment with modifications to that mental model to find the difference that makes the difference. The difference that matters won't be the same for every person or situation. Change can happen quickly and can last when you find the right difference. That is what will lead to your or their desired outcomes.

3

WHY NOT ME?

As a new lawyer, Greg accepted what he now considers "lowball, chicken-shit" offers from insurance companies, because he was too afraid to take a swing in front of the jury. His traitorous brain went into destructive loops of "I'm not good enough," "The other lawyer is way better than me," "I will lose, and everyone will see me for who I really am."

There are times when we look at a situation and think we don't have what it takes . . . and other people do. It might be that, like Greg used to think, you worry you can't really perform at the highest levels in your work. It could be that you want to get in shape. You see countless examples of people with better bodies than yours, but you feel it's hopeless for you. "I don't have the discipline for that," "I'm too lazy," you think with a sigh. Or maybe you need to network more—like the example in the last chapter—but the prospect of it makes you feel like you're being fake. You know there are other people who have done what you wish you could do, but they are not like you. They are gifted at their work. They have discipline. They are naturally extroverted. It's different for you. They are the lucky ones who were born good at those things. At least that's how it feels.

Reality check, folks. We all suffer from imposter syndrome. Fortunately, precisely where some of us see dead ends, NLP sees opportunities. Rather than losing hope when seeing others succeeding where we are not, NLP points us toward how to learn from their successes.

Possibly the most alluring foundational belief from NLP is "If it is possible for someone in the world, it is possible for me."

Let's analyze this statement. Does it really mean that we can accomplish pretty much anything and everything? There are, of course, some physical limitations. Neither Greg nor Josh will ever be centers on a professional basketball team, given our ages and heights. But when it comes to anything that depends on how you think, feel, behave, or interact with other people, the answer is probably yes. Maybe if we argued for an hour we'd find that there are one or two situations where it's not 100 percent true. But what really matters is whether this is a useful belief. So let's try a few thought experiments.

Consider the opposite. What happens when you believe that what you want is out of reach for you? What would Greg's career be like if he never tried his hand at going in front of a jury against an insurance company? What would your health be like if you believed it was hopeless to get in shape? How would your business grow if you gave up on networking as something only others could do, and just didn't do it? There is such a thing as a self-fulfilling prophecy.

In psychology research, it has been shown that when you believe you can't do something, you behave differently from how you otherwise would, and you end up bringing about the thing you don't want. For example, let's say you think you're just fundamentally not good at public speaking. You hate it. It's not who you are. In this scenario, you have a belief that you can't change this ability. Have you ever tried to feel better by telling yourself, "At least I'm not as bad as so-and-so"? Many people, when they don't think they can improve, try to feel better by consoling themselves that at least they are better than someone else at something they do. It's a classic move, and we've all done it. Research shows that when we think we can't change, we tend to look for people doing worse so we can feel better.[1] That makes us feel okay about not trying to change anything.

But our behavior is likely to be very different if we believe we can get better at whatever skill we wish we could take on. When we believe we can change, research shows we look for people who are doing better than us because we want to learn from them. Successful people are no longer threatening, we no longer try to avoid thinking about them, and instead they become role models we try to study and learn from.[2] That difference in behavior is going to make a difference in whether you change, isn't it?

There are other effects, too, of believing you can't change.[3] You might avoid feedback about any kind of failure, because it feels like an insult and makes you defensive. It feels like a comment on your fixed personality. People who think they can change, however, appreciate feedback because it is useful information for course correction. If you think you can't change, you tend to avoid new things that require effort. If it's effortful, you take that to mean you're not good at it, which can hurt your ego. If you think you can change, on the other hand, you see effort as evidence you're getting better, like when there's "good" pain after a little exercise. Avoiding effort and corrective feedback . . . how could that not get in the way of progress? Seeking effort and corrective feedback, how could that not help you make progress?

Research also shows that people who are sensitive to rejection behave in ways that get them rejected more often. And people who believe therapy will work for them behave in ways that make it work. In fact, believing you can change yourself in therapy is a strong predictor of whether you change. In short, your belief about whether something is possible for you will have a big effect on whether you do it.[4]

Now, take a moment and consider what would happen if you really did believe that if it's possible for someone, it's possible for you? Right now you can reflect on a real change you'd like to make. You may choose to reflect on the goal you thought about in chapter 1 when we introduced the well-formed outcome.

If you believed that the changes you seek were really, fully possible for you because if someone else has done it, you can, too . . .

How would you think and behave differently from how you've been thinking and behaving?

How would you interpret the meaning of your efforts and "failures"?

Would you seek and study role-models? Who, specifically?

How would you react to others' success?

What else is different when you approach situations with this belief?

Would there be anything wrong with approaching every situation with this belief?

Wiser people than us have landed on versions of the same truth.

Napoleon Hill in his 1937 classic, *Think and Grow Rich*, wrote, "Whatever the mind can conceive and believe, it can achieve." Henry Ford said this differently, but just as succinctly: "Whether you think you can or you think you can't, you're right."

We invite you to explore taking on the belief "If it's possible for someone in the world, it's possible for me" as something you just see as a given in any situation. It becomes a self-fulfilling prophecy.

And here's one more reason why we—and other NLPers—think this belief is so empowering. If it's possible for someone in the world, it's possible for me *because* anyone can take on any aspect of a mental model that works for them.

If you have a well-formed outcome you can accomplish it, because many others have, and success leaves clues. Let other people show the way. Try to understand their mental model and you can expand your own possibilities. There's more than one way to skin a cat. Learn what the key differences may be between your approach and that of someone who is already successful.

NLP is about adding options in your mental model. You can get started now, just with these beliefs and a healthy curiosity. But as this book progresses, we'll give you more and more tools for understanding someone's mental model (your own or someone else's) and expanding or enriching that model.

Be Like Neo

We considered calling this chapter "Be Like Neo." In the movie *The Matrix*, the main character's name is Neo. He learns that what he thought was his real life was just a computer simulation (a model of the world). This turns out to be quite freeing, because he also comes to realize that he can simply change the simulation (the model). At one point, Neo must use martial arts to fight. A coder who is also free of the simulated world changes the code a bit and Neo suddenly says, "I know kung fu!" Those of us who saw the movie will probably remember Keanu Reeves's face (who played Neo) as he said this, showing bewilderment and delight. If you haven't seen it, the movie is awesome, and you should. If you have seen it, we're happy to have some other Gen Xers joining us.

The matrix is science fiction. As far as we know, we don't live in a simulation, and you can't suddenly know kung fu. But we encourage you to start being more like Neo in this respect: start looking at those around you who have skills you want. If it's possible for them, it is possible for you. Imagine you were on a shopping trip for skills.

Here is just a brief list to give you an idea of what kinds of skills you might want to pick up. Presumably, the full list is long—perhaps infinite—and particular to your needs.

- Staying cool under pressure
- Good at making tough decisions
- Being present
- Gaining trust
- Following through on commitments
- Showing up on time
- Knowing how to dress
- Being vulnerable
- Enjoying public speaking
- Building a practice or business
- Having and holding boundaries
- Aging gracefully
- Being patient
- Doing sales or business development well
- Tolerating risk
- Seeing the humor in things
- Having fun

Josh and Greg both delight in doing this kind of shopping. In NLP, we call it modeling—making a model of someone's mind and then using it to expand or enrich your own mental model. For example, Josh was at a cocktail party thrown by a large organization. It became clear that a person he was speaking with, who he had only just met, was very good at making tough decisions quickly. This person was not burdened by it, did it a lot, and had a good track record with such decisions in their very senior position in the organization hosting the party. Josh thought, "Ooh, I struggle with that," and so asked, "It seems like making tough decisions quickly is a real strength of yours. Would you mind if I interviewed you sometime to learn how you go about it?" The senior executive was flattered and happy to help—a common reaction when you tell someone you are so impressed by something they do that you want to learn how they do it. Josh learned a lot of useful things, but the one piece that really made the biggest difference for him was a belief this executive had which was, "Decisions are easy. If it's hard to make a decision, it's because I don't have all the information I need." So, from then on, when a decision felt hard, Josh would ask, "What information would I have to have in order to make this decision easy?" That set him down a very useful path. It transformed his decision-making.

Right now. Go ahead and pick a skill you'd like to have. It doesn't matter whether you're good at it and looking to get better, if it's totally new for you, or even whether you don't yet believe it's possible for you.

How would you describe the skill?

Who does it well? It could be someone you know personally, or have never met, living or dead.

Do you already know anything about their mental model for this skill? For example, how they think, feel, and what they believe?

What do you imagine is different about their mental model and yours for this skill?

How can you learn more about their mental model for this skill? For example, interview them, read a biography, observe them.

Congrats! Just by reflecting on these questions, you're already starting to discover and expand your mental model. If you'd like to go deeper with it, we've offered a guided set of steps and questions to interview someone and to help you learn and adopt aspects of someone's mental model in Appendix B.

In NLP, what we try to do is to find someone who has done what we want to do, and then learn about their mental model. We look for the ways it differs from our own. That's where there are opportunities to change or enhance our own mental models.

We look to how others before us who are already succeeding have approached things. We try to create a model of their way of perceiving the world so we can learn from it. Even if you seek to do something that's never been done before, there are people who have done things that have never been done before. You can learn about the mental model of someone who did something that's never been done before.

For now, whenever you catch yourself feeling like something is out of reach, remember that the fact that someone else did it means you can. Get curious about the mental model they have that made it possible. This will be a journey in constructing, expanding, and revising your mental models to allow you maximum flexibility in life. That can make you limitless.

To be fair, believing that if it's possible for someone, it's possible for you is not everything, but it can be life-changing. Life is magical, but not magic. If you have never tried a jury trial, you will probably not obtain a multimillion-dollar verdict in your first attempt. Or if you are terrified of public speaking, you will need to take several steps before you achieve your desired outcome. But taking on this belief is often critical in leading to these outcomes. It may be one of the greatest gifts you ever give yourself. We invite you to make it a belief you presume to be true in all situations.

If you are not ready to believe that how we experience the world is not the same as reality, and if something is possible for someone in the world, it's possible for you, then we encourage you to at least act for now as if you believed these things. You can try it on for a few days and see what happens, or not.

4

ALL I NEED IS ALREADY WITHIN ME

Perhaps you are open to the idea that *if it's possible for someone in the world, it's possible for you . . .* in principle. But when you look at what you want in life you feel there is a gulf too large to cross. "Could I ever really be happy?" "Will I ever find someone to marry and have children with?" "What if I'm not good enough to succeed in my chosen profession?" "Could I really conquer my fear of public speaking?" "Do I have what it takes?"

No matter your goals, who you are, or where you are starting from, there is a belief from NLP that can be the difference between action and inaction. The belief is that *each of us has the resources to meet our next developmental challenge.* In other words, all you need is already within you.

Lao Tzu's famous quote "A journey of a thousand miles begins with a single step" has been going viral for millennia. The wisdom he captured in this metaphor helps us all quickly refocus away from the daunting future and onto the manageable present.

This NLP belief helps us follow Lao Tzu's advice by putting our attention on what we are capable of right now that can actually move us in the right direction.

For instance, at the time of this writing, Josh wants to learn to paint. He doesn't appear to have any intrinsic skill. When he puts brush to paper, it looks bad. It feels hopeless and he imagines being embarrassed when people see his work. But he has the resources to learn to paint. He has the capability now to find a great class, and the time management skills to fit it into his schedule. He has the belief that it is possible to get from here to there—he believes this because he's seen others make dramatic gains in painting after taking classes. His son and daughter had made amazing gains already by the ages of eight and five through classes, for instance, in learning how to study the colors and shadows they were looking at. Josh has the experience to know that there is almost always a learning curve to any new skill—slow for a while before you start to really take off. This helps him be patient. He has the ability to shift from worrying about being embarrassed to feeling proud of himself for being adventurous. He has the ability to set learning rather than performance goals. He has the skill to ask great questions when he is feeling stuck. And perhaps most important of all, he has the ability to find others who have gone on this journey and then discover their mental models and strategies for success.

In these ways, all he needs is already within him now.

This is true no matter when "now" is. In the future it will still be true. As a result, when people embrace this belief, they often begin to trust their future selves more, and find they are more open to taking the risks they should be taking.

When we were planning this chapter, Greg said to Josh, "This is the core belief that *everyone* should adopt." He has found that this belief permits him to break free of potentially any of the limiting beliefs that he's accumulated throughout his life. Those limiting beliefs were like heavy luggage he carried around. They led to inaction on so many fronts. This core belief didn't just lighten the load, but annihilated many of those limitations for him. He feels that it gets him past the thought of "I'm not good enough," which used to constantly burrow, rodentlike, into his reserves of self-confidence.

At this point, *all I need is already within me* has become part of how Greg unconsciously shows up to most situations. He has made it one of the resident programs that guides his behavior.[1] What's more, he has found that the more new challenges and goals he takes on, the truer this belief becomes. For instance, with each new business—a law firm, a network of veterinary hospitals, a tequila brand, a network of men's health clinics, and now this partnership with Josh to make NLP more accessible—Greg has developed resources that help him take on new challenges. One of those resources is the psychological freedom to take classes without needing to know precisely what they will lead to, and another is the confidence to know he can handle any outcome.

Greg is not alone. Many people throughout history find versions of this belief to be powerful and hold it as fundamentally true. The idea has been used in various forms in ancient philosophical and spiritual texts, such as the *Upanishads* and the *Tao Te Ching*. As an illustration, the *Tat Tvam Asi* ("Thou Art That") section of the *Upanishads* suggests that turning inward to our divine nature is the surest path to achieving our goals, desires, and happiness.

Research has now also shown that the effects of this belief are reliable—when people believe they have the resources to change, they are significantly more likely to do so. This is true whether it is a personal or professional change. And the opposite has been found, too—even when people do have the resources, if they believe they don't, they don't take action and don't change their situation.[2]

Neuroscientists have discovered that when we connect with inner resources—like our core values—that activates a combination of brain centers that have to do with our sense of self and reward, and supports positive behavior change. When the reward center is active, we are drawn to investing more time and effort—we want to feel that rewarding feeling again. It is a virtuous cycle, in which we continue to feel rewarded, focus on the inner resources we need, and take useful action in the world. In this research, the participants used self-affirmations to deepen their connection with core values—which are a kind of inner resource—as they thought about the future, and this led to changing their behavior in an adaptive way.[3] We invite you to also use affirmations to connect with your inner resources, and to recognize the various ways that all you need is already within you.

Affirmations are positive statements that are repeated over and over again, until the speaker begins to unconsciously believe his or her own words. At the start of the day, just after you finish getting dressed, pause and say, "All I need is already within me."[4] Repeat it ten times before you start work. At the end of the day, before you get in bed, say it ten times again.

We encourage you to think it often. Repeat the affirmation when you're exercising, walking your dog, or taking a shower. Write it on your bathroom mirror. Make it your phone's lock screen and your computer's screen saver. Tattoo it on your forehead if you have to. We are joking, but you know what we mean.

This can help you be ready to remember it when you need it—when you face a daunting challenge or goal. For instance, public speaking terrifies many people. They often have some version of "If I speak in public very bad things will happen to me" playing as a continuous loop subconsciously. It would be quite different if they had "All I need is already within me" playing in their mind.

When you find yourself confronted by a daunting challenge or goal, you can choose what to believe. The choice is between looking at the gulf that is presently too large to cross, or at the steps and resources you will rely on along the way. Every time you take on something new or challenging, you could look ahead and feel you don't have what it takes, or you could look to the present and see that you always have what it takes to take the next step. It is a choice of where to focus.

Let's look at a practical illustration of this principle.

Right now, we invite you to do a little experiment. Your aim will be to notice what happens—to discover whether there is a useful difference for you. Think about a challenge or goal about which you have some doubts, feel overwhelmed, or even a little hopeless.

Now reflect on these questions, which should help you focus on the resources you have now to take the right next steps:

What are the first few steps?
What's stopping you from taking your next step?
How do you need to develop yourself so you can take that step?
What would happen if you were to believe that you have the resources to develop yourself in that way?
Is there some aspect of this goal or challenge you are not so good at yet? Is

there a class you can take? A book you can read? A YouTube video you can watch?

Who else (whether or not you know them personally) has made progress on this kind of goal or challenge?

What resources would be useful in making progress? A resource could be internal—e.g., curiosity, confidence, energy, or perhaps a belief that how someone experiences the world is not the same as reality, *or,* if it's possible for someone in the world it's possible for me. *A resource could also be external—e.g., a person who could offer advice.*

What does it feel like when you believe that all you need is already within you now?

There's really no limit to what you could do, is there?

As an illustration, let's apply the above tools to the dreaded topic of public speaking. What would be our first step? We could ask a friend for help, read an article or a book on the subject, take a recorded or live public speaking class, or hire a public speaking coach. What would stop us? That's right—nothing we can't get past with the tools in this book. We could also google famous people who overcame stage fright and became dynamic speakers and performers, and then *model* them. We believe that everyone who is reading this book has all the resources that they need inside of them to eventually take any of the above steps.

5

THERE'S NO FAILURE, ONLY FEEDBACK

f you've started to embrace the belief that all you need is already within you, you are likely to start taking action toward your goal, if you haven't already. However, there's a decent chance that something you try won't go exactly as you might have hoped.

The story goes that before inventing the light bulb, Thomas Edison made over one thousand unsuccessful attempts. When asked by a reporter how it felt to fail one thousand times, Mr. Edison reportedly responded, "I didn't fail one thousand times. The lightbulb was an invention with one thousand steps."

It's impressive that Mr. Edison held this view. Most of us can see the wisdom in it. But when we fail at something, it's hard to think this way. The quote stands out because it is so different from how most people do it. Unlike Edison, a lot of people take failure very personally. They take failure to mean something about them was flawed or not up to the task. They doubt themselves. They wonder whether they were naïve to think they could succeed. They worry they have gotten in over their head. Instead of inspiring us to be like Edison, the quote sometimes has the unintended effect of making him seem superhuman, because that attitude feels so out of reach for so many of us—even though we know it would be nice if we could do it.

How can we be more like Edison and carry on in the face of failure?

NLP offers a foundational belief that helps. It's kind of radical. The belief does not just claim that failure is okay, or that you can learn from failure. It's not about grit. And it's not just about trying to make yourself feel better. Instead, the belief is that *there's no failure, only feedback.* There is no such thing as failure.

Consider how that would affect you in a moment of self-doubt. For example, when Greg graduated from law school, he was excited to try his first jury trial. But when the verdict was handed down, he lost. He doubted himself. He wondered whether trials were really for him. Maybe he would rather draft documents. However, rather than giving up trial work and becoming a wills and estates lawyer, he took it as a first step toward being a trial lawyer. What he had done did not work. So he corrected course and kept going.

Think of it like a GPS. When you drive past a turn, the GPS does not give up and turn off in despair, or get angry at itself, or complain to its friends. It does not label missing a turn as a failure. It simply recalculates the best path given where you are now. Or imagine a plane that leaves New York City and intends to fly to Los Angeles. Because of turbulence, weather, and visibility, the plane veers off course. Through pilot skill and GPS equipment, the plane is always course-correcting. Life is no different. As long as we have a definite outcome in mind, we are constantly course-correcting to reach it.

Greg recalculated and found the best route despite "weather," "traffic," and "missed turns."

When we say to ourselves, "There's no failure, only feedback," we are doing something psychologists call reframing. A good way to think about reframing is with art—when you take a painting or photo that's in an ordinary frame and move it to a much nicer frame, you can change how you see the art. The frame you place something in can really bring out a different experience—it can make it look important, ugly, whimsical, stately, modern, classic, elegant, or simple, for example. Another good example from art comes from the size of the frame—like when you crop a photo. Josh has a photo of his youngest son as a baby. With a small frame around it, just showing the baby, it looks like he's crying. But zoom out and put a bigger frame on it, and you see he's being tickled by his siblings and laughing hysterically. The frame provides a context in which to make sense of the painting or photo. In the case of a psychological reframe, we take an idea and look at it in a different context—we metaphorically put a new frame on it. It turns out reframing can have a big impact on how you interpret information, which can have lasting effects on your emotions and how your brain processes a situation in the near and long term.

For instance, in research studies, when someone is shown a picture of a person in a hospital looking ill, they will have substantially different reactions in terms of their thoughts, emotions, and how their brains function depending on the frame they put on the situation. People who take the picture to mean there is someone who is suffering a great deal and may soon miss out on life or leave behind others who will miss them may feel fairly bad, and there will be activity in relevant parts of their brains indicating that emotions were stirred. However, people who take the picture to mean that this person is quite fatigued, but they are taking care of themselves and will be in a better place in the future due to their efforts, come away feeling less bad, with less aroused negative emotional brain systems. Moreover, once people make new less negative meaning of something several times, the effects last. They will continue to have a different brain response on future dates when encountering the same situation.[1]

The facts remain the same, but the meaning we attach to those facts can change a lot depending on the frame we use. In the example above from the research, we're talking about the same photo—same facts. For Greg, the fact was that he lost his first trial. There was a period of time when the meaning he made of that was that he was a failure, he was not a good fit for trial law, and he should pursue other kinds of law. But later Greg reframed the meaning of his loss as *feedback about what the job was like*, whether it held something for him, and what he should do differently to succeed.

Whenever we put ourselves out there and try to do something new, we run the risk that we may not do it well. People who choose to use a feedback frame process information about how they performed differently from those who use a failure frame. Even before one second has gone by after getting information about performance, the differences can be seen in the brain. When using a feedback frame our brains give more attention to the information coming in and use it to improve future performance.

Whereas when people see the information as judgment about themselves or whether they failed, then the brain does not capture or use the information coming in as effectively.[2]

Consider some moment of self-doubt you've had. For example, maybe you felt like you said the wrong thing and embarrassed yourself, and then doubted whether others liked or respected you.

What if there was no such thing as failure? What if that was simply useful feedback? In what ways would that shift your attitude, thoughts, feelings about that situation?

One simple way to make this reframe your own deeply held belief is to make it a mantra. Every time you experience judgment or a sense of failure that limits you more than you want it to, say to yourself: "There's no failure, only feedback." Or, here's a variation some people prefer: "I don't fail, I learn and then I win." Pause and say it to yourself in your moments of doubt or rejection, or when you do not achieve an outcome you had hoped for. Say it when you mess up, when you feel despair, when you get angry at yourself, when you are angry at the world, when you feel embarrassed, when something breaks, when you feel out of control, and when you feel you've let someone down, for example.

Right now, think of something that did not go as you would have liked. Tell yourself, "There's no failure, only feedback." Notice what changes when you do.

Ultimately, this reframe from failure to feedback is a way of looking dispassionately at the obstacles life throws in front of us. When we're truly able to see it dispassionately, it boils down to this—every action we take causes a result. Notice that there is no claim about good or bad. Just that everything has some result.

By labeling the result as feedback instead of failure, we are presupposing it is possible to keep moving forward. We are giving our unconscious mind a boost to keep moving forward, too—there is a shift in how we feel and our motivation.

While the idea may seem like a stretch for many people, it is within every one of us already, so it may be more attainable than it at first seems. If our child falls learning to walk, do we throw up our hands and say that's it and buy him or her a wheelchair? If our job requires us to learn new software, do we quit after one or two attempts? Learning to walk is something we believe the baby will get to under normal circumstances—we presuppose it is true, we don't doubt it—it just takes time and practice. Holding on to our job may not be as innate, but most people don't really see it as an option to quit their job every time there's something annoying that happens . . . so they will find a way to learn that new software. These are times when many of us have behaved as if we believed there was no failure, only feedback. Each of us has experiences of simply course-correcting and moving on. You can take a moment now and call to mind a time when you course-corrected and moved on.

You're capable of this, aren't you? We're all capable. Now we invite you to apply that idea to every context and make it conscious.

When Greg decided to stay on his path of becoming a trial lawyer, he also did a number of things that helped him reinforce the belief that there was no such thing as failure, only feedback. He believed that with the right resources and mental model he could become an excellent trial lawyer (chapter 3: "Why Not Me?"); he presupposed that he had the inner resources to take every step he needed to become a premier trial lawyer (chapter 4: "All I Need Is Already Within Me"); he modeled other top lawyers by reading their books and attending their seminars (chapter 2: "How We Experience the World Is Not the Same as Reality"); and more.

You can think of this book—and NLP more broadly—as a symphony, with each chapter being an instrument that uniquely adds to the music. As you progress you may find, as Greg, Josh, and many others have, that as you build your repertoire of mindsets and skills from NLP, the whole becomes more than the sum of its parts.

HOW MY MESSAGE LANDED MATTERS
MORE THAN WHAT I MEANT

magine it is the late 1800s and you are a fly on the wall at 221B Baker Street in London, England. We see a cozy second-floor flat with two men seated across from each other. They are the greatest literary detective of all time, Sherlock Holmes, and his trusted confidant, Dr. John Watson. By flickering fireplace light, Holmes is holding and staring at a piece of yellowish parchment Watson has just handed to him. To Watson's great alarm, he had found it inside his right overcoat pocket just before setting off to see Holmes, without the faintest idea who could have left the ominous note there.

"It says, 'I'll get you at seven'!" Holmes exclaims with a wry smile, tossing the note on the fire.

"Whatever does this mean?" a concerned Watson asks, watching as the threatening words crumple in the flames and vanish into smoke.

"Does anyone have reason to murder you?" Holmes responds, with some impatience for his dim-witted colleague.

"Probably quite a few, given my association with you," says Watson, mustering the bravery that stood him well throughout the war.

"Ah, Watson," sighs Holmes. "Ever so ready for danger. I would admire you, were it not for my pity."

"Whatever do you mean, Holmes?" Watson pleads.

"You say you found the note in your right overcoat pocket as you left the office to come here. You keep your office key in that pocket."

Watson startles at Holmes's correct assertion as to where he keeps his key.

"Hence you reached in to retrieve it as you left in order to bolt the door," Holmes continues, somewhat uninterested. "Your fiancée visits you on Tuesdays, of which today is one, at the office for lunch. Does she not? Tonight is the festival of bells at Wembley—the sort of thing people of your inclination and tastes delight in. The parchment was watermarked—clear to see when held up to the fire—with roses, a common ladies' selection at Fenton's Stationery, which is a short distance to her house, and the penmanship delicate and precise, as is your fiancée's preference.

"Watson!" shouts Holmes at his friend, whose face still betrays confusion. "She means to invite you on a lovely stroll this evening to listen to the bells! Your intellect dazzles me at times, my dear friend."

Given Watson's circumstances, it was not unreasonable for him to be concerned the note could be a threat. Without Holmes identifying all the evidence to point toward a different meaning, that communication was not clear. We don't usually have Sherlock Holmes with us when communicating, unfortunately. Perhaps if we did, there would be no miscommunication. But, alas, we don't, and so there is lots of miscommunication.

Josh periodically speaks to business school audiences or other young professionals and a common question he gets is "What advice do you have for us?" One of the answers he almost always gives is this belief from NLP: *The meaning of your communication is the response you get.*

You can think of this belief as a special case of *there's no failure, only feedback.* When communication "fails," you can learn to take it as feedback, and course-correct. We gave it its own chapter because it is so useful for communicating well with other people, and most things in life involve communicating with other people.

In fact, we'll go so far as to say that we believe that many, if not most, communication issues dissolve when you take this belief to heart.

Have you ever been involved in a disagreement that went something like this?

"You clearly said [X]."

"Oh, but that's obviously not what I meant."

Who's right? Both? Neither? Great communicators know that the truth is it doesn't really matter, because neither answer is useful if you want to communicate effectively. What is useful, on the other hand, is to pay attention to what actually has been communicated—not what should have been communicated—and then try to move forward.

It is best to act as if the meaning of your communication is the response you get. It leads to thinking about successful communication not as making your point well, but as trying to understand whether the other party got the message you intended. People who do this are much more likely to get others' perspectives, to check in, to follow up, to treat the communication as a two-way process rather than a onetime, one-way event. They get curious about the questions "What have I actually communicated?"; "What led to that?"; "What really needs to be communicated?"; and "How else can I communicate?"

The benefits of taking on the responsibility for the message being received as intended include:

- Communicating with greater clarity much more of the time
- Shifting from giving mixed messages (e.g., body language and tone versus words) to consistent messages that people can trust
- Adapting as needed to any audience

And, when communications don't go as initially hoped:

- Shifting from blame to problem-solving
- Shifting from assuming what others think and feel to finding out
- Letting go of anger and defensiveness when others suggest we had bad intentions or communicated poorly
- Finding it easier to say sorry and move on
- Spending less effort and time arguing over who is right

Let's flip it around—that often helps bring the message home. Suppose you feel you've been insulted or treated poorly. You get upset in response.

How do you feel when the person who insulted you or treated you poorly tries to argue why you shouldn't be offended, or you're just being too fragile, or it's really your fault it all happened anyway?

It doesn't really open you up to having a thoughtful and productive conversation, does it? But if they accepted your understanding of reality and shared some responsibility, you'd respond much better, wouldn't you?

Here's an example that may feel familiar to a lot of people. It's about the struggles between two partners in a relationship—we'll call them Noah and Kim. Noah, seeing that the sink has been left a mess with bits of food in it, says, "Can you please try to wash out the bits of food from the sink when you're done cleaning dishes?" Kim snaps at Noah, "It's never enough. Nothing's ever enough for you," and storms out of the room.

What just happened?!

Noah probably thought it was annoying that the sink was a mess. Let's assume he had brought this up a number of times before, too. He thought he was asking her to take his request seriously and remember to clean it. Despite what Noah thought he was communicating, however, what Kim received was "I don't care what you've done [e.g., clean the dishes], it's never going to be enough. In fact, nothing you can do will ever be enough."

Noah has a choice—option one is to try to explain why Kim shouldn't be upset and why it's her fault she took his message wrong. Option two is to accept that she took the message the way she did, and treat it as his responsibility. We're not interested here in which is fundamentally right. What we want to draw attention to is how different Noah's next move is likely to be in the two cases. Let's take a look at each and you can decide which you think will help Noah get his needs met.

CHOOSING OPTION ONE, Noah follows Kim and, through a closed door, shouts all the reasons why it's understandable that he would say that, and she shouldn't be mad. He asks her to please not be mad and not make a big deal out of this. "How does this possibly mean you're never enough?" he asks, rhetorically. "That's crazy."

CHOOSING OPTION TWO, Noah walks to the closed door and says, "Sorry. You are much more than enough. I really appreciate that you did the dishes, by the way. I should have said that. If you feel like talking, let me know."

Unless Noah is looking for a fight, option two should be the better path for getting just about any positive outcome.

This is not an occasional issue that comes up, either. All of us miscommunicate, probably many times a day. When you understand a bit more about how the mind works, you start to realize that you should expect that your intended message will not land as you imagined most of the time. That's not a bad thing or a good thing. It's just a thing. But it is a thing, so there's no point wishing it wasn't.

For our purposes, the key lesson is that just because you said something, don't expect that others got it the way you intended. In fact, playing the odds, you should assume they only got part of the intended message, at best. What they did get had a lot to do with their mental filters.

A great example of mental filters are what psychologists call cognitive biases. These include the unconscious biases that many people have probably heard of that are often addressed with inclusion and diversity work, as well as many more forms of bias in our thinking. Scientists have been studying cognitive bias for half a century, including work that has received the Nobel Prize.[1] The main takeaway as far as we're concerned here is that our biases *bias* how we perceive the world. A classic example is called the confirmation bias. All people—anyone with a brain in their head, because it is just how brains and minds work—make use of this bias when taking in new information. The confirmation bias works like this: We always start out with some beliefs about the way things should be. Then we pay attention to information that *confirms* our beliefs, and delete or discount information that doesn't fit with our beliefs.[2] It happens unconsciously—we just think we're being reasonable. So, for instance, if someone thinks all the drivers in Los Angeles are bad drivers, they will pay lots of attention to, and remember, those cars that did something unsafe on the highway, and will pay little attention to the vast majority who drive safely.

There is a host of other biases—dozens have been researched[3]—that illustrate the ways our beliefs, emotions, attitudes, expectations, stereotypes, and so many other factors both conscious and unconscious filter the information we allow in, and what we take it to mean.

It leads to situations like these: An expert hears a message, gets worried based on what they heard, and says, "Do you realize what this means?" and the other person doesn't, of course, or the expert wouldn't need to say that. Or vice versa, the novice gets freaked out and the expert reassuringly says, "This is just a bump in the road." How could they take such different meaning from the same input? The background knowledge and experience they have colors—or biases—what information they notice and what they take that information to mean.

Fortunately, there is a useful solution for communicating well even when your intended message may not be getting through as planned—presume that the meaning of your communication is the response you get. Take that responsibility and you will take the right steps to find out what you are communicating and ultimately get the right messages across.

Greg makes a living communicating. He daily communicates with clients, insurance adjusters, lawyers, judges, and juries. The way a message is received will determine his clients' future, which could include prison or millions of dollars. The stakes are high, and Greg understands that the responsibility for the ultimate message is his. When we say responsibility, we don't mean blame. We mean ownership, we mean taking command of what you communicate. Not just hoping for the best. Greg finds that this belief takes him out of victim consciousness by taking away his ability to blame the listener for "not getting it" and places him squarely in the role of creating the narrative.

Greg understands that effective communication requires planning. Words make a difference. He is very conscious of the actual language that he uses when trying to convey a message. For example, "You are mistaken" and "You are wrong" can convey a similar message, but will likely have a different effect on the recipient. Greg also uses tone and tempo to better convey his intent. Since early childhood, we have been conditioned to react differently to quick and loud talkers as opposed to the slow and quiet ones. Our body language also impacts how our message is received. Some gestures, like hands on hips or the pointing finger, often appear aggressive and can elicit a different reaction than if we stand with our arms wide open as we address our intended audience. Rather than hoping for the best or trying to guess what will work, often before an important presentation Greg will present to a focus group to find out if the response that he gets from the audience is likely to be the one he actually intends.

In short, don't assume that what you're putting down is what they're picking up. Get curious about what's actually coming across, and ask for feedback. If you see that you are losing your audience, ask a question. "You seem unconvinced. Are you not convinced?" "Is there a disconnect?" "What is your take on this?" These are just a few of many questions available to us to gauge how our message is doing. With the knowledge you'll gain, you'll find it far easier to communicate what needs to be said.

To make this belief your own, follow these three mental steps:

1. Be open to the fact that you always communicate something, whether you know it or not. In other words, recognize that everything is a message.
2. Shift your intention from communicating your point to finding out what you have communicated.
3. Get curious—both about what is and is not being communicated, and what the situation looks like from the other side that could make sense of that.

Many readers will find it helpful to take a moment at this point to think about how to put these ideas into practice. You can start by calling to mind a difficult or important conversation. It could be one that happened recently and isn't resolved, is ongoing, or is coming up. For example, perhaps there is some feedback you'd like to give someone and you don't know whether they'll take it well.

What message would you like for this person (or people) to get?

What is one way they could take it wrong or get upset as a result?

Picture yourself in that conversation—in your mind's eye, imagine seeing them or hearing them get upset or taking it wrong.

Now imagine trying to find out what you have communicated. What happens when you get curious about what the situation looks like from their side?

What would you do or say if you understood their perspective and took responsibility for having communicated what they thought you communicated?

How will you be more likely to get the conversation to a good outcome when you take this approach?

Given how easy it is to communicate something besides what we intend, the best way forward is to stop deluding yourself into thinking others must understand you all the time. Instead, this NLP belief invites you to discover what you actually communicate, and to take responsibility for that.

IF AT FIRST I DON'T SUCCEED, I MUST TRY *SOMETHING ELSE*

W e expect that many readers will see the first half of this chapter title and think we're going to finish with "I must try again" or "I must try harder." Trying again or trying harder is fine advice in some circumstances. It's not this advice, however. Instead, the end of this chapter title is "I must try something else."

The advice to try something else is based on one of NLP's more counterintuitive ideas—*in any system, the element with the most flexibility exerts the most influence.* Some people think that being flexible means that other people can walk all over you. Sometimes people equate being flexible with being passive, always giving up your agenda for what others need. Many people intuitively think that the one with the most grit, or the one who sticks to their guns, or the one who refuses to budge is the one who gets their way. In the movies that makes for a nice narrative, but in real life those situations are rare. Most of the time, the person who is able to adapt to the situation on the ground is the one who gets their needs met.

Everyone has had the experience of trying to get through traffic to an appointment on time. If you only know one route, you need to just take that route and hope for the best. Back in the days before GPS, if you knew a lot of routes, you could try an alternative (and it felt great to think you were outsmarting other drivers). Now, with GPS, we can be even more flexible (even if we don't feel like we're outsmarting anyone)—GPS can even find routes that might have been longer at a different time of day, but because of traffic, are faster now. Captured in this simple experience is the idea that being flexible can make you more likely to meet your needs.

The attitude to have in mind is this—if what you're doing is not getting the result you want, try something else. And then something else, and then something else, and so on. As Albert Einstein said, "Insanity is doing the same thing over and over and expecting different results." We'll go out on a limb and share that we think Einstein was a bright guy. It stands to reason from his point that it would be saner to try something different—be flexible in your approach—if you want to see a different result. Note that this is a little different from the classic trope that success is 1 percent inspiration and 99 percent perspiration. Of course persistence matters, but that oversimplifies and can lead to the equivalent of banging your head against a wall to try to get it to move. If you want your persistence to pay off, make sure to keep learning, adapting, and trying something different as you go.

Anyone can do it. Josh's young son succeeded at this, getting his father to agree to something he was planning to say no to. It was after dinner on a school night. The family had built a fort in the living room earlier and it was still up. His son really wanted to keep it up and sleep in it overnight. Josh said, "Sorry, not tonight. I don't want the living room to be a mess in the morning. And I don't think you'll sleep all night if you sleep here, so I'll get woken up." Josh was just grasping at straws, but the point was that he knew it was a bad idea and was just trying to come up with reasons. His son persisted in asking and Josh persisted in saying no. Then his son changed his approach. If he promised to clean it all up in the morning, could he? No. He changed again—if he got ready for bed really fast, could he? No. But rather than getting attached to any of these ideas, he tried something else and changed his approach again. "Could I climb in and pretend to sleep for fifteen minutes, and then we can take it down before bed?" This meant a slightly later bedtime than Josh had been insisting on, but still manageable for Josh. Bedtime would go fast enough, and there would be no mess within an hour. Ultimately, his son's need for the fantasy of sleeping in a fort was what mattered to him most. He let other things go and paid good attention to his own needs and Josh's stated needs. His son got his needs met and it was a good and memorable evening for both. Josh even climbed in to pretend to sleep for a bit, too. It was really cozy.

The Cambridge English dictionary defines flexibility as (1) the ability to bend or to be bent easily without breaking; or (2) the ability to change or be changed easily according to the situation.

Notice "without breaking" and "according to the situation." These phrases are where the power sits. Life happens. We don't always get what we want. But, as the Rolling Stones advised, "If you try sometimes, you just might find you get what you need . . . oh, yeah." Every situation is unique to some degree, so what worked in the past may not work in the present. The person who is able to stay open to what the present situation has to offer can adapt to meet that situation.

Research shows that people who are more psychologically flexible perform better at their jobs, and experience better mental health.[1] Researchers have also explored a host of mechanisms by which this happens. It seems the way it works is that a person gains clarity about what they value, and then learns to be flexible in the path to get there. The people who do it best get good at accepting the facts of their circumstances rather than resisting them. They are the ones who can most nimbly find a way to pursue what they value. This approach is the cornerstone of a form of well-researched therapy called acceptance and commitment therapy, or ACT. ACT performs reliably well in controlled studies at helping improve mental well-being and coping with difficulties across a fairly broad range of contexts and cultures.[2] It is the kind of psychological flexibility taught in ACT that we are inviting you to take on as well. You commit to something you value, and you accept—or at least learn to tolerate—and adapt flexibly to whatever life throws at you as you pursue it.

For example, suppose you value supporting your family. You might have a goal of connecting with your sister every few weeks. At times this will be easy and joyful. But at other times this will require you to carve out precious work hours when busy, or tolerate some negative feelings about something she did. It may mean finding ways to engage with her in-laws who have whack-a-doodle political beliefs. It may mean a late-night call when she needs someone to talk to. If you commit to the goal that you value highly of supporting your sister, you will succeed best if you are able to accept the changing situation you find yourself in, and be flexible in how you go about achieving that goal. If you are inflexible in how you go about it, you might insist she call at a reasonable hour every time, or insist she find ways to invite you over without the in-laws more often. It's easy to see how you would connect with your sister less often in that case, isn't it?

To be flexible in pursuit of a goal yourself, try this: Call to mind a goal you're working on. It could be the goal from chapter 1, or something else (e.g., "I want to create a digital version of my classes to sell").

Now think through these steps:

Step 1: Clarify your ultimate need.

What is the reason you want to achieve your goal? In other words, why is it important to you? Another way of asking is, what's the ultimate need you're trying to serve? For example, "I want to find a way to generate some passive income."

Step 2: Accept your situation.

What's one problem or challenge to getting your goal? For example, "My partner thinks we should go in a different direction."

Step 3: Flex.

Holding that ultimate need in mind, what other ideas do you already have about how to get there? Some people might say, "I don't know." Well, in that case, answer this instead: If you did know, what do you think might be some ways to get there? For example, passive income can come from subscriptions, rent, licenses, or other digital assets besides digital classes.

Some readers could look at the example we gave and say, "Sure, you were flexible about some things, but you were still being rigid about the ultimate need—to find some way to have passive income." This is an important consideration. Were we being rigid? That comes down to your approach when you can't meet your need. We cannot always meet our needs or attain those things we most care about. In those cases, we try to accept that we can't. A great way to do so is to reconnect with an even higher need. For instance, if passive income is not possible for you in the near future, you can appeal to the reason why it was important to you—perhaps to work less and enjoy your life more. Well, there are many other ways to meet that need of working less and enjoying life more. The key is to get in touch with what you ultimately care about (your values), so you can most easily roll with what your situation offers you.[3]

Let's look at another situation to see this in action, in a real, day-to-day professional context, one that Greg finds himself in regularly. Greg is aiming to convince a judge of his position.

Step 1: Clarify your ultimate need.
Greg's ultimate need: he wants the judge to rule in his favor.

When Greg is conscious of his destination, he can be more flexible about what really matters in the end, and alternative ways to get there. Note that in the way he frames this aim to himself, he frees himself from being too attached to any one legal argument, style of presentation, or set of assumptions about how to make that happen. Greg holds this aim in mind as he works, so he can reorient when setbacks occur.

Step 2: Accept your situation.
In this line of work, the specific judge can make a big difference. So Greg should aim to understand his audience in order to accept and adapt to his situation.

For example, Greg can become curious about the following:

a. "Who am I communicating with?" The judge has a reputation in this district for being very detailed. Greg has a history with presenting in her courtroom and has found that she insists on precision and sticking to the facts. She also cares about being spoken to with deference, in tone and language.
b. "What does she want?" Greg can feel confident of at least one thing—she ultimately wants to make a fair ruling and not be overturned on appeal.

Step 3: Flex.

Here, Greg will start seeking to create rapport with the judge. He aims to communicate that he also values what she does—by offering details, and speaking with deference. He aims to notice how she reacts, and if he is not succeeding, he changes the way he addresses her—verbally, and with his body language.

Then Greg will aim to make respectful, cogent legal arguments, based on sound legal principles. Usually, Greg will have several cohesive arguments to back up his main one if it fails. As the interaction unfolds, Greg will be open to what he hears, and think about alternative pathways. So, for instance, if the judge rules that Greg can't use the word "orange," Greg is flexible enough to offer "citrus," "fruit," or "great source of vitamin C" as an alternative.

In these ways, if Greg can be the element in the courtroom with the most flexibility, he can exert the most influence. If at first you don't succeed, don't just try again; keep your larger needs in mind and try something else.

8

ASSUME GOOD INTENTIONS

Josh was standing in front of a group of leaders from across various organizations, teaching a one-hour session at a conference. A woman in the audience interrupted and made a statement. The gist of it was, "This is irrelevant for me. It's not useful or realistic." A short time later, she asked another question, and again another. Each time, she sounded dismissive and like she was annoyed to be hearing what she was hearing. Each time, Josh took a moment to acknowledge her concerns, understand her resistance, and offer a useful answer, without getting too sidetracked for the rest of the audience. Finally, it got to a point where Josh felt it was becoming a distraction for others there. So he paused and said to the woman, "It seems to me like you are very interested in figuring out whether these ideas can be useful for you. You seem to be putting a lot of effort into that, and are not yet seeing how it can work." At this point, her tone shifted. Josh had won her over. She clarified that she very much believed in the general ideas, but really struggled with whether she could apply them or would be met with too much resistance in her organization. The exchange helped the whole audience get more out of the session.

What Josh did was search for her positive intention in being disruptive, sounding negative, or acting dismissive. He spoke to her positive intention, not just to what she said and did on the surface. People don't put in the effort to ask questions or pose challenges if they are not trying to work out in their head whether something makes sense. There is a positive motivation behind it to understand and assess the value of what they are hearing.

In NLP, there is a belief you can bring to every encounter in life that will dramatically improve your likelihood of getting past difficulties. The belief is that *every behavior has a positive intention.*

Whenever you encounter resistance, get curious about the other person's positive intention first.

Do this in a meeting, in a relationship, when doing sales, in a negotiation, when arguing a legal case, when teaching a class, while talking with your kids—really any situation where you are met with resistance.

Sometimes that resistance comes from inside. You may want to start a business, for example. But a part of you keeps sabotaging your hopes by saying it won't work, or telling yourself you don't have what it takes.

The same applies in all these circumstances. Get curious—what is the positive intention in that resistance or that self-sabotage?

The claim here is not that sometimes there is a positive intention. It is that *every* behavior has a positive intention. That word "every" is going to make some readers resist the idea. Could it really be *every* behavior? What about times when someone is just flat out being a jerk, or seems to be lying to try to win a court case, or bullying your kid at school, or being a condescending and micromanaging boss? Those are obviously bad things and sometimes they are done just to be mean . . . right?

It's true that people can be mean. It's true that people do try to hurt others. We're not saying those things don't happen. We're saying that at some level, there's a positive intention driving that bad behavior, and if you put in the effort to find that positive intention, you have a powerful tool.

Let's unpack some of these examples to help with that.

- *A witness appears to be lying to try to win a court case.* Lying is a shady thing to do in most circumstances, in just about anyone's book. It can be cruel, heartless, unethical. All of that is true. In a legal proceeding and under oath, it's especially egregious. But even in this extreme situation, there is a positive intention behind it. Very few liars lie for the sake of lying. There is usually an outcome that the witness is trying to achieve, and unfortunately, they feel that such an outcome is not attainable without resorting to lying. They may want to avoid jail time so they can spend more time with their kids, avoid losing money so they can have a good retirement, or save face so people they care about will still like them. They may even be lying to themself so they can maintain a positive self-image. Spending time with kids, having a good retirement, having people like you, maintaining a good self-image—these are all positive things.

- *A bully at school.* The bully often feels mad at the world. They've often been treated poorly by someone else and felt powerless. Bullying someone can make them feel powerful. It might even win them other bully friends. But it's a terrible way to feel powerful and make friends. At the same time, wanting to feel powerful and to make friends are positive things.

- *A condescending and micromanaging boss.* Anytime you show your work, the comments are always, "Why is this part done so poorly?" or "How could you have messed this piece of it up after we talked about this?" or some message like that. It's a bad way to lead. But the intention is probably that the boss wants to have control over the outcome, and to make sure the quality will always be consistent. Aiming for quality control and consistency are positive things for a boss to want.

- *Self-sabotage.* You may want to start a business, but you keep giving up on the idea when you tell yourself you don't have what it takes. Your positive intention is probably to make sure you are financially stable, or to be a responsible adult in your own and others' eyes. Being financially stable and responsible are positive things.

We are not saying that bad behavior is okay or should be tolerated. What we are saying is that people rarely act out purely for the purpose of hurting the other person. People generally don't lie for the sake of lying, steal for the sake of stealing, or bully people for the sake of bullying.

The problem for the lying witness, the bully, the boss, and the part of you sabotaging yourself is not that they (or you) are inherently flawed and bad people. In fact, they and you all are motivated by positive intentions. The problem is that they and you are going about getting those positive things in bad ways. Good intention; not a good way of going about it.

So, how do we find the positive intention? We suggest using the question "Why is it important?" Below is an example of how to find the positive intention with a lying witness in a legal proceeding.

Why is it important to the witness to lie? Because she wants to win the trial. Why is it important to the witness to win the trial? Because she does not want to go to jail. Why is it important to the witness to avoid jail? Because she wants to make sure that her family is provided for. And here, it seems like we've landed on what sounds like a highly important and motivating positive intention—to make sure her family is provided for.

By changing our view of the witness from a liar to a concerned family member, we are able to see where her mind is and what motivates her. We can leverage this information to guide and motivate her to alter her behavior to move in a positive direction. By using the simple question "Why is it important?" we are able to home in on what the witness really desires below the surface. If you keep asking "Why is it important?" you can get to the positive intention behind why the witness, or anyone else, is doing what they're doing.

Find a way to serve the positive intention, and you can change those behaviors.

To see this in another context, consider the boss example. Maybe you have a boss like the one we described. Maybe you manage someone who acts like this to their employees. Maybe you are coaching a boss like this. Or maybe you are a boss like this. No matter which of these is true, you can go a long way by searching for that positive intention. Once you are clear on the positive intention, the next step is within anyone's control with some effort. Help that boss find an alternative approach to getting the positive outcome they seek.

The boss's positive intentions are quality control and consistency. When you uncover that, you can help her find a better way to work toward that positive intention. Until now, she has been getting exactly the opposite of what she truly wants. When she acts in that critical and micromanaging way, she has made her employees feel disengaged. Whatever intrinsic motivation the work had for them initially, after being treated that way by the boss a few times, they got the message that they were not respected. They came to feel that only the boss mattered and believed she would never see their true value. They started to think of the work as just a paycheck. At that point, they began to care less and put in less effort, so more errors were likely to show up in their work.

A better way to achieve quality control and consistency would be one that does not cause all the disengagement and resentment. For example, many successful bosses who achieve quality control and consistency—but don't micromanage—focus more on the system than on the specific pieces of work people produce. They put their efforts into creating a system in which the boss's judgment about good and bad quality isn't needed; a system that anyone qualified who is in the job could follow. The boss lays out the goals, and the principles for deciding what is good and bad, the must-have steps to take, and then steps back while others meet those goals, apply those principles, and take those steps using their own judgment. Note that this is just one answer. We don't have to have all the answers, but it helps to have a method for finding a good answer. The method we're offering you here is to speak to their positive intention. Speaking to the positive intention opens the doors to creative breakthroughs.

The same principle applies when it comes to inner resistance—e.g., the person who is sabotaging their own business dreams. To make progress, he must honor how important being financially stable and responsible are to him. Starting a business is not black and white. There are shades of gray. He can consider ways to take smaller, safer risks as he takes the first steps in the business before he takes bigger steps, if and when he becomes ready.

This idea of looking for the positive intention behind a behavior echoes ideas that go all the way back to Freud's time in psychotherapy. Freud talked about "defense mechanisms" like denial. Being in denial wasn't just something self-destructive a person did—it was something meant to protect them from certain thoughts and feelings. Protecting them is a positive intention. Understanding that protective intention was useful in finding breakthroughs, and in finding more adaptive ways to self-protect.

In the 1950s, chair work—popularized by Gestalt therapy—was introduced, and its success led to it being incorporated in various ways across many of the different modes of therapy since.[1] There's a version for internal conflict—i.e., when a part of you wants to do something but another part of you doesn't. In that case, it is possible to let the different parts of you talk it out. As if it were different people sitting down to talk, each part of you gets treated, metaphorically, like a person with a seat at the table. Each part, metaphorically, takes a different chair and turns toward the other to speak their point of view. It's a metaphor, of course. But people are pretty good at acting as if there are two different people talking it out. Each part listens thoughtfully and seeks to understand the other side. Then you can find a way to accept each part, and the value they bring you, and stop fighting with yourself.

This idea of self-acceptance shows up across many areas of successful psychotherapies. Once you accept yourself, it turns out, you can become more likely to change.[2] Finding the positive intention can be a great tool for self-acceptance, because it helps you move away from inappropriate negative self-judgments.[3]

As a simple example of this in everyday life, Josh found at one point that he was putting on weight. The solution was obvious, but he wasn't doing it. He had gotten into the habit of eating dessert after dinner each night—ice cream, cookies, cake. If it was not in the house, he wouldn't eat it, but he kept buying it, and kept being frustrated by how his clothes fit. Part of him wanted to stop eating dessert. But part of him kept wanting it, and that part, which he saw as the saboteur, was winning. He rationalized it as just being tired at night. He tried to convince himself to just put up with it—doesn't everyone get heavier as they get older? But he kept feeling frustrated by the weight. Eventually, he paused to listen to the different parts of himself. One side he knew well said, "Stop eating dessert and you'll feel good about how you look and feel. It's easy. Just do it." The other side was a bit of a surprise to him. When he took a moment to listen, Josh discovered that the saboteur had positive intentions—he wanted the fun to continue at the end of the night, and he felt like he deserved a reward after a hard day. Once Josh understood those positive intentions, he set his mind to finding new solutions. Starting that very night, all he did when it came time for dinner to end was to ask himself, "How will I have fun tonight, and how can I reward myself after a hard day?" With that, he found it much easier to skip dessert and started taking advantage of his evenings in better ways, too. He took off the weight within a month and kept it off, and hasn't had much dessert since.

A version of this concept has made its way into a number of professional domains, too—it goes by the name of secondary gain. It has been a valuable asset to doctors and lawyers, among others, in understanding why certain behaviors persist that may be causing problems for the very person doing them. Patients will sometimes fail to take care of themselves because they want more time with their doctor or therapist. While being unwell is a loss, it has a secondary gain—as a result of staying unwell, they get attention. Getting attention from these caretakers is the positive intention.

As a lawyer, Greg can attest that lawyers who consider secondary gain can have a real advantage. Real trials are different from the way they are depicted on TV or in movies. During his thirty years of trial practice, Greg has rarely seen a witness recant her testimony and admit to lying on the witness stand when confronted. However, if the examining lawyer is open to understanding the witness's positive intention while exposing the lie, the lawyer can score major points in front of the judge or jury by showing compassion to the witness, while discrediting the witness's testimony.

Try this right now. Remember a recent time when your partner, one of your kids, or someone close to you said something to you in an annoyed or angry tone.

At this moment, you can step back from that memory and think about what the positive intention was behind it. What was the positive intention?

Ask yourself, "Why was that important to them to say or do?" as many times as it takes to get the answer.

Perhaps they shouted at you to hurry up or you'd be late to an event. Why was it important to them to do it? Was it to make sure you got somewhere on time? Was it to feel stress-free? Was it because they wanted to share some special time with you, and wanted to be in a good mood for it? Likely they made it hard to be stress-free and enjoy the special time. But the intent was there. Everyone has something worthwhile they are trying to do—they don't just set out to suck.

How does it affect you to see that positive intention?

Next time they do something similar, and you remember that positive intention, what will you do or say differently?

9

IF I KNEW THEN WHAT I KNEW THEN

Warning: if you follow the guidance in this book, you will likely make many changes in your life. When you do, you may look back and think something like this: "How could I have been such an idiot in the past?" Since that will likely come up for many readers, it's worth getting ahead of it now.

We'll offer you one last foundational belief. It is relevant if you have ever felt shame, cringed at your past actions or decisions, or dwelled on the past, second-guessing your decisions and criticizing yourself. Hey, it's cool—we all do it sometimes. Josh sometimes gets so lost in rehashing an old embarrassing episode that he doesn't realize he's doing it until he says something out loud as if he were back in the conversation. Then when his wife hears, she has a blast poking fun at him (which often helps him laugh at himself, too, after he stops being embarrassed he was talking to himself).

People inflict these feelings of embarrassment and self-loathing thoughts on themselves with the best of intentions—e.g., to avoid similar mistakes or missteps. But the effect is that it often stops us from trying new things. It's a miserable experience. And it drains a ton of energy and attention. It's a seriously unpleasant punishment we give ourselves. So, a really common reaction to this kind of self-punishment is just to steer clear of things where we might feel that way afterward. As a result, it is a serious impediment to change and personal growth.

The foundational NLP belief that we'll introduce in this chapter can be a big help. It's this: *People behave in the best ways they know how and make the best choices they can, given their mental model of the world.* Remember that their mental model includes their understanding of the situation they find themselves in, their feelings, their values, their beliefs about their capabilities, how they think others would react, and so on. Given that mental model, people always take the best choice of action psychologically available to them. But also remember, the mental model keeps changing as we go through life. We make progress in life by expanding and enriching our mental models.

In his coaching, Josh sometimes finds his clients looking back after some positive work and wincing at the thought of their old habits, saying something like, "If I knew then what I know now . . ." Josh offers them instead the necessarily true reframe: "If you knew then what you knew then, you'd do it exactly the same."

You can try on this reframe right now yourself. Think of something from the past where you wish you had done things differently.

What changes when you remember, "If I knew then what I knew then, I'd do it exactly the same"?

What happens when you take this to heart: "Given my mental model of the world back then, I behaved in the best way I knew how, and made the best choices I knew how"?

For many people, what happens is a combination of self-compassion and a readiness to let go of the past. They tend to shift their attention to the gains they've made and feel better about making changes.

The same kind of thing happens when we apply this belief to others who we are trying to help make a change. When we believe that they behave in the best way they know how, and make the best choices available to them given their mental model of the world, we are likely to approach them in ways that help them change.

This belief trains your attention on understanding their mental model and helping to enrich or expand it. And it takes your attention away from just being annoyed with them or giving up on them. It gives you that extra reason to dig deep and try to unpack the mental model in which their behavior and choices actually are their best options. This will help you find the positive intention behind their behavior. And it will do more, as the positive intention is just one component of the mental model.

For example, Josh was once coaching a high-level executive of a company who had a reputation as being someone you didn't want to work for—she could be harsh. Some people were fine with her, but it took a toll on other employees' morale and was causing friction. The company didn't want to lose her, though, because she was extremely valuable in driving some of the business units that brought in the lion's share of their revenue. The sponsors of the coaching work did a 360 and a bunch of measurements in an effort to give her greater awareness of how she was perceived. It turned out, however, that she had excellent awareness. Her own scores and answers were spot-on with everyone else's. Awareness wasn't the issue. In Josh's experience, it seldom is, actually.

So, Josh got curious about what kind of mental model made sense of the situation. How could it be the case that she was fully aware of exactly how she behaved and the choices she made—even how that affected others—and yet did those things and made those choices anyway? Of the many relevant things that emerged, one important belief was "I'm the only one that gets shit done around here. This is what you have to do to get shit done. People might not like it, but it works." And it did work for what the company most needed her to do. No one else in the company had done, or could do, what she could to run the business. After many years that was well understood by most people involved.

The only way she knew how to make the business as successful as it was involved behaving how she had been behaving. Because Josh took this approach with her—presupposing that this company executive was behaving in the best way given her mental model—Josh was able to win her respect and build rapport. The company executive felt understood, appreciated, and like she was not being asked to choose between profit and being nice. Josh focused on what she was succeeding at doing, and how important that was, and honored the fact that neither she nor anyone else had found a better way at that company yet. And through this approach, Josh was able to open her up to wanting to experiment with new ways to get her needs met. She took to it quickly and within months had made major changes to how she led. Years later, the company was still very happy to have retained her, profits were strong under her, and most people who worked under her wanted to be on her team. Even some people she had to give bad news to continued to have good relationships with her.

In psychotherapy, there is a concept called unconditional positive regard. The idea is that if the therapist appreciates, respects, seeks to empathize and really understand the other person's perspective, and has compassion for them and their situation—no matter how the patient behaves—that is a strong predictor of successful therapy. And across multiple studies, there's a reliable, meaningful effect where unconditional positive regard predicts successful change.[1]

This NLP belief is one way to help you appreciate, respect, seek to empathize with and understand the other person's mental model, and have compassion for them in any context. In other words, this belief may help you have unconditional positive regard. We believe you'll find that those things flow from embracing this belief.

At this point, we've covered a number of beliefs and their implications. Here's a quick cheat sheet so you can see it all in one place:

CHAPTER 2: How We Experience the World Is Not the Same as Reality
If you want to see change, understand and enrich someone's mental model.

CHAPTER 3: Why Not Me?
If it's possible for someone else, it's possible for me, because I can learn from their mental model.

CHAPTER 4: All I Need Is Already Within Me
Everyone has the resources to meet their next developmental challenge. This means we can always take the next step toward our goals, at every stage.

CHAPTER 5: There's No Failure, Only Feedback

There is no such thing as failure. Everything is an experiment, and all outcomes are useful if you choose to take them as feedback for course-correction.

CHAPTER 6: How My Message Landed Matters More than What I Meant

The meaning of your communication is indicated by the response you get. Be curious about what you actually communicated, not just what you intended.

CHAPTER 7: If at First I Don't Succeed, I Must Try *Something Else*

The person who is most flexible is most likely to get their needs met. Commit to what's important to you ultimately, and be flexible in how you get there.

CHAPTER 8: Assume Good Intentions

Every behavior has a positive intention. Speak to the positive intention and you can get past resistance.

CHAPTER 9: If I Knew Then What I Knew Then

People make the best choices and behave in the best ways they know how given their mental models of the world. Aim to discover why someone's behavior makes sense in the context of their mental model, and you will be well on the way to meaningful change.

These beliefs together can be taken as a mindset you can travel through life with. To help this mindset sink in a bit more, it may be helpful to pause and reflect on several things. These questions can help you make these beliefs more accessible in your mind from day to day.

Which of these beliefs have you found yourself thinking about the most, or putting to use?

If you put a belief to use, what was different from how things used to be before you had this belief in mind?

Have you told anyone else about any of these beliefs? If so, why?

Pick one (or more) belief that has resonated for you.

a. How would you describe it to someone else?
b. Why is it valuable to believe this? How does it benefit you? How does it change your thoughts, feelings, or behaviors in a useful way?

NLP contains more foundational beliefs than the eight we've shared.[2] The others largely are variations on these themes. The nuances in these variations can be valuable. But we've highlighted these eight because we believe that together they can make you limitless, and they tap into what we see as the key aspects of the broader wisdom of NLP's foundational beliefs.

What comes in the next section of this book is a set of tools for discovering someone's mental model of a situation. They enable you to understand someone quickly and deeply, getting at the stuff that really guides their thoughts, feelings, and behaviors. The eight foundational beliefs not only have value in and of themselves, but they'll also enable you to use the coming tools most effectively.

HOW TO UNDERSTAND SOMEONE'S MIND

You're about to learn ten tools for quickly discovering some-one's mental model of the world, one in each chapter of this section. The first one—be curious about their mental model—is like the key to the front door of someone's mind. The remaining nine specifically help unlock the different rooms inside.

Also, a quick welcome to those readers who are starting the book here—we know some of you want to get right to the concrete tools you can use to understand people quickly. The book is designed for that, also, so you should find these tools accessible and valuable without any background. There's a glossary at the end of the book, as well, in case you want to quickly look up a term. After learning these tools, you may want to go back and read about the foundational beliefs in section 1. These were mind-blowing and eye-opening for us when we learned them. Whether or not you have that reac-tion, though, they will help you use these tools masterfully, and will multiply what you are able to do with them.

10

BE CURIOUS ABOUT THEIR MENTAL MODEL

Curiosity may have killed the cat, but people aren't cats. A healthy curiosity about another person's view of the world will allow us to be more flexible in our encounters, and consequently make us better communicators. If you simply got curious about someone's experience and perspective and asked questions, you'd go far.

As this section of the book progresses, we'll do much more, however, and point you toward specifically which things to ask questions about that bear the most fruit. But first, we'd like to help you take on the right attitude of deep, open, unattached curiosity that great NLPers adopt. That attitude will help you at every step of the way.

Steven Leeds, one of the directors at the NLP Center of New York, will sometimes do a demo when teaching an NLP technique. He's been practicing and teaching NLP for forty years and is truly a master. It can seem like magic how he seems to always know just the right question to ask for someone to have a breakthrough. His secret—which he happily shares—is to be curious.

A story may help us explain what Steven means, specifically, by being curious. When Josh was in his twenties he did a lot of improv comedy. Improv comedy is a show where the audience comes up with a scenario and some relationships, and then the actors just make up a whole scene right there on the spot, and it's often hilarious. It's like the TV show *Whose Line*

Is It Anyway? The way it works in a lot of comedy venues is that you take classes to learn the skill, and some people from those classes get invited to perform for the live paying audiences, or even eventually join the main group. Josh loved it but got held back. While his friends were invited to take more advanced classes and perform, he was told he wasn't ready, but could repeat the classes as often as he wanted.

To be fair, he would often come up with things that were really funny, and get both the other performers and whoever was in the audience to laugh. But that was actually the problem. He would come up with an idea, fall in love with how funny he thought it would be, and then focus on finding a way to deliver his line. He was quick, too, so he could do it a bunch of times in a single scene. It would derail the scene. It stopped the other performers from being able to do their part. The reason is that when he got attached to his own idea, he stopped noticing what was happening in the scene. Eventually, he learned that an improviser's job is not to be funny. The improviser's job is to notice what the other performers are doing and saying, and offer the next thing that seems most obvious to say or do in that moment. The context makes it funny. If you're a funny person, it will probably be a touch funnier, but it will be funny with anyone doing it well. This form of attention is a kind of radical curiosity. It's about being fully present at each moment and wondering what is coming, rather than trying to predict it or steer it.

Steven Leeds, just like everyone else, has plenty of ideas when he's working with someone—about what they think, how they really feel, how they should change their behavior, what may be the main problem that needs solving, and what will help them. But he knows that these are his ideas, not facts. He will ask whether he is right, but he stays open to any answer and honors it as a real answer.

That attitude of curiosity is central to finding out what someone else's mental model is—to finding out how they experience, understand, and think about themself and their situation. Remember that our aim in NLP is to understand someone else's mental model for a situation, because that is when we can help them find ways to change. So being curious in this way is perhaps *the* foundational skill in making all of NLP work.

This kind of curiosity is something probably all of us have experienced at some point. Remember your early childhood. What was the first question your parents asked when you were sad, upset, or crying? It was probably "What's wrong?" or "What happened?" or a variation thereof. They were genuinely curious about what happened, and their desired outcome was to make it better. When your parents did that, they understood that they could not make it better without first understanding what it was.

When Greg is interviewing a new client and wants to get hired and paid (that's how lawyers pay the bills), he needs to be curious and understand the actual outcome that the client desires. Without this understanding, Greg will be speaking to the client based on what he believes the client's model of the world to be, and sometimes—or often—be dead wrong as a result. For example, if a client's child is injured at the local playground and her goal in hiring a lawyer is to make the playground safer, promising her a large financial recovery without a pledge to actually make the playground safer may cause the client to seek different representation.

The opposite of this kind of curiosity is believing we know the answer. John C. Maxwell, a renowned American author and lecturer, said, "The greatest enemy of learning is knowing." If we believe (often erroneously) that we know something, we are more likely to disregard any information that will conflict with or challenge what we think, even if true.

It's better to let go of the need to feel you are right, and just aim to find out if you are—you'll be more effective at communication and at helping people change. You can't lose with this kind of curiosity. You either learn something new or confirm what you believed.

We are not suggesting you approach all moments in life with this level of curiosity, either. For example, a plumber who sees a clogged drain can quickly glance at the situation and then often be very effective by believing he *knows* why it is clogged. He does not need to spend time exploring all options with an open mind. Nine times out of ten it will work out. That's good for business. It saves time and he's able to be highly productive. But there are many situations in life where it pays to suspend judgment—especially when we're dealing with people.

In the earlier example we were talking about improv comedy. For improv, curiosity is practically an extreme sport. But people limit themselves by believing they have the answers or falling in love with their own ideas, in all kinds of situations, not just in improv. Here are a few that may help some readers recognize it in their own behavior:

- Have you ever found yourself waiting for someone to finish making their point so you could then make yours?
- Have you ever gone into a situation thinking you know what the problem is, and then focused your energy on showing you were right?
- Have you ever been involved in an argument and been determined to win no matter what was said?
- Have you ever been in love with your creative idea and focused your attention on getting your idea included in the final product?

These are not bad things to do or to want, per se. Everything has a time and place. But these are experiences where we have the opposite of the kind of curiosity that's needed to make NLP really work.

To bring this home a bit more, right now, you can pick one of those situations we mentioned above where you may have gotten attached to your own idea. Think about an example from your own life. For example, when you may have just waited for someone to finish talking so you could make your point.

Imagine how things would have gone had you gotten curious about what the others involved were saying or putting forward. Really curious— like you wanted to actually understand what made sense about their point of view.

What might you have learned?

How do you think it would have affected them if you had been curious in that way?

How would it have opened them up to listening more to your point, or to thoughtfully considering your ideas?

To take on deep curiosity, do what Stanford neuroscience professor Jamil Zaki—author of *The War for Kindness*—taught Josh: something called perspective getting. The typical advice we hear is that we should engage in perspective taking. Perspective taking would mean that you imagine what it is like in someone else's shoes—imagine their inner experience and what they must think and feel. But it turns out that when people try to do perspective taking what they come up with is frequently no better than guesswork. We may be able to make a little progress with perspective taking. But the real wins come when we ask what their experience is—perspective getting.[1] Perspective taking can give you some great hypotheses—for instance, "If I were in your situation, I think I'd be mad and feel like it was unfair." Perspective getting goes that extra step of asking, and being open to any answer, "Is that the case for you?"

It takes some practice, but with practice, deep curiosity is a skill we can all master. The opportunities this skill opens doors to are amazing. As with any skill, the people who master it fastest and best are often the ones who love doing it. You can learn to love being curious. It requires starting to notice when you don't fully understand, and getting excited about the opportunity to find a new way forward.

The steps include (1) learning to recognize that you don't fully understand; (2) asking questions; (3) being open to any answer; (4) updating your thinking to really incorporate what you've just learned.

For example, Josh was interested in getting better at networking and catching up with friends. So he was interviewing his friend Jake, who is great at doing that, to see what he could learn. In NLP, we'd say Josh was trying to "model" Jake. He was trying to understand Jake's mental model for catching up and networking. Then Josh could incorporate what he learned into his own mental model for networking and catching up with people. Remember the NLP presupposition—if Jake can do it, so can Josh.

One behavior Josh learned about was that Jake reaches out to people every day. Josh made a note—"need to do it every day"—and felt like he had learned something. The conversation moved on. Over the next few minutes, it dawned on Josh that he didn't know what that meant in a lot of ways. How many people? How much time does he put into it? Through what channels? Does that include people he has reached out to recently with no answer? Does that include friends and business leads, or does he mean he reaches out to business leads every day? So Josh paused the conversation and asked for clarity. It turned out the answer was twenty minutes a day. At most a few people. Mostly people he knew personally—some days friends, other days business leads, often both.

Then Josh felt his stomach tighten a bit at the prospect of having to put himself out there and carve out time for all this, even if it would really be only twenty minutes a day. It sounded stressful, and like it would be hard to know if he was succeeding or wasting time. He realized he worried about feeling foolish, too. Josh found himself assuming Jake must just be blessed with thicker skin than him. In short, as Josh tried on what he knew of Jake's model, it didn't fit. He couldn't see how to get there yet.

So Josh took a step back again and considered what he didn't know for sure. He asked Jake to hold on and to answer things like "How do you know if you're just wasting time?" and "Do you ever feel foolish? I think I would sometimes." Jake's answers were surprising for Josh, and really helped to flesh out the mental model. Regarding wasting time, Jake said he canceled meetings when he didn't think there was much value, and he didn't reach out to someone in the first place unless it was either a fun personal connection or there was something he wanted to learn. With that approach, he rarely felt like he wasted time. Regarding a thick skin, it turned out Jake was not immune from emotions. Instead, he said, he did feel foolish sometimes. But he had learned to remind himself that people are usually happy to see his name pop up. Historically, he's found that most people like him. So there was no need to feel foolish because they generally wanted to catch up with him.

To Josh, that sounded nice, but he didn't think it would work for him. He imagined telling himself, "It will be fine because most people like me," and "They'll be excited to see my name pop up." Sure enough, it didn't work. Josh just didn't believe that most people he would try to network with would be excited to hear from him. He imagined them being annoyed, and that trying to network would actually make them like him less. . . . Something didn't add up. So Josh asked, "Why do you think most people like you and would be happy to see your name pop up?" To which Jake had a ready reply, "Because I like them." Josh was glad he asked. In truth, Josh likes most people, too, and somehow this belief clicked. It made sense that if he liked them and would be happy to see their name pop up, they would probably feel the same. Now Josh felt like he could believe people usually would be happy to see his name pop up. So Josh decided to focus his outreach on people he liked, or who were introduced to him by people he liked. That seems obvious in retrospect, but was news to Josh at the time. It was one of those differences that really made a difference given Josh's previous model of the situation.

Josh also watched Jake's body language and tone of voice as he spoke. For instance, at one point, Jake gave some advice with a bit of hesitation in his voice. The advice was that it is a good idea to reach out to some cold contacts, even without an introduction, so you can expand your network more quickly. Josh picked up something as being a little off. Jake's body language and tone of voice were not congruent with the idea that this was good advice. Josh was tempted to just write down the advice and move on. But he realized he had a doubt, and instead said to Jake, "I noticed what seemed like hesitation in your voice when you said that." Jake replied that he was just trying to think of some good advice, but the truth was it wasn't part of how he regularly did things. He had tried that and it rarely worked for him, so he just did it once in a while when he had a special reason to. They had a good laugh and moved on.

What Josh was doing was to pause whenever something didn't add up. He was trying on Jake's mental model and, when it didn't work for him, he asked a question. And when Jake said something that was not congruent with his body language or with something else he had said, Josh asked a question. When Josh asked questions, he was interested in Jake's beliefs (thoughts), his emotions and motivations (feelings), and the concrete steps he took (behaviors). Some psychologists call these the three pieces of the pie—the three big components of experience—your thoughts, feelings, and behaviors.

In this example, Josh was modeling Jake. But being curious in this way is key to breakthroughs in any kind of communication: managers with employees, salespeople with leads, parents with children, partners in a relationship, lawyers with clients, and so on.

Right now, take a moment to think about a situation in your own life involving another person that you might approach with deeper curiosity. Is there some breakthrough you are seeking with someone in a work or personal context—e.g., changing employee behavior, moving a sales lead forward, getting your kid to do their homework, asking your partner for more intimacy, etc.?

You can do a little mental prep now that should serve you in the aim of staying curious about the other person's mental model whenever you do engage with them. We'll go through each of the four steps we outlined earlier in the chapter.

Step 1: Learn to recognize what you don't understand.
With that situation in mind, what are some things you don't fully understand?

Step 2: Ask questions.
What questions would help you understand better?

Step 3: Be open to any answer.
Imagine how they might answer. What happens when you accept that what they said is true for them and serves them in some positive way?

Step 4: Update your thinking to incorporate what you've just learned.
Mentally try on what you came up with in step 3. How would you operate if your mental model were more like theirs? What new questions does this bring up for you, if any?

Curiosity may kill the cat, but it makes us NLPers stronger and better. Without curiosity, we are likely doomed to a mundane existence of sameness. We're unlikely to expand our horizons without being curious as to what lies beyond them. Most great discoveries were probably preceded by a curious seeker asking him or herself, "What if?" Searching for congruence (e.g., do the words match the body language?) and asking about the pieces of the pie (thoughts, feelings, behaviors)—like Josh did with Jake—are great ways to be curious and gather useful information. However, those are just the tip of the iceberg in terms of how you can unpack a mental model.

In the chapters that come after this, we'll tell you what specifically you can be curious about in order to quickly and more fully discover someone's mental model. As you do so, you'll also see how helping them change their thoughts, feelings, and behaviors becomes much more straightforward.

11

JUST THE FACTS

There's what someone says or does, and then there's what we take it to mean; they are not the same. In this chapter, we'll share with you why and how to keep these two things separate in your mind.

Most of the time people don't separate these two things. Often, our default is to assume that whatever way we interpreted something that we saw or heard is the only way to interpret it. However, we can learn to make it our default to separate what happened from what it means. When we do, we dramatically expand our ability to understand others quickly and accurately.

Imagine you're sitting on a jury with your best friend. There is a police officer testifying—he says he saw the three accused people at the scene of the crime. Suppose you come from a long line of police officers, but your friend's father was wrongfully convicted and imprisoned because a dishonest cop lied on the stand. You both will see and hear the same witness saying the same things. Will your interpretation of what you see and hear be different? It's pretty likely.

Later on, in the jury room, you might state that it seemed like a straightforward case—after all, if an officer (someone you trust like family) actually saw the accused at the crime then what is there to wonder about? Your friend, however, looks at you like you're a traitor. He feels a great injustice is at hand and his emotions are rising. He counters that the officer (someone he automatically distrusts) was obviously lying to cover for his buddies or his own negligence. The story was thin and he had no direct evidence, he adds.

In NLP we call the things that you hear or see the sensory information. And we call what you take it to mean the interpretation.

In the courtroom example, perhaps the officer who testified said, specifically, that he saw the three people accused leave the scene of the alleged crime and flee. He also coughed and seemed to have a dry throat when he said it. Let's suppose he was looking at the ground when he said it, too. The sensory information includes his words, his cough or dry tone of voice, and the fact that he was looking at the ground. You might interpret a dry throat and looking down as discomfort at being put on the stand. Your friend might interpret the dry throat as lack of confidence because it was a made-up story, and looking down as avoiding eye gaze because it's hard to look someone in the eye when lying.

By separating the sensory information from your interpretation, you can much more effectively understand the thoughts and feelings of the people with whom you interact, and you can often change the outcome of an interaction.

Let's compare a typical approach to one in which you separate facts from interpretation. A typical approach many people take is to argue about whose interpretation is right—if you argue with your friend about whether the officer was trustworthy, it would likely lead you both to lean more heavily into your stated positions. Now your pride is on the line. People don't like losing an argument. They tend to look for ways to convince themselves they were right and that you were obviously wrong. No one likes to look bad by having come to a wrong conclusion, so both sides dig in.

However, you can much more effectively engage your friend by separating the sensory information from the interpretation.

A great way to do this is to:

1. Point out the sensory information.
2. Ask how else it could be interpreted.

It can be helpful to repeat step 2 several times, as it increases the odds they'll see new possibilities.

You might start by saying, "The officer said he saw those three leaving. You pointed out he was looking down and he coughed. How else could we interpret that—why else could he have been looking down and coughing?" Your friend might then say, "Well, he may have a cold. And maybe he looked down because he feels uncomfortable with public speaking," and, reluctantly he adds, "That's very common, actually." Ultimately, your friend may be right, you may be right, or there may be a third interpretation. By separating the sensory information—just the facts—from the interpretation, you are both more likely to recognize what filters you are seeing the situation through. You are both more likely to recognize what meaning you are projecting onto the officer's testimony. And as a result, you are both more likely to find a better way forward.

The conversation would likely lead you to realize that you could be a little more skeptical and should probably look for solid evidence to corroborate or discount the officer's story. And it may lead your friend to recognize that not all cops are the same as the one who lied about his father, and that there is other evidence he could look at to consider whether this officer's testimony is false.

Steps 1 and 2 can lead people to become more open to seeking the truth, and steer them away from getting their pride caught up in the matter.

Try this little thought experiment. Have you ever been speaking to someone about something personal and they sat back and crossed their arms, as if to show they were in judgment, or did not seem very open toward you?

How else could you interpret them sitting back and crossing their arms?

Have you ever felt a little cold and crossed your arms to keep warm while talking to someone?

The thing is, you never really know the reason why the arms are crossed. What NLP invites you to do is to suspend judgment until you find out why the arms are crossed.

Here's another example of a personal relationship that may resonate for a number of people.

Josh's daughter, who had just turned five, was home for the week from preschool. The winter vacation was over for everyone else, but as preschools do, they were taking an extended vacation. Neither Josh nor his wife could take another week off at that point. But they felt guilty and wanted to make her happy. Josh's wife had a fixed schedule, but he had some flexibility so had arranged to have a couple of hours each day to do something with his daughter. He would work the rest of the time. Josh felt stretched thin, and like it still wasn't enough. Even with this schedule, he was sure his daughter would want more time and not understand why she couldn't have it. And it was understandable—his daughter didn't have good plans apart from those two hours. There would be a lot of playing quietly alone, or going to the park with a sitter and her baby brother. And too much TV.

At dinner the first day of her break, she asked Josh, "Why do you have to work?" Instantly he felt squeezed in all directions. After jumping through hoops to be with her, she was being ungrateful. "Was nothing ever enough?" he thought to himself. He started to get irritated and explain to her she should be grateful they can spend any time together this week. And thankfully, before he could start lecturing her, she followed up with questions showing she was curious about his work—the importance of money and the value for other people of doing the writing and teaching he does. It turned out she was not asking for more time.

The facts:

- She asked, "Why do you have to work?"

Josh's interpretation:

- "It's never enough. She's not being grateful. I'm being squeezed in all directions and won't be able to work enough. She is upset."

It turned out there were other interpretations of those facts. The truth, in this case, was that she was interested in learning about Josh's work, and how it benefits the family and others. All of Josh's initial interpretations were wrong in this case.

Josh could have paused and asked himself, "How else could I interpret her question?" And then maybe said to her, "Why do you ask?" or "What would you like to know?" In this case, he didn't have to because she took care of it so quickly.

If we take a closer look at how perception works, it helps explain why you should not just assume you got it right when you were trying to understand someone. Research from neuroscience and psychology shows several reasons why perception is never just a reflection of the facts, but always a combination of sensory information and interpretation—always affected by the filters each person perceives the world through.

First of all, it may help you embrace the fact that we commonly misinterpret what we perceive, to learn that research has fairly consistently shown over the last few decades that people often are wrong about what they think happened in a situation, even if they are confident about what they think. For example, they may confidently misremember whether a sign at the scene of a car crash was a stop or yield, what kind of hair someone had, and even whether a building or a person was present at some location or event.[1] Emotions have been shown to color what we think happened, too.[2] One study even showed how it's possible to directly stimulate a part of the brain involved in memory—to link fear to a new context—and in that way create a false memory.[3] The research has been convincing enough that eyewitness testimony no longer has the same value it once did in court.[4]

This simple visual illusion helps show how we see the world through mental filters, and not objectively. How can two people look at the same picture and see something different?

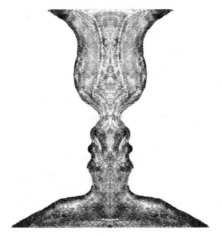

Is the picture above a chalice or two people facing each other? The answer is it depends, and what it depends on are the mental filters the observer sees the world through.[5] If you've just been thinking about faces, you may be more likely to see faces. If you've just been thinking about wine, you may be more likely to see the chalice. It's part of a larger pattern seen in studies in which knowledge that is active in the brain influences what we later think, feel, or pay attention to.[6]

There's a fun parlor trick that illustrates this. Answer these questions quickly:

- What continent is the Sahara Desert on?
- Do you like black-and-white pictures?
- How many stripes are on the American flag?
- What's an animal you can see at the zoo?

Did you answer "zebra" for the last question? A lot of people do. Africa, black and white, stripes, zoo. These are all ideas associated with zebras. So the neural circuitry associated with zebras gets primed. It becomes easier to access.

Initially, we take in the data through our senses. We use our eyes to observe the visual, our ears to hear the auditory, our skin to feel the tactile, our taste buds to experience the gustatory, and our noses to experience the olfactory. And already, even at this early stage of perception, when our senses interact with the world there is a problem. The problem is one of accuracy—we are constantly filtering and deleting the majority of the information that continuously assaults our senses.

Remember from chapter 2 that sensation exists to serve our needs, not just to catalogue what's out there. Our senses help us navigate the world. For that, we don't need to capture everything, and we don't need to be exactly right. Instead, we need to capture what's useful. And, as a result, we don't process most of what's out there.

What happens to all the other information we don't process?

Well . . . we ignore it. We pay attention to or focus on those things that are important to us. Our eyes, ears, probing fingers, etc., provide us valuable information based on which we can make decisions that will help us survive, meet our goals, or make our lives better.

So our brains focus our senses on those pieces of information that are relevant to us. One way to think of it is that we see what we are motivated to see.

Our motivations can be unconscious—we may not be aware of them—but they still color what we perceive. For example, we are exposed to thousands of cars daily as we traverse the roadways throughout the world. Yet, it is doubtful that we pay attention to a specific car unless our mental filters direct our attention to that specific car for a particular reason. That reason could be anything relevant to our needs or interests—a reckless driver could affect our safety, an odd color could make us reflect on whether we would ever be so bold, a more expensive or less expensive car than ours could bring up issues about our sense of self-worth, a fascination with exotic cars could be a source of fun, an offensive bumper sticker could tap into our sense of right and wrong, a frustration with gas pollution might stir a concern for global warming, or simply a model of a car that we are interested in buying might get us to consider our finances.

The key message here is that we have filters in place that determine what we even pay attention to.

These filters are different for everyone because they are amalgamations of our personal experience and they reflect our values, goals, capabilities, and other factors unique to us. For instance, Greg remembers his father saying, "Guys who wear bow ties are a special kind of asshole." Greg is aware now of how there must be many exceptions to the rule, but his knee-jerk reaction is always to dislike or distrust them.

Once our unconscious mind points us to what is important, our senses take over and decode the information as pictures, sounds, smells, feelings, and tastes—i.e., the world we experience. And when we experience that world, we don't doubt it—instead, it is just our version of reality.

Here's a quick game you can play to get better at separating facts (sensory information) from interpretation.

a. Picture yourself asking a question at a busy store, and the salesperson rolls their eyes.
→ Pretty rude, right?
○ How else could their eye movement be interpreted?

b. Imagine you're working hard to get things done on time so you and your partner can join friends for a dinner reservation. Your partner calls out, "You need to stop doing that. It's 6:40! We're going to be late."
→ Do they think you're stupid or just incompetent? You feel it's unfair to be judged as being bad about timing, and you shout back about how they are the one making you late.
○ How else could their comments be interpreted?

c. Imagine you are presenting or leading a meeting. You notice that one of the most senior and relevant people in the audience is looking at her phone more and more and not paying attention to you. Eventually, she even starts talking to others quietly and referring to the phone.
→ She does not care at all about your presentation, does she? Obviously, she realized pretty quickly this was a waste of her time, and moved on. It's clear that this whole presentation was a disaster.
○ How else could her behavior be interpreted?

d. Now think of something someone did that bothered you at some point.
○ How else could you interpret what they said or did?

When we simply accept our interpretations as reality, we can get into trouble. Many years ago, Josh was talking with a mentor of his and he opened up to this mentor about something personal he was feeling a bit anxious and embarrassed about. The mentor made a face of disgust. Josh felt awkward and doubted himself around this person for about two years. One day they were talking again and Josh brought up something he had been thinking about but really was not anxious or embarrassed about, so he felt safe to speak. The mentor made the same face. Disgust made no sense in this context, and Josh was now a bit more advanced in his NLP training. So Josh noticed something didn't make sense. He said to the mentor, "You just made a face that looked a little like this. What were you thinking?" The mentor chuckled, and said, "Oh, that. Yeah, I've been told that I make that face from time to time when I'm concentrating and very interested." The sensory information was that there was a particular facial expression during a certain point in the conversation. The interpretation of disgust was wildly off. When Josh paused to get curious about how else he could interpret the sensory information, he came to understand his mentor better, which vastly improved the relationship because Josh no longer felt awkward or the need to be reserved.

Sigmund Freud was famously (mis)quoted as saying, "Sometimes a cigar is just a cigar." Whether he actually said it is immaterial for the purposes of our discussion. But it may help to remember that trope when you get stuck. Sure, the cigar might be a phallic symbol. But it might not be. Separate the sensory facts from the interpretation. Get curious about how else the facts could be interpreted. It may feel like an extra step to pause and separate the two, but it is actually a shortcut to truly understanding someone.

12

DON'T SHOULD ON YOURSELF!

I f we listen carefully in the right ways, getting curious about someone's language choices, we can learn where the speaker lives. Not their street address, of course, but the mental and emotional world they inhabit. For instance, people often say things like this: "I have to get to work"; "We can't be late!"; or "I shouldn't have said that." Through these communications, they sometimes give clues to their beliefs, thoughts, and feelings to those who are willing to pay attention to what they say and how they say it.

The words in those examples above reflect someone's mode of operating. Words or phrases like "should," "have to," "couldn't," "must," and "can't" indicate a relationship a person has to a certain task. If they say, "I have to go to work," that often reflects the fact that it may feel like a burden, obligation, or responsibility to them. If they say, "We can't be late!" it often reflects the fact that they may feel very stressed about the consequences of being late—like looking bad, seeming rude, drawing too much attention, feeling like they let someone down or like they are irresponsible. When someone uses this kind of language, it can pay to listen for it and get curious about how they truly do relate to the task at hand.

This kind of language both reflects someone's mode of operating and can influence it. Right now, think about something on your agenda for this week for which you're thinking, "I have to do this."

Now consider . . . what would have to be different for you to think, "I get to do it"?

What happens when you switch your mode of operating from "have to" to "get to"?

Here's another example. Picture this: You've been promising your daughter that you'll finally make it to one of her performances. She is clearly excited and you know it means so much to her. Then something comes up at work. You feel awful, but you let her know, "Sorry, honey, I can't make it to your play tonight after all. It turns out I have to work. I'm so sorry."

Now let's replay it again, but instead you say this to her: "Sorry, honey, I am choosing to skip your play tonight. It turns out that although I work all the time and haven't been to your plays, I have the chance to do a little more of the same work. I'm so sorry." Imagine saying that, and picture her reaction. It probably feels like a punch in the gut.

Sometimes just shifting the language evokes a meaningful shift in the way something feels, how we think about it, and what seems possible. The language can change the meaning quickly and profoundly at a deep and personal level.

We owe much of our understanding of the power of these language shifts to cognitive psychology and rational emotive behavior therapy. There's a fun story about Albert Ellis, one of the pioneers in these types of psychology, on this point. He was once voted by psychologists as the second most influential psychologist in the field, and the renowned Albert Ellis Institute is named after him. Josh once had the good fortune to see Ellis do a live demo with volunteer patients. Ellis was maybe ninety at that point and almost deaf. So he shouted just about everything he said, and did so in a bit of a New York accent. When he would hear a patient saying "I should" or "I shouldn't" too much he'd shout a version of one of his famous lines—something like "You're should-ing all over yourself!" or "Don't should on yourself!" For example, when people say things to themselves like "I shouldn't have said that"; "I should be further along in my career by this age"; "I should be a better mother," etc. There's a sense of intense self-judgment, negative emotion, low self-esteem, and feelings of failure that often go with "should." It is seldom a useful mode of operating.

As Ellis was quick to highlight, there's nothing wrong with feeling bad or wanting to behave differently. It's getting stuck in the hopelessness and self-loathing that often accompanies "should" that he helped people move away from. For instance, he would see it as a win to help someone instead think something like "I'm sad that I said that." It helps shift the mind to a place of acceptance. Ellis was not saying you have to be happy all the time. But from self-loathing to acceptance is often a big and useful shift.

Research has shown that in both personal and work situations,[1] people hold themselves back by telling themselves things like "I should be running my own company by now," or "I shouldn't need to rely on anyone," or any number of other "shoulds" or "musts." These thoughts are called limiting beliefs. They are beliefs about yourself, what is possible, and about how the world works that limit you from behaving in the most useful ways. For example, if someone says, "I shouldn't need to rely on anyone," then they are likely to create negative meaning anytime they perceive someone else as being useful or helpful to them. In response they may dismiss or insult others' support as not useful, or may avoid taking help that would be rational to take. That will, of course, make life harder.

However, research also shows that when someone replaces a limiting belief with one that is more rational or more useful, they often change their feelings and behavior. They also change what's happening in the brain. In general, parts of the brain that are associated with conscious control influence the reactive and emotional centers to calm.[2] When we rethink something in a way that makes it less emotionally negative, parts of the prefrontal cortex (critical for executive functions) become more active, and the amygdala (critical for the fight-or-flight response) becomes less active.[3]

If you started with the limiting belief "I shouldn't need to rely on anyone," then a more useful belief could be "I'm better when I accept help" or "Everyone gets help from other people. Doing it all alone is a myth." After replacing the limiting belief with one of those alternatives, you'd be more likely to accept help and acknowledge the people who meaningfully help you, wouldn't you? That will, of course, make life easier.

One note of caution as you start noticing "shoulds" everywhere. The word "should" doesn't always mean someone is operating from such a place. But it often does, and a great NLPer will get curious when they hear it. Does it represent a limiting way of operating? Or is it just a way of talking about what's on the agenda? Either answer is fine—being curious is about staying open to any answer. However, when you hear "should" and get curious about someone's mode of operating, you often can open doors to change quickly.

In NLP these words that reflect someone's mode of operating are called modal operators of necessity, and modal operators of possibility. There are a bunch of them—"have to," "should," "need to," "must," "ought to," "can't," "couldn't," for example.

When you hear these terms and get curious about what's behind them, you can ask just a few simple questions to discover much about the person's mental model.

We like to call these cartography questions. Cartographers make maps, and these questions help you make a map of how someone thinks, feels, and is likely to behave. In other words, they help you discover important parts of the other person's mental model. These questions end up being some of the great workhorses in NLP.

When you hear words like "should," "have to," etc., ask these cartography questions:

- "What's stopping you?"
- "What would happen if . . . ?"
- "Why is that necessary/impossible?"[4]

So, for example, when Greg said to Josh the other day, "Let's each draft another chapter by next Wednesday," and Josh said, "Wednesday . . . oh, I can't," Greg was able to follow up and ask (not rhetorically, but with curiosity), "What's stopping you?" This question helped Josh get specific about why he reacted that way. He had a feeling of piling on one too many things. He knew that adding one more would be stressful. But that also led Josh to think about what those things were and to realize that it made sense to choose to draft a chapter and to put off one of the other things on his list.

Or when Josh said to Greg, "People are telling me we really *should* be raising our prices for classes," Josh was feeling a mix of anxiety that he was leaving money on the table, and feeling discomfort that he would price some people out who wanted to be there. It felt like a stressful decision Josh would rather just avoid. Greg was able to ask, "What would happen if we did?" This took Josh past the point of uncomfortable avoidance and onto a more useful mode of operating. "If we did, we would *get to* earn what we think we are worth. And we *can* find ways to help people who can't afford it fully to have access."

You can experiment with these questions right now as you think about the ways you talk to yourself. Think of a situation in your own life where, although you want to do something, you feel that you can't. A slight variation on this is that you want to do it and feel that you really should do it, but you just keep not doing it.

With that situation in mind, now ask yourself, "What's stopping me?"

As you answered that question, did you start to notice any useful thoughts or ideas about things you might do differently?

For fun, let's come back to Sherlock Holmes, who we last saw in chapter 6, to see how someone might use these cartography questions in a conversation. This time Holmes is confronted by master criminal Professor Moriarty, who has just voiced his desire to kill Holmes.

MR. HOLMES: Why do you want to kill me?

PROFESSOR MORIARTY: I *have to* kill you. ("*have to* kill"—mode of operating)

MR. HOLMES: Why do you have to kill me? (cartography question)

PROFESSOR MORIARTY: If I kill the greatest detective of all time, I will be considered the greatest criminal of all time.

MR. HOLMES: What will happen if you don't kill me? (cartography question)

PROFESSOR MORIARTY: I will still be considered the greatest criminal of all time.

MR. HOLMES: So you don't have to kill me to be considered the greatest criminal of all time?

PROFESSOR MORIARTY: I guess you're right—I *don't have to* kill you. ("*don't have to*"—mode of operating)

MR. HOLMES: What a shame it would have been to lose a great sparring partner by killing me, and gain nothing in your reputation as the greatest criminal mastermind.

As we see above, Mr. Holmes, through effective use of cartography questions to understand Dr. Moriarty's mental model, not only creates clarity for both himself and Dr. Moriarty, but in so doing leads Dr. Moriarty to realize that he does not need to kill Sherlock Holmes to get his needs met. Asking the cartography questions ultimately moved Dr. Moriarty from one belief to another.

Just as happened for Holmes, asking these questions creates the space for people to move from impossible to possible, or, from *need to* to *don't need to*.

The steps are these: (1) Listen for the mode of operating in someone's language; (2) get curious; (3) ask cartography questions. It is not a silver bullet, but it is a tool in our quivers that can help us understand someone's mental model of the situation they are in, and ultimately help them move from unproductive states to productive ones.

Let's be honest—every one of us is should-ing all over him- or herself somewhere in their life. Whether Greg believes that he should spend more time with his kids, or Josh thinks that he should spend more time networking, if we dig deep we all can find something in our life that we should be doing differently—the mother who feels she should go back to her pre-family career; the workaholic who should slow down; the office worker who should write that novel; or you doing whatever your destiny should be.

Modern culture is replete with heroes and antiheroes who should but aren't. In the movie *Good Will Hunting*, Matt Damon plays a math prodigy who should be an academic superstar, but instead works as a janitor at MIT. With the help of an NLP-trained (maybe) therapist played by Robin Williams, Matt's character overcomes his demons, makes his "should" a "can," and follows his true calling as a mathematician.

So what should or shouldn't you be doing in your life right now? Let's move beyond that feeling of should or shouldn't. If it's a should, what's stopping you? If it's a shouldn't, what would happen if you did it?

Note that sometimes the answer you'll come up with will make you want to stay the course and you will decide not to change anything. If so, you are making progress because you are moving from stressing about it and should-ing on yourself to accepting it and making decisions. As cognitive therapists often teach patients, we don't always get what we want, but we can learn to tolerate that, feel sad for a while, and then continue on with a good life. When you can do that, you can handle anything that comes. It is a step away from self-loathing and anxiety, and toward new opportunities in life.

After answering these kinds of questions, you should, no pun intended, understand your model of the situation better, and you should understand better what limitations are preventing you from making a change.

In *Return of the Jedi*, Luke Skywalker says at one point, "I'm endangering the mission. I *shouldn't* have come." Luke realizes that Vader can sense his presence and can track them down. He starts to second-guess himself and worry. Alas, Luke did not have Greg and Josh to guide him. Had we been there, we could have asked, "Luke . . . what would happen if you didn't come?" Naturally, Luke would have replied, "I would not face Vader, and this war would rage on forever because no one else can stop him. Thank you, Greg and Josh, I see that it is better I stay and fulfill my destiny. If I don't he will continue work on the Death Star and become too powerful." We're just having fun with Star Wars and Sherlock Holmes, of course. But these simple questions and answers many times have been the difference between "should-ing" all over ourselves, and accomplishing what needs to get done.

The language patterns called modal operators of necessity and modal operators of possibility are part of a collection of common language patterns you can learn to spot that can reveal a lot about what's going on in someone's mind. In NLP, this collection of language patterns is grouped together and called the meta model. We're not including the entire meta model in this book, but instead we focus on what we see as five of the most useful aspects of the meta model for everyday communication in this and the next several chapters.

Each language pattern in the meta model provides a clue about how a person is thinking and feeling about the situation they are in. What NLP teaches us to do is to learn how to spot these language patterns, get curious about why the person spoke that way, and then ask the right questions to find out more.

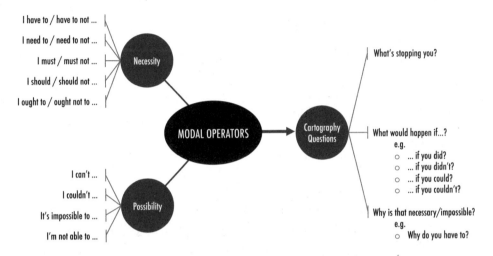

Figure 1—Modal Operators of Necessity and Modal Operators of Possibility

Think of each modal operator as a mode of operating. They can reflect and influence our relationships with the tasks we do. They are like rules for the game of living—they tell us what moves are allowed and what moves are off-limits. Some people find it helpful to see two buckets: (1) necessity: a sense of need or obligation; and (2) possibility: a sense of whether, or to what degree, something is possible or impossible. The cartography questions can help you understand the mental model of the person you are speaking with. The first two cartography questions, "What's stopping you?" and "What would happen if . . . ?" are often used in NLP to help the person answering to shift from a limiting mode of operating to a mode in which they experience more options and possibilities. The third question is not typically taught along with modal operators. We include it because we believe a "why" question can be helpful in terms of understanding the mental model of the person you are speaking with. However, a "why" question may not be useful in helping them to make this kind of shift. When they do shift, you might hear in their language that the modal operators of necessity and possibility have been replaced by terms like "I get to . . ."; "I can . . ."; "I could . . ."; or "I'm able to . . ."

13

SOMETHING'S MISSING HERE

How did you let this happen?"

This is a rather simple-sounding question, and when people hear it they usually feel that they need to give a good answer, and fast, in order to save face. A lot of people will just start trying to explain themselves. But have you ever been unsure what exactly you were being accused of? Josh and Greg certainly have, as have many people. That's no accident, because the accusatory question leaves out an important fact—specifically, what happened.

When important information is missing, it can be hard to communicate effectively. With a question like "How could you let this happen?" it's not obvious at first that some important information is missing. So an easier example may help.

There's a really fun game called Mad Libs. It goes something like this: fill in the blanks with your own words, and then read the whole paragraph and have a good laugh.

The restaurant was kind of _____, don't you think? Maybe _____ eating is not _____ enough. But the _____ was _____. I don't think I'll _____. This is my _____. Don't _____. Good night.

There are a lot of ways someone could fill in the blanks. We're going to guess that no one else filled it in this way: "The restaurant was kind of smelly, don't you think? Maybe revenge eating is not passionate enough. But the soup was chicken. I don't think I'll date you. This is my boyfriend. Don't call. Good night." When it's a game like this, it's obvious that something is missing, and equally obvious that you can't really know the author's original intention.

What is often surprising to people, however, is that most conversations are also missing a lot of information. But in a conversation, we tend to fill in the blanks with our assumptions without even realizing. Not only do we not know whether we're right or wrong, we're often not even aware we filled in any blanks. However, the missing information often holds the keys to understanding someone's mental model about a situation—what they think and feel, and what they see as possible.

When someone leaves information out of what they are saying, we call that deletion in NLP. You can learn to notice when information is deleted and then ask a useful question or two. That can reveal a great deal about what's really going on in someone's mind. It often helps them gain clarity while it helps you gain clarity, too.

For example, "Sorry, how did I let what happen?" is a reasonable response to the question posed in the first line of this chapter. Especially if you can ask without sounding too defensive.

Deletion generally occurs when a necessary fact is left out of a sentence and it is unclear what was done, and possibly also unclear by whom, to whom, and/or why or how. "I am not happy" is a great example. How can we attempt to make a person happier if we do not know what is making them unhappy?

In a realistic conversation, we have to actively look for the speaker's deletions and actively inquire, or else risk a missed opportunity or even a serious miscommunication.

Let's look at a simple check-in conversation between a husband and wife in the evening at home, some version of which happens nightly in many households.

WIFE (WITH SOME EAGERNESS TO LEARN THE ANSWER SHOWING IN HER BODY LANGUAGE AND TONE): Well?!

HUSBAND: Well, it was . . . (pause) . . . At least it's done . . . and I'm tired. Don't worry. You don't have to.

WIFE: No. Come on. Tell me.

HUSBAND: It's no big deal. You know, you try stuff and you learn. I just shouldn't have . . . But now I know. Next time I'll do a test run first. The instructions were too long and confusing. So we didn't even really get to do the whole . . .

WIFE: Ugh. Yeah, that sucks. Sounds like you made the best of it. . . . Want to get some dinner?

Let's analyze this simple conversation. It sounds pretty normal. If you haven't had a conversation somewhat like this yourself, you've probably seen conversations like it on TV. Wife and husband seem to have successfully communicated. It kind of feels like we know what the husband is feeling—apparently something did not go as planned at work. It also has the feel that the wife is a caring person, or at least wanted to seem caring. And there's a sense that the husband was just going through the motions to humor her, probably because he values the relationship, but he mostly just wanted to get the conversation over with and move on with his night. The wife finally accepted that, gave him some sympathy, and suggested dinner.

But look at how much information was left out.

"Well!?" *What does this refer to?* Husband took a guess—his event. But maybe he was self-absorbed because he was bummed about his event. Could Wife have been wanting Husband to notice something about her—a new haircut, a reaction to her new website, a response to that ridiculous thing her mother texted the two of them in the afternoon? All the information about what "Well?!" refers to is deleted. Had Husband noticed that the information was missing and tried to clarify, he could have had a totally different conversation, and probably could have left both of them feeling better. What if Wife was asking for his reaction to her mom's text, for example? They both could have rolled their eyes, had a good laugh, and avoided all the negative vibes about Husband's work.

"Well, it was . . . (pause) . . . At least it's done . . . and I'm tired . . .

Don't worry. You don't have to." There are many deletions—It was *what?* I'm tired *of what—physically tired, tired of doing something?* Don't worry *about what—about how I feel, about how it went, about the other people involved, about how this affects our finances?* You don't have to *what—give this issue attention, care about me, try to problem solve?*

"Tell me." *What—how you feel, what you did, when it ended, whether we should talk about this?*

"I just shouldn't have"—*have done what?* "Now I know"—*know what?*

Suppose Wife was actually asking about Husband's event, and really did want to show she cared. Had she picked up on even some of the missing information and tried to clarify, she could have done a better job at showing she cared. For example:

WIFE: You're tired? Yeah, well, I guess we didn't sleep well last night.

HUSBAND: No, I mean I'm tired of all this.

WIFE: What do you mean by "all this"?

HUSBAND: I'm so over doing these kinds of user testing events. I'm tired of this job. I don't want to spend the night complaining, but it's time for me to find a new project or position.

WIFE: Are you serious about it being time to find a new position?

And from there, it's not hard to imagine the conversation going quite differently from the first example. If that is what was on Husband's mind, then Wife's questions probably would also have the effect of showing Husband she really cared.

People who notice what's missing or unclear and get curious about it get to the heart of the matter quickly. Coaches and therapists who do this often surprise their clients with how quickly they help them find breakthroughs. Lawyers who do it often guide judges and juries to see things from their perspective. Negotiators who do it often discover win-wins that seemed elusive to others. Partners who do it are often great at providing the support their partners crave. It is a small behavior change, but it opens doors left and right to powerful communication and influence.

Research has shown that people often delete information, and doing so affects their thoughts, feelings, and behaviors. In cognitive therapy, for example, therapists help patients identify how their thoughts may be distorted. One of ten typical distortions they will look for is called mental filtering, in which the patient mentally deletes or ignores relevant positive information. For instance, a person who interviewed for a job might have received a warm reception and good feedback throughout the interview, but then dwells on one statement they made that didn't come out right, ignoring or forgetting the other 95 percent of the interview that went very well. They feel like it went terribly as a result. Mental filtering is often associated with unwanted thoughts and behaviors, and negative feelings.[1] Cognitive therapists help people change by identifying the distorted thoughts—e.g., thoughts that delete or mentally filter out relevant information—and replacing those thoughts with more useful ones. In the previous chapter and elsewhere in the book, we've also pointed out how research on cognitive biases, false memories, and motivated perception all show that people routinely ignore, leave out, dismiss, or don't notice relevant information without even realizing it. It's how the brain works. It is not a problem, necessarily, but is a useful fact to be aware of.

One way to explore whether relevant information is missing in the way someone is thinking is to pay attention to how they speak about their situation. In cognitive therapy, either the therapist can take note of the way the patient describes their situation, or they can ask them to articulate or write down what they are thinking.[2] Their language often reflects their thoughts.

Other evidence shows that the language we use both reflects and affects how we think in many realms[3]—e.g., what we think is morally right, how much money an insurance company owes someone, or whether to make a big decision in our lives. While at times it is just semantics, it really is often more.

Paying close attention to what's deleted in the way someone speaks can give you a clue about what might be going on in their mind. For example, they might be avoiding thinking about something, or they might be thinking about something different from what you think they are thinking about.

For the pattern of deletion, the cartography question is "What does this pertain to?" (As noted in the example below, there are many variations on this question, but they all aim to get at the same idea.)

You may find it helpful to do a little practice right now. Here are five phrases many people are likely to hear sometime this week. Get curious about what's missing, and consider how you could ask follow-up questions to gain clarity about what the sentence pertains to.

1. "I just can't."
2. "We need to do better."
3. "Whose responsibility is it?"
4. "I get that you're upset. Tell me why."
5. "I've got a big day tomorrow. I need everyone's help."

ANSWER KEY: (1) "Can't do what?"; (2) "Do better at what?"; (3) "What are they responsible for?"; (4) "Why what? Do you mean why this happened or why I'm upset or something else?"; (5) "Help with what?"

There are other good ways of asking similar questions. These are just examples.

Over the course of the next day, see if you can find at least one example of a deletion where the missing information might make a difference. Look for it in a conversation or an email. When you spot a deletion, get curious and ask a follow-up question or two.

A note of caution: when you learn about the pattern of deletion and any of the meta model patterns, it is tempting to start noticing them in every conversation and asking for clarity a lot. We would advise against that. It will get annoying to other people. And the closer someone is to you, the more they probably expect you to just be able to read their mind, so it could be even more annoying for people close to you. What we've seen, however, is that with some practice, it is possible to do it and not overdo it. At the core of doing it well is being very curious. In your mind, make it a game or a goal to notice when you don't really understand. Notice when you think, "Something's missing here." Then use your judgment. If gaining clarity would really help you know where to go next in the conversation, then ask a clarifying question.

In this chapter we've introduced the idea that information can be missing, and we've focused on *what* is being deleted—"What does this pertain to?" However, other information can also be deleted, too.

In the next two chapters, we'll dive into specific cases of missing information that can make an enormous difference in how well you can communicate and influence change.

14

WHO, SPECIFICALLY?

There's a common joke that goes like this. One person says, "You know, they say [. . .]," and then dispenses some wisdom. Something like "They say you should drink red wine because it makes you healthier," or "They say you should start saving money when you're young." And the other person says, "Who are *they* anyway? *They* seem to know just about everything, and *they're* often telling you what you should or shouldn't do."

But there's a reason we use this way of talking. When we vaguely refer to "they," we're implying that this is accepted knowledge by a large group of people. There is a feeling of authority behind it. And it's easier than remembering your sources. Saying "they say" usually goes by unnoticed because it works. But as soon as someone makes the joke "Who are *they* anyway?" the spell is broken.

After a quick laugh—usually a polite one, because everyone has heard the joke before—the first person might answer something like "I don't know, I read it somewhere online" or "The guy at the wine shop told me." The sense of accepted knowledge and authority are gone; the feeling that you should follow the advice diminishes, as "they" becomes the guy at the wine shop.

"They say" would be just a cute quirk in language if it didn't reflect a much more broadly used pattern in how we communicate with ourselves and with others. The broader pattern is that we often leave out information about who, specifically, we are referring to. In NLP we call this language pattern the lack of referential index.[1]

It matters because when we speak of "they" or "people" in general without getting specific, it often reflects a mental model in which a large group (maybe even the whole world) feel or think something. It reflects that there is some norm out there to follow. And, if you don't like what *they* say, then this language pattern also suggests there is a sense that fighting against it would be a large and daunting task, made all the more so by how vague is who, exactly, you would fight against.

Following norms is no small thing for human brains. One of the powerful forces researchers know about for attitude and behavior change is the simple act of letting people know what the norm is.[2] Showing people what the norm is includes both describing what most people in their group do and saying what people in their group think you should do. In one really surprising study, even when the norms pertained to a different group you don't like—e.g., a liberal hearing about how a group of conservatives behave, or a conservative hearing about how a group of liberals behave—people tended to shift their behavior toward the norm.[3] If you've had friends who moved to a different part of the country, you may have seen their attitudes and habits shift a bit. Clearly there are times we can fight these tendencies, but it feels very awkward and takes a lot of courage. The urge to conform or to fit in is just a natural force.

Let's look at an example. Kara had been working for other people as a business strategy consultant for fifteen years. She was always a star employee and a real asset to her boss. However, in her heart, she never wanted to work for someone else. But she always worried about stability and being responsible, so she was afraid to go out on her own. One Sunday, with work on her mind, she was complaining to her friend Manny about it all. Manny said, "You should just quit and start your own company." To which Kara almost instinctively replied, "People would think I'm so irresponsible. . . . People would think I'm crazy. I have kids in school, a mortgage, and my own school debt."

Manny empathized. He joined her in talking shit about her boss and the system. That helped her feel better. But then Manny said something else. What he said did more than make her feel better—it helped free up Kara from that stuck state of mind she was in. He said, "I'm wondering something, though. Who, specifically? You said 'people' would think you are irresponsible and crazy. I'm wondering who, specifically? *I* wouldn't think that."

At first, Kara responded, as many people do, by digging in and just saying, "Everyone!" But Manny was persistent and patient. "No, really. Who, specifically, are you picturing?" And after a moment, this question got Kara to think. She came back by saying it was really her mother and her husband whose reactions she worried about.

Once she had moved in her mind from "people" to her mother and her husband, it became a solvable problem. She was no longer feeling like she would be going against the norm and what's considered responsible by "people." "People" can imply everyone in the world (or at least everyone in the culture or extended group she's part of)—that's overwhelming and very abstract. It has both a strong feeling of helplessness to it and is hard to think about.

Kara realized she needed to have a conversation with her husband about what he really thought and whether he would support this move fully. Regarding her mom, she recognized after a while that her mom would worry if she did it, but that her mom would worry no matter what she did. Kara would need to do some extra work to reassure her mom, but that was manageable.

When Manny asked "Who, specifically?" he was picking up on an important language pattern he had learned about in NLP—the lack of referential index. Recall that John Grinder, one of the founders of NLP, was a linguist. Part of his and Bandler's gift to the world, and one of NLP's great strengths, is the ability to see linguistic patterns (and not just hear words) and understand how they may map onto someone's experience of whatever situation they are speaking about.

When people speak, they reveal a lot of clues about how they may be thinking or feeling about an issue. When the language is vague, for example, it often means the experience is vague. Kara's language was vague and made sweeping generalizations about all people—no wonder she felt like the world was against her. Manny noticed that Kara was saying, "People would think . . . ," and having a strong emotional reaction of hopelessness in response. He saw that her language was vague and was generalized to all people. So he knew the odds were decent that her thinking wasn't really clear or accurate on the issue. The simple question "Who, specifically?" led Kara to both move from overgeneralizing to getting specific, and from being vague to getting clearer. In doing so, she freed herself from the pressure of perceived norms, and focused just on her concerns about two people.

So, in this chapter we offer you the next cartography question: "Who, specifically?"

There's a variant of this cartography question as well: "According to whom?" Kara could have said something like this instead: "It's completely irresponsible. . . . That's crazy. I have kids in school, a mortgage, and my own school debt." To which Manny could have said, "You said it's completely irresponsible. According to whom, specifically? *I* don't think it would be irresponsible."

This would also likely lead Kara to focus on her concerns about her husband's and her mother's attitudes.

In NLP, we'd say the language pattern Manny was picking up on this time is called the lost performative. The information about who is performing the action in the sentences is missing. It's just stated as if it were fact that it would be irresponsible. But being irresponsible is a judgment, and thus has to be judged by someone.

What Manny did, and what you can learn to do, too, is to recognize the language patterns that suggest the speaker might not be clear in their own mind about the people involved. If it helps to use the names of the NLP ideas, lack of referential index and lost performative, then do so. Whether or not you use those names, the key here is to get curious about someone's mental model when you're not sure who, specifically, they have in mind.

We invite you to pay keen attention when listening, and to identify the missing "whos" and "whoms." You may be surprised to find how often such information is missing. When you start getting curious, you may also find, as we have, that it is both fun and liberating to be able to quickly unpack what someone's mental model really is, and to help hold a mirror up for them as well.

It may help to try this out on yourself right now. We all engage in self-talk, and we're frequently not so nice to ourselves. Yes, research shows it's not just you—we all do it.[4] We're referring to the ways we silently speak to ourselves in our mind's ear. (And occasionally out loud, too.) Here are some really common ways people talk to themselves that can be limiting. Do any of these sound like something you've said to yourself?

- "You can't show up looking like that."
- "Nobody will want to talk to you."
- "People won't take you seriously."
- "You can't do that—it would be so embarrassing."
- "Everyone will look at you like you're crazy."

Think of a time you said or thought something like that.

With that situation in mind, notice what happens when you ask yourself these questions: "Who, specifically?" and "According to whom?" For example, "Who, specifically, thinks you can't show up like that?" "Who, specifically, will not want to talk to you?" "It would be embarrassing—according to whom?" Get specific in your answers about actual people.

Distorted thinking—like the vagueness or overgeneralizations in this chapter and deletions in the last chapter—seems to show up in almost every mental model in some way or another. The game here is in spotting those in someone's (or our own) language and getting curious whether it reflects their (or our) mental model. It opens doors.

Here's an example in a day-to-day business situation. Imagine you're in a real estate negotiation.

CONVERSATION 1. **A negotiation for a piece of real estate with an asking price of $1 million.**

BUYER: The real estate market is soft. You'll never get your asking price.
SELLER: Well, what do you think is a fair price?
BUYER: It's $800,000.
SELLER: That's very far from what we're asking. Maybe there's some middle ground we can discuss.

CONVERSATION 2. Same facts as above. Same opening line. But the seller asks a different question.

BUYER: The real estate market is soft. You'll never get your asking price.

SELLER: According to whom? Who or what leads you to say that?

BUYER: It's all over the news.

SELLER: I've seen that news, too. So I've spoken with the brokers of all five other similar-sized properties in this region that have been on the market this year. Despite all the noise from the talking heads about general trends, this particular residential market is very strong and prices are actually going up due to lack of inventory.

We think the seller in Conversation 2 appears to be on track to negotiate a higher price because she took the time to understand the buyer's lost performative, or who or what her belief of a soft real estate market was based on.

As you engage with other people, just like the seller in this negotiation did, keep an eye out for statements where it's not clear who is being referred to. Then ask, "Who, specifically?" or "According to whom, or according to what source?" Often, though not always, it will help both you and the speaker to understand their mental model better. As a result, you may be more likely to discover the difference that makes the difference.

Putting the last two chapters together, here's an example where someone inquires about both what and who. Suppose Greg is in the middle of a deposition and questioning a witness. He might hear the witness say something like, "The problem is that there's no trust." Greg could nod along, believing he understands, or he could recognize that something's missing here. He could follow up and clarify the ambiguity by asking things like, "Who doesn't have any trust? Is it mutual? Who does this person, or do these people, not trust?" And "What do they not trust will happen?" Or "What do they not trust each other to do?" These kinds of questions will help Greg get to the heart of the issues and feelings between the parties much more quickly than he would otherwise if he simply let the deleted information go by without asking a follow-up question.

And it's not just *what* and *who* that are frequently missing in the ways people talk. In the next chapter, we'll see what else is often missing.

15

HOW, SPECIFICALLY?

Suppose you're with a friend from work and they turn to you and start complaining—starting up the same old conversation you've had a thousand times—and say, "This place is toxic. There's just no trust at all." You might find yourself feeling annoyed at having to hear it; you might find yourself wanting to complain, too; you might find yourself sighing with resignation as you pause to lend a supportive ear; or you might have some other reaction. Regardless, your friend is stuck in a negative space, and it's often not clear what to say that would make any difference and help them move on with their lives.

One option is for you to problem solve. To problem solve, you might reply something like "You deserve better. You should put your resumé out there and find a new job"; or maybe you're tempted to problem solve by helping them turn that frown upside down and seeing how it's not as bad as they think.

Another option is for you to commiserate and empathize. "Yeah, this place sucks. Whatever trust there once might have been, it's all gone now."

Those are common and logical things to do. One approach aims to help your friend fix their problem. The other aims to help your friend feel understood, like they are justified, and that they have a friend in you.

However, the problem doesn't usually go away. How many of us have had conversations quite like this over and over, with little or no progress?

No matter how much problem-solving or empathy is offered, not much seems to change. Not that problem-solving and empathy are bad things—there is a time and a place for both. But from an NLP perspective, there's something else that needs attention in this situation.

What needs attention is the fact that it is very unclear what your friend from work really thinks and feels. Your friend's statement was "This place is toxic. There's just no trust at all." The sentences are grammatical so they sound meaningful, and since you work with them and know them, you probably would have some sense of what that means. But there's actually a lot that is unclear. And if it's unclear to you, it probably is unclear to them as well. That makes it hard to make progress. How can you make progress on a problem if you don't know what problem you are solving? How can you get from here to there if you don't know where here and there are? How can you move ahead if you don't know what's holding you back?

The tools in this chapter will help you discover what problem needs solving, where "here" and "there" are, and what may be holding someone back. They do so by helping to reveal key parts of someone's mental model. Toward these aims, we present the next cartography question. This question can cut through vagueness like a knife and provide helpful clarity. The question is deceptively simple for such a powerful tool: "How, specifically?"

So, a different approach when your friend complains "There's no trust" is to get curious about how, specifically, they understand the situation. "How, specifically, do people at this company not trust you? How, specifically, do you not trust them?"

This line of questioning tends to lead to new lines of thinking rather than rehashing the same old patterns and complaints. What the question does is shift their focus. It helps them specify just what the problem is rather than only feeling like there is a large and hard problem. It opens up new ways of thinking about the situation they are in, and new ways of relating to that situation in terms of their feelings and beliefs about what it means for them. It does this by helping them think about the processes and actions they can engage in, rather than just thinking about what's wrong. In this particular example, it takes the focus off of trust as a thing to either have or not have and turns it back into a process, and not an all-or-nothing thing.

From a linguistic perspective a word like "trust" is what's called a nominalization—a verb that has been turned into a noun. But even though we can use the word "trust" like a noun in a sentence, it isn't really a thing you can touch or see or have. It is a vague concept. That's because trust is really an action—it's a thing you do. When people speak with nominalizations, they are turning a verb into a fixed thing, and focusing away from the actions one can take and onto a thing to have or not have. But when that thing is just a vague idea, that usually leaves them stuck.

Poets nominalize all the time—turning verbs into nouns. It stirs up powerful emotions, and puts the listener into kind of a trance-like state. William Blake wrote: "Cruelty has a human heart, and jealousy a human face." Cruelty and jealousy are not things or people, but they are used that way grammatically. The words, at least to us, evoke a sense of a person with bad intentions. It's powerful. Langston Hughes wrote: "Hold fast to dreams, for if dreams die, life is a broken-winged bird that cannot fly," and "What happens to a dream deferred?" While we roughly know what a "dream" refers to, dreaming is really a verb—*to dream*. Dreaming is a process or activity. People hearing the nominalization are free to project all kinds of meaning onto the word. It is a slightly confusing way to talk that takes the mind away from action and onto a feeling of how things are in some fixed sense. It's a wonderful mindf**k that's put to really good use by these poets. That's great for poetry, but not great for clarity.

Here, we're doing the opposite of what those poets do. We're taking a nominalization and turning it back into a verb, an action, a process. It softens the emotions as it increases the opportunities to take action. It also breaks those actions into smaller steps by focusing specifically on what really needs to be addressed.

It would be reasonable for a skeptic to wonder whether this is all just wordplay. Does it really change the experience a person has when they think of something as a fixed object versus as an action or a process? Or are we just fooling ourselves when we note that it seems to feel different to think of a thing versus an action? It turns out that the brain, in fact, behaves differently when processing object words (typical nouns) versus action words (typical verbs). There is a network of brain regions, specifically involving lower-temporal areas, that is more active with object words (on the sides of the brain, closer to the ears), while a set of regions involving frontal or frontoparietal networks seems to be more active with action words (the front and upper back of the brain).[1] These different networks reflect the different ways that we relate to object and action words. Action words activate parts of the brain that have to do with movement, and engaging with the world or interacting with others, within a specific context. Object words activate parts of the brain that have more to do with identifying meaning or knowing what things are in a relatively fixed sense.

Also, nominalizations in particular (e.g., "The Dance") are more confusing for people than more straightforward action words—they tax the mind. These words activate a part of the brain called the inferior frontal gyrus more heavily than regular action words (e.g., "Dancing"). Activity in that region helps us sort out just what it is that a word pertains to when it doesn't really fit well into an action word or an object word category.[2]

The question "How, specifically?" helps guide the person hearing that question out of a stuck mental state and to refocus them instead on actions. It helps them to unpack the particular behaviors they can engage in and ways of interacting with others that are available to them within their individual context. In this way it focuses them on simple steps involved in moving from where they are to a more preferable outcome.

Your friend could reply something like this when you ask "How, specifically, do people at this company not trust you? How, specifically, do you not trust them?": "My boss [a specific person] doesn't trust me to make decisions about what to recommend to potential clients [a specific action]." And "I don't trust my boss [a specific person] to know a good sales opportunity [a specific action] if it bit him on the ass." With those answers from your friend, you can understand much better what they actually think and feel. Any empathy or problem-solving you offer now will be much more targeted and likely much more useful as a result.

You may find it helpful to ask yourself this question now to get a firsthand sense of how it works. Do you need to reach a decision about something, but you struggle to do so? You can pause and call to mind an example of something like that now (e.g., "I need to make a decision about what health care plan to sign up for.").

"Decision" is a verb that's been turned into a noun. It's not a tangible thing. Turn it back into a verb with this question and notice what, if anything, happens. How, specifically, are you deciding?

Here's another one to try. Do you have some problem with a relationship you are in? It could be a personal relationship with a partner, friend, or relative; or a professional relationship, like with a difficult colleague or client. You can take a moment and think of an example now.

"Relationship" is a verb that has been turned into a noun, into a fixed thing. But it's not a fixed thing. Let's turn it back into a verb and see what happens. How, specifically, have you been relating to this person, or failing to relate? How, specifically, would you like to relate to this person?

For many people, answering "How, specifically?" leads them to think about their process—e.g., of deciding, or of relating—instead of just thinking about what problem they have. They remember (or discover) that it is a process.

At times, people do speak in terms of verbs, processes, or actions, but there is still a lot of vagueness about what they really mean or how they arrived at their conclusions. For instance, if someone says, "I want you to show respect," it remains unclear what would count as showing respect. "How, specifically?" can help in those cases, too, by helping both you and them gain useful clarity about what they mean. After reflecting on the question "How, specifically?" people frequently find they can make adjustments to their process or to their thinking that help.

Here are four language patterns that NLP teaches us to listen for that all beg the question "How, specifically?" See if any of these sound like things you've said or heard recently.

1. Nominalization

We've talked about this one already. That's when something that really should be a verb (an action) gets turned into a noun (a thing). Here are a few more examples:

   a. "We have made a list of our *values*." → "How, specifically, *do you value* those things?"

b. "I'm feeling like my *freedom* is limited here." → "How, specifically, *are you* not *free?*"

c. "We provide *solutions.*" → "How, specifically, will you *solve* my problem?"

2. Unspecified verbs

Someone describes an action, but it really could be understood multiple ways.

a. "*Planning* ahead is hard." → "How, specifically, do you plan?"

b. "We're *obsessed* with customer service." → "How, specifically, do you obsess about it?"

c. "I *run* a business." → "How, specifically, do you run your business?"

3. Mind reading

The person speaks as though they know what someone else thinks or feels.

a. "She doesn't want me around." → "How, specifically, do you know she doesn't want you around?"

b. "I can't do that. They will think I'm annoying." → "How, specifically, do you know they will think you're annoying?"

c. "My father is always judging me." → "How, specifically, do you know he is always judging you?"

4. Cause and effect

The person makes a statement that one thing caused another, but it's not clear how.

a. "The evening was going fine, and then you made me feel like an idiot." → "How, specifically, did I make you feel like an idiot?" (One person does not have the power to change another's feelings on their own, so there must be something missing in this cause-effect link.)

b. "If I don't get into the right college, I will be devastated." → "How, specifically, will that devastate you?"

c. "At this age, it's too late for me to get in good shape." → "How, specifically, does your age cause you to not be able to get in good shape?"

Let's unpack one of these examples a bit more to see how asking this question can open doors for you. Your son says, "If I don't get into the right college, I will be devastated." You, as a good parent, know that it would be disappointing and could bring up a host of negative feelings or self-doubt were that to happen. At the same time, you want to teach your child that life goes on and what will equip him best in this world is to be able to handle situations and emotions like this, and still thrive in life. So you do not try to tell him it's no big deal. That would discount both his feelings and what you and he believe to be true. And you don't try to tell him, "I'm sure you'll get in." That would set unfair expectations and just reinforce his worry that it would be a big problem not to. Instead, you get curious and ask, "How, specifically, will that devastate you?"

This leads him to open up about how he worries about what his friends would think of him, and that he has heard he'll never make as much money if he doesn't get into the best college, and that he worries he would be letting you down. Now you know what the conversation is really about. You could choose to probe deeper into any of these—e.g., "How, specifically, do you know I'd think you let me down?" or "What, specifically, makes you believe I'd think you let me down?" When he answers that you went to a good college and you told him how important education is, then you are in a position to have a very useful conversation. You might tell him how you feel like he's made you proud by showing how much he cares about education, and that college acceptance is not in his control. What matters is how much he chooses to learn wherever he goes to college.

A note on how to ask the question well: it may seem unnecessary to actually say the word "specifically." We encourage it, however. It tends to guide people toward specifics. It can also help you as the asker focus on trying to learn the specifics. Some variations on the question can work, too. Instead of "How, specifically, is planning ahead hard?" you might ask, "What, specifically, is hard about planning ahead?" So long as you are curious about how, specifically, they think, feel, or behave when you ask, that's what we're going for.

Some readers may also be concerned that it could be hard to spot the language patterns. In fact, it often is at first because we're so used to speaking in these ways that we don't think twice when we hear these patterns. Though with a little practice, the patterns do start to just pop out at you. This story offers the key to making it work: A skilled NLP trainer was working one-on-one with a great student who was super motivated to master NLP. As they spoke about a challenge the student was working on, the trainer asked various questions. A number of times, the student had valuable insights into her own challenge when the trainer did so. At one point, the student stopped the trainer, and half-exasperatedly said, "How do you know when to ask a question and what the right question is?" The trainer paused and smiled and told the student the secret: "I ask something when I don't know the answer or don't understand." The student was very much ready for this secret. Are you? Doing this well calls on you to try not to use your great intellect, penetrating intuition, ability to read people, or to psychoanalyze. Instead, it works best when you just listen to what someone says, without reading between the lines, and notice when it doesn't quite add up for you.

In other words, the game here is to recognize when you don't fully understand why someone is mentally stuck, and just try asking how, specifically, they are going about doing whatever they're doing.

In the next chapter, we offer one last language pattern to listen for, and cartography questions to ask for unpacking what someone really thinks or feels.

16

DO THEY REALLY DO THAT ALL THE TIME?

A long time ago in a place called Sparta, the leader of the Spartans, King Lenny (short for Leonidas), was a powerful and admired leader who had a reputation for never losing. He had a younger, lesser-known brother whose story is largely lost to history, who was known as Prince Luzalot. Luzalot was not a name given to him at birth—this was a name that he earned by *always* losing *every* encounter that he became involved in. This was the family lore. Lenny wins everything and Luzalot always loses. Fortunately for Luzalot, his dad, King Andi (short for Anaxandridas), was a progressive monarch. He noticed his son's dejected attitude and arranged for him to be psychoanalyzed by a fellow monarch, King Eddie (short for Oedipus), who moonlighted as a Freudian psychotherapist with training in NLP. The prince related to King Eddie that *all* of his problems stem from *always* losing and *never* winning. King Eddie diagnosed Luzalot as suffering from unproductive use of universal quantifiers, or absolute beliefs. King Eddie and Luzalot proceeded to examine the prince's life in more detail. Luzalot's model of reality began to transform as he started to realize that he did not *always* lose, and that, in fact, he sometimes won. Upon seeing the truth, the family agreed he would henceforth be called Prince Winabit.

While the events in the above paragraph are made up, these kinds of family myths are very real. They are one of many areas in life in which we tell ourselves stories that something or someone is always one way and never another. We use universal quantifiers to describe the person or situation—words that make statements total and absolute. They are words like: "all," "every," "always," "everyone," "everybody," "never," "none," "nobody," "nothing," and "no one." They capture the idea that something is without exception. These words have a powerful effect on us, for better or for worse, and they are seldom accurate.

When we say things like "always," "never," "everyone," "no one," or other universal quantifiers, we're very likely overgeneralizing—often by quite a bit. That's not a benign thing to do. One of the core teachings from cognitive therapy (which has received a good deal of research support over the last roughly fifty years—perhaps more than any other therapy) is that when people have distorted thinking, like overgeneralizing, it can cause them strong, frequently unwanted or limiting emotions, thoughts, and behaviors.[1] For example, men who are violent in their marriages are more likely to overgeneralize, as well as think other distorted thoughts, than men who are not violent in their marriages, in response to an anger-causing situation.[2] And people who are highly socially anxious and somewhat depressed have been shown to overgeneralize, as well as have other distorted thoughts, more than a control group.[3] They might tell themselves something like "I *never* get any respect" or "*No one* will want to talk to me." Imagine if you deeply believed either of those two statements. The first would make a lot of people feel mad or dejected. The second would make a lot of people feel anxious and want to avoid a social situation.

Overgeneralizing can be very persuasive—both to the speaker and to the listener—because it creates a sense of conviction or certainty. Universal quantifiers are words that take overgeneralization to an extreme. They make it seem like there is no possibility that the statement is false—often this happens unconsciously or is just felt if we are not paying attention. But the impact is real. The beliefs reflected in such words can be positive and empowering (e.g., "*All* I do is win," "You must *always* be charitable," "*Everything* will work out") or negative and disempowering (e.g., "*All* lawyers are greedy," "*Everyone* on welfare is lazy," or "I'm *never* good enough").

Given their impact, universal quantifiers can be a great clue into someone's internal beliefs of how the world works. That's why universal quantifiers form one of the language patterns we teach people to notice in NLP, and to get curious about.

Every day, lawyers, doctors, salespeople, parents, and many others use universal quantifiers in a variety of situations. They may or may not be conscious of choosing these words, but when they use them they really can make a difference in how the speaker and listener think.

For example, a lawyer may use a universal quantifier to make a strong argument in court, such as "The law ensures that *all* people have the right to a fair trial." This statement uses the universal quantifier "all" to create a sense of certainty that the law does indeed guarantee everyone the right to a fair trial, regardless of the statement's veracity. But is this statement really true? The fact is that "all people have the right to a fair trial" does not equate to all people having a fair trial in the real world. Some litigants have it more fair than others. The harsh truth is that not all trials are fair, be it due to a biased judge or jury, or one of the parties being able to afford a superior legal team. It is a well-known fact amongst criminal lawyers that rather than being presumed innocent as guaranteed by the US Constitution, criminal defendants are sometimes presumed guilty by the fact finders, be it judges or juries. Perhaps that plays a part in the striking percentage of guilty verdicts. According to the Pew Research Center, in 2022, 83 percent who exercised their right to a fair trial in federal cases were found guilty.[4] And 90 percent of defendants avoided trials altogether by pleading guilty. A conviction in a trial can have a harsher penalty, and the odds are not good for being acquitted. No one can know whether all those defendants were actually guilty. The socioeconomic and psychological reasons for this phenomenon are beyond the scope of this book, but it seems reasonable to suggest the law may not *always* ensure fairness for *all*.

A parent might say to their young child, "*Never* talk to grown-ups you don't know." This statement uses the universal quantifier "never" to create a sense that this is a rule that cannot be broken.

If a salesperson says to us, "*Everyone* loves this product line," it suggests there is universal agreement that buying it is a good idea. Were we not to love this product line, we would need to go against common sense.

This is where a skillful listener armed with a healthy curiosity can steer the conversation in a more useful direction. For this, we offer you one more type of cartography question to discover the thoughts and feelings and beliefs that may be hiding behind a universal quantifier. When you hear a universal quantifier, just say it back, with curiosity, and make it a question:

"Always?"
"Never?"
"Everyone?"
"No one?"

Another version of this is to restate the whole belief as a question, and not just the universal quantifier. For example, "Everyone has equal opportunity?"

If repeating the question does not accomplish the task, you can follow it up by asking them to specifically search for even one counterexample. "Really . . . there's never been one time when . . . ?" or "Is there anyone who doesn't have equal opportunity?"

It can look like this:

JIM (VISIBLY IRRITATED AFTER GETTING BACK FROM THE DOCTOR): Everyone at that office is so disrespectful.

MIRANDA (CURIOUS): Everyone?

JIM (STILL IRRITATED): Just about. Okay, not everyone, but the people at the front desk were. And the doctor didn't seem to care at all.

MIRANDA (STILL CURIOUS): There wasn't anyone who was respectful? The doctor didn't care at all?

JIM (VISIBLY STARTING TO RELAX A BIT AND MOVE ON): That's not true entirely. The nurse was very nice and the woman who did the billing at the end was sweet. And the doctor was fine, but just didn't really say much when I told her how I was treated when I showed up.

Miranda could have just taken Jim's statement at face value. But instead, she heard the universal quantifier, recognized it may have been an overgeneralization, and got curious. In so doing, she came to understand better the truth of what Jim was thinking and feeling, as well as the truth of what actually happened. As she did so, Jim also understood the truth of what actually happened better. His thoughts became less distorted as he moved from overgeneralizing to being more accurate. His emotions also softened. He was able to move on from that stuck, unpleasant state he was in.

It's not always necessary to specifically restate the universal quantifier or repeat the belief as a question, although that is very often a great way to do it. What matters most, however you do it, is to be curious about whether it is an overgeneralization and steer them toward exploring counterexamples if they don't do it on their own after your first question. For instance:

ELANA (FRUSTRATED): You never think about my needs. You're never there for me when I need you.
JUSTIN (AFTER TAKING A DEEP BREATH TO RECENTER, SAYS WITH CURIOSITY): First of all, I'm sorry I wasn't thinking about your needs. . . . Is it really true that you feel I've never considered your needs or been there for you?

If the questions do not lead others to where they need to go, you can also offer your own counterexamples to the speaker's universal quantifier(s). In the everyone-has-equal-opportunity example, you could state, "Can we agree that a billionaire's son has more opportunity than a child born to parents on welfare in a low-income neighborhood?" or "Can we agree that everyone deserves equal opportunity, but unfortunately that doesn't always happen?"

In the following real-life example, a lawyer—let's call him Greg P. to keep it anonymous—effectively notices a disempowering universal quantifier during the jury selection phase of a trial, gets curious about it, and guides the process to a better outcome.

JUROR: All lawyers are greedy.
LAWYER: All lawyers?
JUROR: Yes.

LAWYER: Are there *some* lawyers who aren't greedy?

JUROR: Never met one. (With a smile)

LAWYER: What about the lawyers who volunteer for the indigent or public defenders who work for very low wages, are they greedy also?

JUROR: I guess not.

LAWYER: So *some* lawyers are not greedy?

JUROR: Some are not.

LAWYER: So can we agree that not *all* lawyers are greedy?

JUROR: I guess we can.

LAWYER: You don't know me yet. But can I ask you to keep an open mind about me, and give me a chance to prove to you that I am not one of those greedy lawyers?

JUROR: Sure, I'll give you a chance.

By noticing the universal quantifiers, getting curious, and asking for clarity, Greg was able to change the narrative for both parties. He was able to both understand and change a bit of the mental model of the juror.

To be fair, sometimes universal quantifiers are accurate and that sense of certainty or conviction is appropriate. We're not suggesting you challenge them just for the sake of it, nor that you assume you are right when you do. It is possible that a person has actually always struggled with relationships or has never felt financially secure, not even once. However, if they are overgeneralizing, you can help change the narrative while you come to a better understanding of what needs attention. If they are not overgeneralizing, you will still come to a better understanding of how extensive and enduring the situation truly is. Either way, by spotting the universal quantifier and getting curious about it, you will be in a better position to take the next most useful step, whatever that may be.

You can experiment right now by applying this to the way you speak to yourself in your mind. Are you someone who has ever said to yourself, "It's never enough" or "Nothing's ever enough"?

Now ask yourself, "Never? Was there really never even one time when I or others felt that what I did was enough?"

You can also think about some pet peeve of yours. Is there a person who always does that annoying thing (your pet peeve)? For example, they always leave the kitchen a mess; or they always take all the credit; or they only ever think about what they want, not what you want; or they always treat you disrespectfully, etc.

Now ask yourself, "Always? Every time? There was never even one time when that was not entirely true?"

What happens when you openly and honestly explore these questions?

Many people find that their feelings shift. As they notice it is not quite as universal as they had been thinking, their anger and frustration subside a little, and their compassion or patience expand a little.

Asking yourself the question can both help you understand the mental model you were operating with and start to expand or enrich your mental model in adaptive ways.

Summary of the Cartography Questions

In chapters 12 through 16 we introduced a series of language patterns that form part of what NLP calls the meta model. When someone uses one of these language patterns, it suggests that there might be information that is deleted, distorted, or overgeneralized in their mental model of the situation they find themself in. For each of these patterns, there is at least one useful cartography question to help you understand the mental model of the person speaking. In each case, the questions are about getting more specific and accurate. Often, just trying to get clarity in these ways helps not only you but also the other person gain clarity, and can lead to a breakthrough for them.

As you may have been noticing, each of the tools we've offered can be used to better understand and change ourselves, too. The ways we talk to ourselves follow the same patterns as the ways we talk to others. You can learn to spot these patterns in your own language, get curious, and probe deeper into your own mental model, too. There's no need to get stuck in the same negative self-talk anymore.

What we've covered in chapters 12 through 16 we've summarized here:

CHAPTER	LANGUAGE PATTERN	CARTOGRAPHY QUESTION(S)
12. Don't Should on Yourself!	NLP patterns: modal operators of necessity and modal operators of possibility (e.g., "Should"; "Have to"; "Can't")	What's stopping you? What would happen if . . . ? Why is that necessary / impossible?
13. Something's Missing Here	NLP pattern: *deletion* (e.g. "I just can't anymore")	What does this pertain to?
14. Who, Specifically?	NLP patterns: lack of referential index (e.g., "People say . . ."); lost performative (e.g., "That would look bad if I . . .")	Who, specifically? According to whom?
15. How, Specifically?	NLP patterns: nominalization (e.g., "We need a decision."); unspecified verbs (e.g., "We obsess over every detail."); mind reading (e.g., "You think I'm dumb."); cause and effect (e.g., "They made me feel worthless.")	How, specifically? E.g.: How, specifically, are you deciding? How, specifically, do you obsess? How, specifically, do you know? How, specifically, did they make you feel that?
16. Do They Really Do That All the Time?	NLP pattern: universal quantifiers (e.g. "Always," "Everyone," "Never")	Repeat the universal quantifier as a question (e.g., "Always?") Look for counterexamples (e.g., "Has there ever been a time when . . . ?")

You might find it helpful to keep the cartography questions on hand somewhere so you can have them as a readily available reference. For example, bookmark this page and glance over them before going into a difficult conversation.

If someone were to master only what's in this table summary—spotting these language patterns, getting curious, and asking cartography questions to create a map of someone's thoughts and feelings—that would be enough to dramatically improve their ability to communicate with others and lead them to change. But in the coming chapters, you'll find there's so much more we can all learn to be curious about, to quickly and deeply understand other people, and, if appropriate, help them change.

17

WATCH THEIR EYES FOR CLUES

ave you ever noticed that when you ask someone a question, their eyes often go off to the side, or up or down, as if they're searching their mind for the answer? When people need to think about what to say, they often look away from the person they are speaking to. This is a well-documented phenomenon in research.[1] In fact, if you want to look straight at your audience or at the camera the whole time you're speaking, it takes practice. Glancing away may be the more natural thing to do.

There are various theories about why people look away, and no consensus on the answer. One idea is that it is distracting to look at someone, so looking away helps you think. Another idea is that, if you have a mental image in mind, you might actually be looking at it in your mind to help you come up with an answer—like when you are trying to remember where you left your keys in your house. A third is that where you look actually reflects what kind of thinking you're doing. NLP embraced the third option. Primarily, the claim is that people look up when they are picturing something in their mind's eye—like picturing a trip to the beach; look in the middle, but to the left or right, when they are hearing something in their mind's ear—like a song; and look down when connecting with a feeling.

We've probably all seen a character in a movie or TV show say something like "Picture this . . . your name in lights!" While they say it, they look up and wave their hand slowly across the sky. They're asking someone to picture something and pointing their attention upward to help facilitate that. It would feel weird if they looked down at their feet, and waved their hand along the background of the street while saying it. Imagine that same character later in the show, when it seems they won't make it to the big time after all. We see them feeling dejected, ruminating in self-talk and lost in their feelings. Chances are that character is looking down, perhaps kicking the dirt as they walk.

Go ahead and play with it right now. Picture, in your mind, the last place you went on vacation. Give yourself a moment to remember it, and once you do, go ahead and picture it in more detail.

Did you gaze up some of the time while picturing it?

Now, try this one. How do you feel right now? Take a moment to connect with how you are feeling physically and/or emotionally. What's going on in your body?

Did you look down for a decent part of the time that you were considering how you felt?

And one more. How does the Beatles song "I Want to Hold Your Hand" go? Just go ahead and hear it in your head.

Were your eyes roughly in the middle (not up or down) and did they go to the side somewhat? Not the whole time, but for a good chunk of time?

Many people find these patterns tend to fit with their experience. But not always.

If you've ever come across someone criticizing NLP, there's a good chance they focused entirely or mostly on the tool we'll share in this chapter. And some of the criticism is justified. We think it's important to honor what's true in those critiques and consider whether the tool should be abandoned. In fact, we considered leaving it out of the book. It's not as useful as many of the other things in NLP, in our opinion, and if we didn't have this tool, it wouldn't affect anything else we teach in this book. But we've decided to include it because a number of people have heard about it and we suspect those readers might be wondering what we have to say on the topic. We also think it's important not to throw the baby out with the bathwater.

The tool we're talking about is to watch someone's eyes when they're talking, or thinking, to get some clues as to their mental model of whatever it is that they're thinking about.

The proposal that NLP's developers made was actually a little more specific than what we outlined above—up for seeing, middle for hearing, and down for feelings.[2] They also claimed that for most people, looking to the left indicated the person was remembering something, and looking to the right reflected imagination—constructing a new idea. (This might help you remember the left/right part of it: a timeline often goes left to right—left is past for remembering, right is future for imagining something new.) And they added one more distinction, too, which is that looking down only pertains to feelings when you look down to the right. Looking down to the left was when you talk to yourself, which is often tightly linked with feelings—e.g., saying to yourself, "I'm such an idiot! Why did I say that?!" often accompanies feeling embarrassed.

Since the 1980s several attempts were made by researchers to find evidence of a one-to-one mapping in which these claims were always true. They failed to support the full set of predictions.[3] One can always make the argument that maybe the studies weren't done just right, so it's an open question still. But we think there's value in saying that they did discover something useful. There probably is not a one-to-one mapping, in which eye gaze always means these things—e.g., if someone is looking up to the right, it does not mean they are definitely imagining something visually in their mind's eye. After all, how could there be such a one-to-one mapping? Sometimes we look up to look away from something yucky like vomit on the ground; other times we look up when picturing something tall in our mind's eye like a skyscraper; other times because of a noise—like an airplane coming from that direction, and so on.

But that doesn't mean there's nothing useful here. However, before getting into what is useful, we think it's important to say a bit more about what is not true.

Some people have latched onto these ideas about what eye movements mean and made outlandish claims. For example, it has been suggested that you can tell if someone is lying by watching their eyes. The logic is that if they have to look up and to the right while answering, then they must be imagining—making it up. Whereas if they looked up and to the left then they would be remembering. For example: "Where were you the night of December sixteenth?" and the person on the witness stand looks up and to the right while answering. Even if you fully embraced the original claims about eye movement from NLP, and moreover, believed it was a one-to-one mapping, this would just be really poor logic. The person on the witness stand might have no recollection because they were innocent and it was an unremarkable day. So they might try to *imagine* where they likely were. Or perhaps, the person on the witness stand was really nervous because they had never been in a courtroom, and they were trying to *imagine* why the prosecutor was treating them this way, or *imagine* what trap the prosecutor was trying to set. The point is, there are endless reasons why a person would imagine something when lying has nothing to do with it.

So, we suggest paring down this tool to just what seems prudent and useful, and recommend you use it for that and nothing more. Because anything more would just be fooling yourself, and actually making you a worse communicator and less effective change agent, thinking you know something when you don't.

Here's what we do know that we think is relevant. There actually are parts of the brain called the frontal eye fields. We have them on the left and right sides of the brain, and they pass signals from various parts of the brain to the eyes regarding where to move. Also interesting for us is that the frontal eye fields appear to work in the other direction—they may pass signals about eye movements to various parts of the brain. For instance, eye gaze can influence how much value we put on something when making a decision. When researchers interrupted the activity of the frontal eye fields, they found that this effect on decision-making went away.[4] So there is at least a neural mechanism by which eye movements theoretically could both reflect and affect brain activity, even if we're not aware of how we're moving our eyes.

More evidence that eye movements can both reflect and influence brain activity comes from the success of eye movement desensitization and re-processing, or EMDR. Studies have shown it to be a successful and reliable treatment for PTSD (post-traumatic stress disorder), working as well as CBT (cognitive behavioral therapy).[5] As strange as it may sound, in the EMDR process, the trauma sufferer reconnects with the traumatic memories while moving their eyes side to side. The theory goes that they connect the traumatic event to many more psychological resources by moving their eyes—that the eye movements actually help them access other resources, like additional information or memories. This may help them to see the big picture, to forgive, to regulate their emotions, and so on. Is the theory about why it works right? No one can say for sure yet. But regardless of the theory, moving the eyes in that way has that documented effect.

Researchers also know that there are at least some circumstances when eye movements do reflect specifically what someone is thinking about. For example, when thinking about something visual, eye-tracking equipment has been used to show that people will move their gaze to different parts of a mental image just as they would to something they were seeing in the real world.[6]

You can probably convince yourself of this through your own experience, too. Picture your living room right now. Take a moment and get an image of it in your mind. As you scan around the living room—in your mind's eye—start from one side of the room and work your way across to the other. Where is the door? Are there any plants? See them. Now look to the couch. Now over to the TV. Is there other furniture? Any art on the walls? How does the ceiling look? Is there a rug on the floor?

Most people probably move their eye gaze around when doing that. It's hard to keep your gaze still, in fact, isn't it?

So, putting it together, there is a neural mechanism that suggests eye movements can reflect and influence how we think and feel; there is evidence that eye movements can help people move on from trauma as part of EMDR; and there is evidence that eye movements reflect specifically what we are thinking about at least some of the time. There are also culturally common ideas that people look up when picturing something, and down when connecting with their feelings. Maybe those are just metaphors, but they might still reflect what's going on internally. Given all that, we think it makes sense not to throw out the idea that eye movements might be a clue to what's going on in someone's head.

But how should you use this tool—of watching someone's eyes for clues? The answer is, don't presume you know what the gaze direction refers to exactly, but do get curious. The direction may often, but not always, mean something useful. You can use the NLP suggestions for what the eye-gaze directions mean as a starting point for understanding the other person's mental model better. You might be wrong. In fact, you should expect to be wrong some of the time. But, it can lead to a richer understanding of what someone is really thinking or feeling.

It might look something like this:

JOSH ASKS GREG: Do you think it's too early to market the next class we're going to teach?

GREG PAUSES AND LOOKS UP—some to the left and some to the right, but a lot of looking up.

JOSH SAYS: Are you picturing something right now?

Notice that Josh does not assume Greg is picturing something, but wonders if he is. He used Greg's eyes for clues, not for answers.

GREG REPLIES: Yeah, actually. Funny you should ask. I was seeing us on stage at this conference I'm going to in Vegas. Huge audience, people loving it.

JOSH: Okay, cool. I'm not opposed to people loving us. But why were you picturing that?

GREG: I've been thinking it would be good to wait to launch the next class, so that it is just after that. We should try to speak at that conference. It would be a perfect audience for us.

In that case, it helped Josh not only get an answer but understand Greg's thoughts and excitement behind his recommendation. In fact, Greg did think they should wait. Greg could have said, "I think we should wait," any number of ways. But this interaction led to a specific and energizing way of thinking about it. Josh was not only convinced, but excited.

Here's another example. A mom is talking to her ten-year-old son as they sit side by side on a park bench during what was supposed to be some special bonding time on a beautiful spring weekend day. He's looking down a lot as he talks and seems to be stuck in feeling down. The mom has learned a bit of NLP, so she gets curious about whether the looking down is connected to him being consumed by his feelings. So she experiments:

MOM, ALSO LOOKING DOWN, TO JOIN HIM WHERE HE IS: Seems like you're having a lot of feelings about something.

KID: [No response, but also doesn't deny it]

MOM, STILL LOOKING DOWN AT THE GROUND LIKE THE BOY: Sometimes I feel like nothing's going my way, and things just feel hard.

KID, GLANCING UP THEN BACK DOWN: Can we do something?

MOM: Look at me for a sec.

KID LOOKS UP AT HER: Yeah?

MOM: You can feel however you feel today. No pressure. All right, let's do something. Look over there—you see those musicians? Let's go listen to them.

KID IS LOOKING UP NOW, and is starting to move on from being stuck in his feelings to engaging in the moment with his mom.

The mom guessed that looking down meant he was stuck in his feelings. She got curious about that. She got curious about whether helping shift his eye gaze would make a difference. She helped him look up and around and get unstuck. Was it the eye movements from down to up that made the difference? We'll never know. She said some things, too. And her tone of voice probably also mattered, as did numerous other things. But it helped the mom have an idea about where to start and gave her some principled reasons to try things out.

At some point, research may be able to help us understand how often the direction of eye gaze corresponds to a certain kind of mental representation—e.g., up for seeing, left and right middle for hearing, and down for feeling; or even the more complex patterns that include left for memories and right for imagination, and down to the left for self-talk.

Until then, we think that when you put it all together, there are a few conclusions that make sense:

1. There is no one-to-one mapping from eye-gaze direction to type of mental representation in which the mapping is always true.
2. It makes more sense to believe eye gaze does have some connection to how we think and feel than that it never has any connection.

3. If there is a connection, we don't know the mechanisms—e.g., it may be an artifact of cultural norms or common metaphors, or it may pertain to some more physiological or neuroanatomical mechanism linking gaze direction to the different kinds of processing.

4. It is reasonable to use the NLP suggestions about eye gaze as a jumping-off point to get curious about whether someone may be picturing, hearing, or feeling something. But don't presume you've guessed correctly—have a conversation with the aim of learning what's true for them.

You can learn a lot about someone's mental model when you discover what they are picturing in their mind's eye, hearing in their mind's ear, or feeling. The more you learn about their mental model, the more you can guide change. One tool you can start using for doing so is to watch their eyes for clues about what might be going on in their mind. If nothing else, using this tool may serve to get you to be more curious, and ask more questions, about what the other person may be picturing, hearing, or feeling, and whether they are remembering or imagining something. Exploring those things could help you get closer to finding the difference that makes the difference for them.

In the next couple of chapters, we'll invite you to get curious about how someone sees themself in relation to their situation. How they see themself can have important consequences.

18

WHO'S DRIVING?

Why did the narcissist and the empath start a podcast together? Because one could talk about themself for hours, and the other could listen for hours.

Narcissists care only about themselves and they think they are superior to everyone else. They attend to their own concerns—"What do I want? Is this good for me? How do I feel?" Others' interests, needs, or feelings are less important to them. Think of the classic movie villain who discards people when they are no longer useful to them. Empaths tend to care deeply about others and are very concerned with their interests, needs, and feelings—"What do they want? What would be good for them? How do they feel?" The empath can forget about or push aside their own interests, needs, or feelings in the process. Think of the exhausted parent who gave up sleep for days to take care of a sick kid who was up at night.

In most cases, calling someone a narcissist is an insult, and saying someone is very empathetic is meant as a compliment. Surely there are many contexts where that makes sense. But in this chapter, we're not interested in narcissists and empaths, per se. We just used those labels of being narcissistic or empathetic to quickly paint a picture that's easy to imagine. Instead, what we're interested in highlighting is the difference between attending to yourself and attending to others. We suspect that many people would agree that for a healthy person, there is a time and place where thinking about yourself is the right thing to do, and a time and place for thinking about others.

Those different concerns—self versus other—are what we really want to draw attention to. In NLP we call this distinction being self-referenced or other-referenced. The idea is that we use either our own needs, interests, feelings, and values or the needs, interests, feelings, and values of others as the frame of reference for determining what is important and what decisions to make.

In the ways people speak and behave, they usually reveal whether they are preoccupied more with their own needs, interests, feelings, and values (self-referenced) or more with others' needs, interests, feelings, and values (other-referenced). In this chapter, we invite you to get curious about this distinction as a way to understand someone better. When we learn to spot in their language or actions where they are on this spectrum—self versus other—we can learn a lot about their thinking, their motivation, and what may be holding them back if they are stuck.

For example, Josh was once coaching a guy who we'll call Marcus who was really stressed out about a job interview. Marcus had been recruited. It was a job that would pay well but Marcus had his concerns about the people, the management style, and a few other things. So Marcus didn't feel good about the prospect. Nonetheless, he felt like he had to interview, and in general he wanted more money and a new role. For a week, what kept Marcus distracted and sometimes up at night was how he could answer their questions and whether they would be impressed by him. If he got past the first interview, there would be more rounds, with even higher-profile people. What would they think of him? He doubted himself. He obsessed about it. It felt miserable to him, and he wished for the time when it would all be over.

Then Josh asked him a question: "What do *you* want to get out of these interviews? You've given a huge amount of energy to thinking about what they might want, which is useful. But you haven't considered what *you're* looking for in these interviews." Josh had a hunch that Marcus was being very other-referenced; thinking almost entirely about what the interviewers cared about, and forgetting about himself. By asking Marcus this question, Josh's aims were to (1) explore whether Marcus really was being other-referenced; (2) help Marcus try out being more self-referenced; and (3) find out if that would make a difference for Marcus.

Marcus had not really considered that side of the equation. But he was able to get in touch with a number of things he wanted to get out of the interviews once he thought about it—he wanted to try to understand who these people really were, and what the management styles would really be like, for example. As he allowed himself to think about it more, he kept uncovering more—he wanted to learn what it would take to find something he saw as a great fit (whether with this company or somewhere else), and get a better sense of what compensation he could feel good about. Within minutes, the interview process changed into an opportunity in his mind.

Marcus shifted into being self-referenced. He was basing his decisions on his own criteria, his own values, his own interests, his own needs, his own feelings. He had been previously other-referenced—basing his decisions and his sense of what counted as success on what other people might think or care about. He was letting them drive while he sat in the passenger seat, with no control over where the car went or how it drove. He was letting them be in control of the interview process, what the interviews were for, and how to interpret what it all meant. Then, when he explored what he wanted, he instead sat himself in the driver's seat. He took control over the purpose and meaning of the interviews.

You can experiment with this shift toward being self-referenced now if you like. Call to mind a situation in which you are very concerned with what others may think. For example, you're hosting a party and you are stressed about what the guests will think of your house; you're embarrassed about something you said and are worried people thought poorly of you; you are going to lead a meeting or present or do a sales pitch and you are preoccupied with how it will be received; you're going on a date; you're providing care, etc.

Now ask yourself, "What do *I want* to get out of this?" For example, "What do I want from this party—is it to have fun with friends?" Remember the well-formed outcome from chapter 1, and pick things you want to get that are within your control.

And ask yourself, "What do *I think* about this?" For example, "What do I think of my house—would I be happy if I came to a party here with my friends?"

For sixty years, there has been accumulating research that feeling that you are in the driver's seat has a wide range of effects. It can affect your level of stress or your resilience in the face of stressors, your work performance, your overall well-being, your experience of pain, your physical health, and even the structure of the brain—linked with the size of brain regions involved in a lot of functions, like self-control, processing reward, feeling or managing emotions, and aspects of thinking. The point is, it can make a big difference when you see yourself in the driver's seat—feeling like you are in control.[1]

At this point, you may be thinking that the lesson is to always try to be in the driver's seat. The example of Marcus interviewing for a job shows how it helps for you to do so. And you might expect people to tell you that you must be in the driver's seat to succeed in life. But that would actually be a limiting way to operate, too.

Pause for just a moment and it becomes obvious that there are times when it is better to defer to others—like when the dentist informs you that you need to have a cavity filled. And we all know people (perhaps ourselves) who find comfort in believing that something else or someone else out there is looking out for us, or has a master plan.[2] Clearly there's a place for letting someone else drive at times.

The real secret is not to become totally self-referenced or totally other-referenced, but to be able to do both, and shift between them as the situation calls for. Remember the NLP belief *the person with the most flexibility exerts the most influence*? This is a perfect example. People who can flexibly adapt to the situation by being self-referenced, other-referenced, or some amount of each may not always be in the driver's seat for any one event, but are the ones who end up in the driver's seat of their lives.

It helped Marcus to think about how his interviewers would make decisions. It helped him even more to also connect with his own needs. To completely forget the needs of the interviewers would be unwise. But Marcus was in no danger of that. In his particular case, he needed to build out the other side of the equation.

The balance between being self- and other-referenced can be compared to the way of the Tao. If the self is the black area of the Tao and the other is the white, the goal is to be the line separating the two. Let's call the line being balanced, and interpret it as striking a healthy balance between your own needs and the needs of others, as well as being aware of your own emotions while also showing empathy and consideration for others. What counts as a healthy balance depends on the situation. High up on the line in the image, balance means more black (self) than white (other). Lower down, balance means more white (other) than black (self).

We've seen an example of when shifting into being more self-referenced was highly adaptive. Now let's see an example of when shifting into being more other-referenced is more adaptive.

Some years ago, Greg felt that the staff in his office was lazy, overpaid, and mercenary. After several very successful sessions with an extremely efficient NLP-trained coach, he realized that he viewed his employees as tools meant to accomplish a job as opposed to human beings. He changed his approach and started treating everyone in the office as family members. He stopped focusing on late arrivals, early departures, and other minor infractions. He started sharing credit, freely handing out praise and bonuses. His work family is now just that—a family. By seeing the "others" in his firm as people with the same challenges, needs, and desires as him, he was able to become more other-referenced in his interactions with them. They in turn did him the same favor.

In Greg's case becoming other-referenced ended up being the best way to actually serve his own needs. That kind of win-win is common. Oftentimes a person resists shifting from self to other (from driver to passenger), because they fear they will not take care of their own needs. But after making the shift, they discover that it was, in fact, a better way to attend to their own needs than what they had been doing.

You can try out becoming more other-referenced in your own experience now. Do you ever find yourself blaming others or getting mad at them (in your mind or out loud) for things they did or did not do?

If so, that's a situation in which you were probably too self-referenced. In your mind, now, see that situation from some distance, as though you were a fly on the wall. Remember the NLP belief *every behavior has a positive intention.* Looking at the situation now, what happens when you consider the positive intention of the person you blamed or got mad at? Why did they do what they did?

For most people and most situations, we find that answering those questions helps create a balance in which they become aware of both their own concerns (being the driver) and the concerns of the other person (being the passenger). Often, people find their emotions calm down, and they have an easier time moving on.

To help bring home the point that one is not better than the other in self versus other, but a balance between the two is best, here's another example. With Greg, we saw how focusing on others' needs helped him serve his own needs. Here's a situation where it is the opposite—where focusing more on our own needs (being the driver) helps us serve the needs of others.

It may come as a surprise to many people that being a veterinarian is very psychologically taxing. Many of us assume they are living their dream of helping animals in need. Surely, many of them are. However, there is a high level of work stress and burnout, as well as substantially increased rates of depression and even suicide as compared to the general population.[3] Veterinarians tend to be overworked and in a difficult environment of distraught pet owners, suffering animals, and limited interpersonal support. Veterinarians appear to also suffer from greater levels of empathic distress—a kind of burnout from too much empathy for those in traumatic situations—even compared to other health care professionals.[4] By concentrating on the needs and suffering of their clients and their furry kids, these professionals sacrifice their own well-being.

However, one factor that seems to be a key difference for those who fare best even in a highly stressful health care environment is self-care—-e.g., taking stress management or mindfulness trainings.[5] Self-care is about honoring and attending to your own needs. It comes from being willing to be self-referenced about how you use at least some of your time and energy.

There are people in many organizations who take on any request they get whether they can handle it or not—they are far too other-referenced (always the passenger), so they fail to set boundaries. They end up totally overworked and stressed out, and they don't get their own work done. Often this leads them to need to postpone deadlines and miss targets for the work that matters most to them, to their careers, and to the organization they serve. But the organization, their career, their coworkers, their clients, and their own sanity would fare much better if they instead set boundaries because they would get their most important work done and done well, while doing less work overall. Josh actually wrote a book on how to do this, called *Two Awesome Hours*.

Is there a situation in which you have not stayed within your boundaries? Perhaps by taking on more work than you know you can handle? Perhaps by giving too much of your energy to someone or some task, and feeling too drained to take care of other important things? Perhaps by pushing yourself to keep up with others when it didn't feel right?

If there is a situation like that for you, you have probably been too other-referenced (being the passenger), letting others' needs and wants drive your behavior. What would happen in that situation if you did honor your boundaries?

What's stopping you from honoring your boundaries?

What would be an ideal way for you to engage in a situation like that, whether or not you believe it is possible yet?

How would maintaining your boundaries help you attend to others' needs more effectively than if you didn't maintain your boundaries?

So let's come back to the narcissist and the empath for a moment. We used the words "narcissist" and "empath" at the start of the chapter. It was part of a joke, sure. But it helps bring home the point that people sometimes attach a stigma to being self-referenced. We've offered the terms "driver" and "passenger," too. That brings up a stigma to being other-referenced. Who—at least in the United States—wants to admit to being like the passenger? No, we all want to be the driver—we want to be in charge, right? There are some people in NLP circles and outside of NLP who talk about healthy narcissism, and contrast it with unhealthy narcissism. Use whatever terms you find helpful or freeing. "Self-referenced" and "other-referenced" are more neutral, but if you want to use them with other people in your life, you'll find you will need to explain what you mean. Regardless of what you call it, learn to spot it.

Imagine a line running across this page. In fact, don't imagine it, and just look below.

Driver / Self-Referenced ◄──────── Balanced ────────► Passenger / Other-Referenced

As you pay attention to your own or others' thoughts and words, you can get curious about whether a shift to the left or the right on this line would make a difference.

Test yourself right now. Which do you think is the bigger issue in each case—too self-referenced or too other-referenced?

1. A person is causing problems by mistreating others.
2. A person is failing to set boundaries with their kids.
3. A person is stressed out about what others would think.
4. A person is micromanaging their team.

Here's what we think are the answers:

1. Mistreating others—too self-referenced
2. Not setting boundaries with kids—too other-referenced
3. Stressed about what others think—too other-referenced
4. Micromanaging—too self-referenced

The point of that test was to help you point your attention toward getting curious about whether someone is self- or other-referenced. Once you do so, you can try shifting that person to the other side and see what happens. Remember that a great NLPer doesn't presume they've got it right, but instead is looking for the difference that makes the difference. There's no failure, only feedback. Oftentimes, exploring a shift from self to other (from driver to passenger) or vice versa (from passenger to driver) can make a world of difference.

19

WALK A MILE IN THEIR SHOES, IN YOUR MIND

S o far in this book, we've offered you ways to try to gather information about someone's mental model as an outsider looking in. Now we invite you to understand someone's mental model in a different way, as an insider looking out.

This tool is extraordinary for at least two things. One is finding a breakthrough in how to communicate with someone, and the other is modeling someone so you can learn how to do what they do.

The tool we're talking about is to take what NLP calls the second-person perspective. If you and your friend are talking, then your perspective would be called first-person perspective. But if you imagine being your friend, feeling their feelings, seeing through their eyes, hearing what they hear, as they look back at you in the conversation, that's second-person perspective. Instead of experiencing things as yourself (first person), you step into—in your mind—what you imagine it is like to experience things as the other.

It may help to clarify how second-person perspective differs from something you've probably heard of, called third-person perspective—the third person is an outside observer, not one of the people involved in the interaction. So it's: first person—*self*; second person—the *other* person who you are talking to; third person—an *observer* looking at both of you. We'll come back to third-person perspective in a later chapter. For now, we're focusing on taking the second-person perspective.

Sometimes when people hear about second-person perspective, they think it is the same as trying to think about what someone else might think or feel. It is not that. The critical difference is that it is about letting yourself *act as if you were* the other person, and discovering how you—as the other person—think and feel. You don't just think about what their perspective might be, you try to experience it.

You might think you'd get to the same answers by thinking about what they might feel and think versus trying to experience it. But much of the time, there is a wealth of information that was hidden until taking the view of the insider looking out—taking the second-person (other) perspective. Somehow, we understand more when we actually see the view from the other side, hear as they hear things, feel as they feel, experience what they experience as the insider looking out. It's strange that this should make a difference. After all, the information must have always been accessible to you in principle—you use the same brain whether you're thinking about what someone might think versus stepping into their perspective in your mind. But taking the second-person (other) perspective can change what we become aware of.

The effects are often so profound and meaningful that this shift from first-person (self) to second-person (other) perspective has become one of the great workhorses of NLP.[1]

Stepping into the second-person (other) perspective as if it were your own can reveal a lot about what may be someone's mental model, both in terms of what you become consciously aware of, and in terms of a deep, intuitive sense of how they might experience the situation they are in. And it does all this fairly quickly.

With the advent of VR—virtual reality—like in video games, researchers have seen an opportunity to study the effects of becoming immersed in someone else's experience. Of particular relevance to us is the research on how this affects empathy—i.e., understanding someone else. For example, in one study, one group of participants had elderly faces in their VR experience and the other had young adult faces. The participants saw "themselves" (their avatars) in a VR mirror and they moved around a room and interacted with someone. The experience of stepping into the body of an elderly person in this way significantly reduced stereotypes about elderly people.[2]

Another study looked at behaviors toward the homeless. What's so useful, in particular, about this study for us is that the researchers looked at different degrees to which people can try to step into the experience of another person when taking their perspective. One group of participants just learned useful information about the homeless. Another group did more. They were asked to imagine a day in the life of a person who was homeless as if it were happening to them, and were given a story to imagine about a person who is evicted and must leave their apartment, ultimately spending the night on a bus in search of shelter. A third group deeply took on the second-person (other) perspective. They were not simply asked to imagine themselves in the shoes of the homeless person in that story. They also experienced things as though they were the homeless person looking out at the world, moving like them, seeing through their eyes, hearing through their ears—gathering their own belongings, riding the bus all night, searching for shelter—becoming homeless for a time, using virtual reality. Both groups who tried to imagine themselves as the homeless person (with or without the help of virtual reality) showed significantly improved empathy toward the homeless. And the researchers also did a separate trial comparing the two conditions over time in which people imagined themselves as the homeless person (with vs. without the help of virtual reality). Those who got immersed in the homeless person's experience the most—with the help of virtual reality—had longer-lasting effects and were substantially more likely to take actions to help the homeless, like signing petitions for housing.[3]

Without a VR headset and a knowledge of programming, we can still follow the same principle—find ways to make your immersion into the second-person (other) perspective as deep and personal as you can.

Don't just try to imagine what the other person must be thinking and feeling. Actually allow yourself to imagine being them, looking out of their eyes at you, or at the situation they find themself in. Take on their body posture as you sit, and even as you stand up and walk around. Take on their tone of voice, mannerisms, gestures. Various studies have shown how posture and movement and other ways of using our bodies affect what we think, feel, perceive, and what information becomes accessible in our minds. For instance, smiling can lift your mood. Blocking a smile-with-the-eyes with Botox injections (which paralyze the muscles) can interfere with emotions and with understanding others' emotions.[4] Also, slumping can make you more depressed, breathing slowly can decrease anxiety, and reading fast can make you happier.[5] And neuroscientists have shown that empathic accuracy—being right about someone else's experience—can be better when our brains and bodies simulate what the other person is going through moment by moment.[6] Our point is not to prescribe any specific movements or things to do with your body, but to help make the case that taking on the physiology—movement, breathing, gestures, expressions, posture, etc.—of the other person really can point you toward understanding or experiencing something different from just trying to think about the other person.

You can use language to guide you, too. Suppose you've been struggling to connect with your mother, so you try to take on her perspective. When stepping into her shoes—second position—don't let yourself say things like "She gets defensive." Instead, imagine being her in the interaction and say, instead, "I feel I need to defend myself." Researchers have found that I/me pronouns versus he/she/them pronouns do matter to how we experience a situation. In research this was tested with stories. A work of fiction, for example, could describe a tense father-son moment in either way.

For example, he/she/them pronouns:

"The young man, no longer a boy, entered the same kitchen he had entered a thousand times, but this time, on returning from the war, he saw the old man for what he was—a withering body and a sad, lonely soul, wanting to feel powerful again."

Or I/me pronouns:

"As a young man, no longer a boy, I entered the same kitchen I had entered a thousand times, but this time, on returning from the war, I saw my old man for what he was—a withering body and a sad, lonely soul, wanting to feel powerful again."

In those studies, when people read stories that used pronouns like I/me, they reported that it transported them more fully into the story, as if they were in that world in which the story took place. I/me pronouns also made people feel more immersed in the perspective of the protagonist—e.g., seeing as if they were in the protagonist's position.[7] The takeaway here includes two things: (1) it's worth insisting on the pronoun shift to I/me when you imagine the other person's perspective; and (2) even something as small as the pronouns someone uses can make a measurable difference on what they experience when trying to take someone's perspective.

One note of caution to help you succeed with this language. Saying, "If I were her, I would get defensive," isn't fully a switch to second-person (other) perspective. While it technically uses the I pronoun, psychologically, it's still mostly first-person (self) perspective. Taking the second-person (other) perspective fully, using I/me pronouns would sound more like this: "I feel I need to defend myself."

To step into their experience, use I/me pronouns, and take on their physiology—try to see and hear the world through their eyes and ears, and feel what they feel. And then take one more step into their experience. Imagine you hold their beliefs, capabilities, values, and identity.

Elsewhere in the book, we have discussed how beliefs, capabilities, values, and one's sense of identity can provide powerful filters through which people see the world and the options available to them in any situation.

Make that part of your immersion into the second-person (other) perspective, too. Beliefs, capabilities, values, and identity are also important parts of the mental model of the other person. What does the other person believe? What are they capable of? What do they think is important? How do they see themself?

As you experiment with doing this work, this caveat may help. You might find that you resist some aspect of the other person's mental model. For instance, sometimes people find themselves judging the other person's perspective negatively, and as a result, are not as open to learning how the world looks from that other perspective. If that happens, you can remember the NLP foundational beliefs that *everyone behaves in the best way they know how given their mental model*, and *every behavior has a positive intention*. For a time, let yourself be open to discovering how they are doing the best they know how and what their positive intentions are. Rather than trying to judge their mental model, or see how you would do things differently, the aim with this tool is to understand their mental model. Presuming positive intent and that they are doing the best they know how will help you focus on understanding rather than judging.

For an example of deep immersion, when Josh was learning NLP as a student at the NLP Center of New York, he and the other students did an exercise. Each student was asked to think of someone who did something well that they would like to learn. There was one professor Josh had studied with who, in Josh's opinion, *always* seemed to have the best questions after any presentation or discussion. The questions got right to the heart of the matter, and even when the professor brought up a shortcoming, Josh felt it was done in a way that helped everyone find a better solution. This professor was a major force in the intellectual life of the department, and was very successful as a researcher. Josh wanted to get better at asking questions and contributing to discussions like that professor did.

In the exercise, Josh took on the professor's body posture. For example, when sitting in a presentation or meeting, the professor sat somewhat lopsided, legs crossed, shoulders rolled forward and head tilted and leaning in toward the speaker, eyes focused on the speaker.

Josh tried looking around as though he was the professor, looking at his own hands and body in this position, looking at other people in the room from this point of view.

Josh was asked to think about his values, beliefs, capabilities, and how he sees himself while acting as if he were the professor. Josh answered such questions using I/me pronouns to help him maintain that perspective of acting as if he were the professor. For example:

- What's important to you when you listen to a presenter?
  "It's important to me to help the presenter do the best work they can do." (value)
- What do you believe about the best way to be an audience member?
  "I will understand the presenter's message best if I think about how to champion their message rather than try to find flaws." (belief)

- What capabilities do you have that help you do this?

     "I'm capable of understanding what this presenter wants to communicate and whether they have done so." (capability)
- How do you think about yourself when you are in the audience at a presentation?

     "I am a helper." (identity)

In the class, they did something else. It was a bit weird, but worth it. It was to have Josh stay in character—like a method actor might—and walk around the block, having a conversation with someone else in the class, as if Josh were this professor the whole time. You don't have to take that last step, but hopefully you can see how it gives even more opportunity to deeply immerse oneself, and experience—not just think about—the other person's perspective.

Sometime later, Josh was in a seminar being taught by that very professor. Josh asked several questions throughout. Afterward, spontaneously, the professor took Josh aside to tell him, "Hey, great questions!"

Could Josh have come to the same understanding without doing this? Possibly. We think it is unlikely, but certainly not impossible. Could Josh have been wrong in his understanding of the professor's mental model? Possibly. And it is good to try to verify what you learn in this exercise when you can. For instance, Josh had interacted with this professor in other ways before, when the professor taught the students how best to go about understanding an article they had read. The professor had talked about the importance of championing the perspective of the author when reading, rather than only looking for holes. This is a counterintuitive approach for most people. But the professor argued that we may miss important contributions when we only look for weaknesses. And when Josh had tried reading articles that way, he found it helped him understand what he read better and think about how to build on it usefully, and surprisingly, helped him spot more weaknesses than he otherwise would have. So it was not much of a leap for Josh to imagine that this professor might have a similar attitude when listening to presenters.

Josh also got the feedback we noted from the professor—he took Josh aside to appreciate how Josh was asking questions. The more you know, or know about, the other person, the more you have to work with when imagining their perspective. If you are able to actually observe them and talk to them, or talk to someone who knows them better than you, you can try to learn what they value, how certain things make them feel, what they believe, how they see themself, and so on. But even when you don't have the full range of information, you often know enough to be able to discover a useful mental model that is different from what you started with by stepping into the other person's perspective in an immersed way.

That event for Josh was decades ago. It was a single event, but the effects were quick and have lasted ever since.

Based on the evidence so far we think it seems likely that the richer the immersive experience, the more it will differ from just trying to understand someone from the outside. If you agree, or at least agree it's worth experimenting with, here's how you can do so.

Think of a person who you have been struggling to communicate or collaborate with. It could be someone with whom you have a work relationship or a personal relationship. For example, if you are the head of a department in an organization, is there a head of another department who you often butt heads with? If you are in consulting or sales, is there a client whose behavior is hard to predict? If you are in a romantic relationship, does your partner sometimes get upset with you unexpectedly, or demand things of you that seem unfair?

How do you see that person in your mind's eye right now? Picture them.

Take a close look at that picture of them. What is their posture—how are they standing or sitting? What facial expressions are they making? What are they doing with their eyes? Notice everything you can about their body—head, neck, shoulders, torso, arms, hands, legs, feet.

Take on their posture and facial expressions to the degree you're able to right now.

Now, in your mind's eye, look back at yourself. (For example, if Greg were doing this and taking on his wife's perspective, he would take on the posture of his wife, and—in his mind's eye—look back at Greg.) Describe the person you see. (For example, "He [Greg] is tall. He looks tired around his eyes, and his hands and legs are fidgety. He looks distracted. His shoulders and neck look tense. He's looking away while we're talking, not at me.") Give this some time—as if you were the other person, looking back at someone else, describe the person you see.

Now, answer these questions as if you were the other person, using I/me pronouns:

- What do you see, hear, and feel?
- What's important to you?
- What do you believe?
- What are you capable of?
- How do you think of yourself/what's your identity?

Now, look back at yourself one more time in your mind's eye. (For example, if Greg is taking his wife's perspective, then he would see Greg in his mind's eye, as though looking from his wife's eyes.) Answer these questions using he/she/they pronouns:

- What do you wish he/she/they understood?
- What would you like to say to, or ask of, him/her/them?
- What do you wish he/she/they would (or would not) think, feel, or do?
- What would you like to say to him/her/them? Go ahead and say it, either out loud or in your head silently.

Now let that all go, and step back into your own perspective. What, if anything, did you discover that could be useful?

In Josh's coaching, this exercise often leads to breakthroughs in working with others. It is not uncommon for executives he's worked with to say that this was one of the most important pieces of work they did. As with anything we teach, however, the best approach is not to presume any one tool will solve your problems, but instead to try them out when they seem relevant in order to find the difference that makes the difference.

For a guided visualization that can help you deeply step into the experience of someone else, Josh has some recordings at www.nlpdifference.com.

One caveat for this tool. Great therapists and actors have learned this.

If you are going to get immersed in the experience of someone who is really suffering, you can lose your objectivity for a time and get quite fatigued as you experience what they are going through to some degree—especially if you do so regularly. Researchers call this empathy fatigue or compassion fatigue, and it is associated with burnout in many helping professions.[8] So it can help to have a plan for how to snap yourself out of it. Perhaps a pinch on your leg. Or set an alarm, when appropriate, to limit the time during which you allow yourself to get immersed in someone's experience, after which you could pause and recenter.

It's old news that there is value in taking someone's perspective. The phrase "walk a mile in someone's shoes" and the idea it represents certainly also predate NLP.[9] We don't think anyone doubts that it's a really good idea to do so. So we're not here to suggest it as some new idea. What we're trying to communicate is that it pays to go all the way. Really explore the world as if you were the other person. Inhabit their mental model as if it were your own, for a time, and it can help you understand at both conscious and unconscious levels why the other person thinks, feels, and behaves as they do. It can also help you a great deal in learning how they do what they do, if that's what your goal is.

HOW TO CHANGE SOMEONE'S MIND (YOURS OR THEIRS)

We know that some readers may be jumping into the book here. Some of you want to get right to the section on changing someone's mind. If that's you, welcome, and we're glad you're here. You'll get a lot out of these chapters. As you read, you'll also notice that we reference the earlier chapters. The ideas and tools we shared in those earlier chapters are also extremely valuable for guiding someone to change their mind. If you like what you find in this section, you will likely enjoy going back to the earlier chapters for more useful tools.

For those of you who have arrived at this section after reading what came before, you have both a powerful set of tools and an excellent foundation for getting the most out of everything that remains. You know how to set a well-formed outcome to dramatically increase your or someone else's odds of success at any change goal. You are equipped with the right mindset to be limitless in your ability to change yourself and help others change when they are ready. And you have the tools to understand the people you are interacting with and to discover their mental models of the situations they find themselves in. With these tools, and this mindset, you already have an exceptional set of resources for leading change. For each person, change happens when we find the difference that makes the difference for them in their specific situation. Up until now, we've shared with you how to explore what that difference may be for each person.

We are excited to now add to your toolkit in section 3. This section starts with two chapters that help open people to change, which is often a very important step to take. These chapters are about how you earn the right to influence. Then the section moves on to seven tools (one chapter each) that are powerful workhorses for change. There are many tools we could have chosen from that are taught within NLP. We did not include a number of tools that are common both inside and outside of NLP—tools such as speaking to someone's values, making a strong logical argument, providing new information, or appealing to an authority—so that we could bring you more of what is distinct. Instead, we have focused on a set of tools that are important in NLP, but not as commonly taught elsewhere. And we've selected tools that often lead to profound shifts quickly. They each provide the person who will change with new ways of perceiving, experiencing, or thinking about the change. And they each invite the person who will change to have a key role in discovering how to change in ways that work for them and in their situation.

20

HOW TO GET ALONG WITH PEOPLE

Consider these three surprising events:

- A parent walks into the school principal's office angry and leaves appreciative.
- A skeptical shopper, just starting to learn guitar, spends a meaningful amount of money on a guitar following a salesperson's advice, and never feels remorse. Instead, over time, the shopper continues to feel like the salesperson did them a service.
- A hopeful and nervous job seeker interviews for a job and leaves feeling like they had a personal connection with the interviewer.

What happened?

All three events have actually happened to real people. What the principal, the salesperson, and the job seeker all understood was that you have to earn the right to influence.

Often we are taught that to be persuasive, we need to hone the perfect message, make the most powerful arguments, or offer the best incentives. But no matter how good your message, arguments, or incentives, they can be worthless if the person on the other end doesn't want to hear them and doesn't trust you.

Before making any arguments or sharing any messages, NLP encourages you to focus on the relationship. You can earn the right to influence by finding a way to get along with the other person as a person. Creating that personal connection helps both you and them communicate with greater ease, and be open to really seeing and hearing each other. It helps you both trust, like, and respect each other.

There's a term for this kind of connection. It's "rapport." You know how you feel like you click with some people, like you "get" each other, or you just get along well? Maybe you can't put your finger on why that happens. But you probably know the feeling. That's often what it feels like to have good rapport with someone.

That said, rapport doesn't have to be all sunshine and roses, either. Rapport is about forming a trusting, open connection. That's true even when the topic is unpleasant. You might have to have a difficult conversation— like laying off a friend who you work with. But if you establish rapport, that can be done in a way where both people continue to be friends in the short and long term. As a CEO, Josh's brother, Kenny, has been able to do that when necessary—it can be done.

In Kenny's case, his friend was a critical part of the growth of the company in its early stages. But they had arrived at a point where they were going to be closing her whole division. Kenny asked what she thought of announcing the layoff together. He suggested they do so with the whole company present. Kenny would sing the praises of her and her team. All of it would be true, real, and honest. Nothing sappy. They would share about the contributions, achievements, and the fun they had had. In the end, Kenny cried that day, as did perhaps most people there. He said, "By the end of the meeting, it felt more like a party for those who were leaving. Because we were being authentic, we trusted one another. And, because of the trust, once we got the tears out, we laughed and let loose." One employee said this was the best layoff he had ever been a part of. People laughed, and everyone agreed.

When we are trying to communicate our position, how the other person receives the information depends in no small part on how they feel about our motives and integrity. If the person we are communicating with values and trusts us and what we have to say, then even the bad news can be received with understanding and respect.

In NLP, we teach people to start by establishing rapport. Whether it is a new relationship or just a new conversation, if your goal is to communicate well or guide someone to change, then start with building rapport.

Over the years, a number of studies have looked at the importance of rapport for successful communication. A review of the scientific literature showed that in therapy and in medical health care, rapport between the care provider and the patient consistently showed up as an important predictor of whether the treatments were successful.[1] It was suggested that this had to do with everything from more accurate diagnoses to patients being open and willing to do their part to make the treatments work. Researchers have found rapport to be important outside of therapy and health care contexts, too. For example, scientists coded interviews with terrorists (who were later convicted), and found that when the interviewer established rapport, they obtained substantially more useful information from the terrorists than when the interviewers took other approaches, like what you might think of as "tough tactics."[2] Another study looked at what makes for the most effective coaches for people in organizations. They found that trying to find a coach who was the best match on paper (e.g., specialties, experience, demographics, leadership competencies) didn't have much impact by itself on how well people felt the coaching went, but the experience of rapport and trust—regardless of whether they matched on paper—between the coach and client did.[3]

Many professionals—lawyers, medical doctors, financial advisors, psychologists, etc.—understand that building rapport with their patients or clients makes a difference. It strengthens trust and helps people feel comfortable sharing personal concerns or goals, which often proves critical to giving the best professional service. For example, when Greg represents an injured client, it can make a big difference if the client shares candidly with him versus holding back certain details. There needs to be a level of trust for the client to disclose all the crucial facts. Greg has found that when he focuses on building rapport when interviewing an injured client, he learns much more of the information he will need to help him do his best work for the client.

From your own experience, think of a person who you don't trust, or who you don't think understands you, or who you feel is disrespectful toward you.

Now recall a time (or imagine one, if nothing comes to mind from memory) when they tried to persuade you to do something you didn't want to do (e.g., to volunteer for a committee, to accept their political beliefs, to buy something, or to agree to some arrangement).

How open were you to being influenced by them?

So, how can we establish rapport? In other words, how can we learn to get along with the people we interact with?

It turns out there's no one set of behaviors that gets people to like you or feel comfortable with you. Counter to what many people think, we're not all drawn to someone who smiles a lot, for example, and is extroverted. Instead, one of the things that does matter is whether we feel like we are in sync with the other person.

Being in sync can happen in a lot of ways. Both people might be reserved; both "too cool for school"; both relaxed in their body movements; both energetic and gesturing a lot; both kind of stiff; both swearing a lot; or even both cynical—misery loves company.

Have you ever had a conversation where you were in sync with someone? It will help to think of a specific example.

Did you feel like they understood you and you understood them? Did you feel at ease with them? Did you feel some level of trust? Were you open to their ideas?

Being out of sync looks different—one person might be cynical and the other peppy and positive; one could be reserved and the other an over-sharer; one cool and the other awkward; one relaxed in their movements and the other energetic and tense; one person really loose and the other kind of stiff; one person swearing a lot and the other using polite language.

On some level, we all know this already. For instance, comedies love to put people together who are out of sync. Think of the stuffy millionaires in the movie *Trading Places*, juxtaposed against Eddie Murphy's character. Or movies and shows like *The Odd Couple*, *The Heat*, *Perfect Strangers*, *Up*, *Lethal Weapon*, and many more—the writers get laughs, and the movie or show has more tension because we all expect that the main characters, who are out of sync, won't get along.

Have you ever had a conversation where you were out of sync with the other person? Think of a specific example of being out of sync.

Did you feel like they understood you and you understood them? Did you feel at ease with them? How much were you ready to trust them and accept their ideas?

Most people find that when they are in sync, they feel more understood, at ease, trusting, and open to the other person's ideas. Of course, there are exceptions to every rule. We suspect you could find instances of when you trust someone, for example, because of your long history with them, even if you are seldom in sync. But, in general, this is a pattern.

We did not come across research that had looked at every specific form of being in sync that we've mentioned. But our examples fall into two categories, and each has research support. One has to do with seeing yourself as part of the same group as the other person or having some personal understanding—that leads to rapport and then better outcomes.[4]

The other category has to do with behaving like one another. The findings can be largely summed up this way. When people are in rapport, they tend to act, and sometimes talk, more like one another.[5] For example, Josh swears more when talking to his good friend Jules, gestures more like him, and takes on a touch of Jules's Canadian accent even. Josh doesn't try to, but his wife notices it.

Have you ever done that sort of thing—when you like someone, or you feel sympathy for them, you start to talk and gesture a little more like them?

Unconsciously, or consciously, we often try to be a little more like them because, on some level, we probably expect them to like us more.

A simple way to think about it is this: people like people who are like them. This is not always true, but it is often true. There's a lot we communicate regarding whether or not we are like another person in how we talk and act. You don't have to have the same background or fashion sense or body type to feel similar. Anyone can build rapport with anyone else if both people are open to it.

Researchers call this kind of syncing up by many different names: convergence, imitation, mirroring, synchrony, or even intercorporeality. No matter what you call it, there's a verifiable phenomenon where being in sync is often associated with rapport. When we perceive that people are in sync with one another, we tend to believe they are in rapport.

In NLP, we encourage people to (1) notice whether or not they are in sync, and (2) look for ways to get more in sync, in an attempt to help build rapport.

The advice that you should search for points of commonality—being part of the same group, or sharing some personal understanding—as a way to get in sync is something you will probably find in many schools of thought beyond NLP. Getting in sync in terms of your behavior is something that, in our experience, is often new for people when they learn NLP. NLP uses the terms "mirroring" and "matching" to describe getting in sync. In NLP, we encourage people to mirror or match, for example, how the other person talks and acts—body language and aspects of spoken language.

A note of caution when first trying this out. Many people, when starting to experiment with mirroring and matching, will accidentally do it too much. Then the experience is more like what happens when a kid teases another by exactly copying everything they say or how they move. It's remarkably annoying. This is not a children's game of follow the leader. The aim is not to copy, but to get the gist of how they talk and act, and subtly get more in sync with that. But you have to start somewhere. Remember, there's no failure, only feedback. If you go too far, pull back a bit. You can always regain rapport. A good guideline for getting started is to try to just do one thing that mirrors or matches the other person. Don't try to sync up in every way.

We also think there's an important concern some readers may have that we should address before you start experimenting. Some people may think of mirroring and matching as being inauthentic. It's true that you may need to talk or act differently from the way you usually do in order to get more in sync with certain people. But that does not have to mean it is inauthentic. We offer a reframe that may help for those who are open to it— many people think of getting in sync as being respectful. It is respectful to meet the other person where they are—to flex a little, so that you show you accept and appreciate their way of being in the world. Many great psychotherapists, who very much have had their patients' best interests at heart, have connected with people in these ways. It has helped those psychotherapists adapt to any audience. We all do it unconsciously—either matching more when building rapport, or mismatching when breaking rapport. What this chapter has to offer is that we can accelerate connection and understanding by also consciously mirroring and matching. We believe that to do it well, it is best to do it out of respect and a genuine interest to connect personally.

We can also offer some specifics about ways to adjust how you talk and act to better sync up with someone. There are many ways people can get in sync that are taught within NLP. We have not included them all in this chapter. Instead, we offer you a list of a few things to focus on that we believe give you a solid foundation and can be very useful.

1. Overall posture
2. Nonverbal movements and use of voice
3. Ways of describing a situation or experience

1. Overall posture

Three main things you can look for are whether they are:
   a. slumped or upright
   b. closed—e.g., folded arms, crossed legs—or open
   c. oriented toward you—e.g., leaning in, facing you—or oriented away

Have you ever seen a scene like this? A teenager is with his parents at the mall. The parents are standing up straight—shoulders back, heads up. They are looking directly at the teenager and are facing him while they speak. The teenager has his shoulders slumped forward, his body twisted a bit away from his parents, and he's looking off to the side while speaking to them.

You can almost feel the mutual discomfort between the teenager and his parents just by glancing at the scene.

The teenager and his parents are mismatched in their postures.

The parents could try to match the teenager by looking away from time to time, slumping their postures a bit, and not always facing toward him.

The teenager could try to match his parents by standing up straighter, looking at them once in a while, and facing toward them sometimes.

Note that they don't need to do it all the time. In fact, matching everything, or matching the whole time they talk, would look and feel weird. When done well, you match some things and you do it sometimes. A helpful guideline one NLP trainer we know uses is to not be at either extreme—of never matching or always matching.

People generally continue to move throughout an encounter, too.

There's no need to change your posture every time they do. In fact, that could backfire, as it could read as copying. It's about capturing the gist of it. The aim is to embody their posture somewhat so that you nonverbally communicate you are with them.

If you'd like to see a video of being in sync and being out of sync, you can find that at www.nlpdifference.com.

2. Nonverbal movements and use of voice

This category has to do with how they move or use their voice—qualities like rhythm, speed, intensity, pitch, and tone.

If you are gesturing or speaking slowly and the other person is gesturing or speaking fast with a lot of intensity, try speeding up and increasing your intensity a bit. If you are loud and they are quiet, try getting quiet for a bit. If you are speaking in a lower pitch than them, try shifting a little higher. If they are tapping their hand or nodding or swaying in a certain rhythm, and you are not, try getting on their frequency in the way you move. If they have a little irritation in their tone of voice, see what happens if you let yourself have a bit of the same in your tone of voice here and there.[6]

One very effective way to align your rhythm or speed with them is to breathe with them. Speak or breathe in sync with their breathing. Other things may sync up, too, as a by-product of breathing in sync. Breathing affects your autonomic nervous system (fight-or-flight reaction, stress response, relaxation, etc.). For instance, a great way to influence your heart rate variability is to change your breathing rate. Breathe slower and your heart rate variability tends to increase (an increase in variability is a good thing in many contexts). Most people know already that deep, slow, belly breathing will reduce anxiety. Breathing is a quick and powerful tool for resetting your physiology.[7]

3. Ways of describing a situation or experience

Imagine you're having a conversation with a single mom you know who works full-time and has three young children. In the conversation with you she vents, "I feel like I can't even come up for air. Everybody needs something all the time. I'm drowning in it all. It's just too much."

How could you respond so that you join her in using her ways of describing things? If it sounds like a nice challenge to you, try coming up with a response before reading our examples.

To match her language, you'd have some options. For example, any of these would likely come across as being in sync:

- "You can't even come up for air?"
- "Seems like you're working hard just to tread water."
- "I know that feeling. Everyone needs something at all times. You're under a lot of pressure."

In the first response option, we focused on literally using some of her words or phrases—"You can't even come up for air?" We made it a question, but it could have been a statement—"You can't even come up for air."

Notice that in this example, there was no paraphrasing. Paraphrasing is when you put what you understand into your own words. That can be very useful for gaining clarity. But to gain rapport, it can sometimes be better to try to use the other person's specific words and phrases.

The second response option picks up on metaphors she was using about being underwater—"drowning in it all" and "can't come up for air." In this option, we've tried to stick with her metaphor by using "working hard to tread water."

In the third option, we joined her in talking about feelings. She said, "I feel like I can't . . ." and we responded with "I know that feeling." We also used "under a lot of pressure," which describes a feeling. Usually people talk about their experiences in terms of what they feel, hear, or see, or some combination. If you notice that someone is using one of those a lot—e.g., our single mom pretty much only talked in terms of feelings—you can try to match that by also talking about feelings as a way to get more in sync.

So the three options we offered that have to do with matching how she described her situation were to match by using:

- some of her literal words or phrases.
- her metaphors.
- her use of feeling versus seeing versus hearing words.

From the outside, it may seem like silly wordplay. And at times it is. But, very often matching someone's way of describing their situation makes a difference in how well or how quickly you build rapport with them.

It may be instructive if we also show what a mismatch—being out of sync—could look like. Remember, she said, "I feel like I can't even come up for air. Everybody needs something all the time. I'm drowning in it all. It's just too much." For those readers who want to experiment, see if you can come up with a response to the single mom that mismatches her, before you read our examples.

A few options that mismatch, and are more likely to come across as out of sync:

- "You're not able to attend to your own needs."
- "It's a losing battle. You've lost before you've even begun."
- "I see what you mean. You're working hard, and there's no end in sight."

The first mismatch is done by paraphrasing. She said, "I can't even come up for air," and we paraphrased it as "You're not able to attend to your own needs." Maybe she meant she can't attend to her own needs when she said, "I can't even come up for air." But maybe she meant that it's all overwhelming. Or maybe she meant that nothing is ever enough. Or something else. She chose her words for a reason. If you can use someone's actual words, the person often feels like you really understand—what comes across unconsciously is that you not only are listening closely, but also think about it the same way they do.

The second option mismatches by using a different metaphor. Her metaphor was being underwater. We changed the metaphor to being at war—"It's a losing battle. You've lost before you've even begun." Now it's a metaphor about war. That can be jarring for some people. It can be like walking through a house in the suburbs, opening a door, and suddenly being in the desert with no neighbors in sight. The whole mental scene can shift. It's not that it's bad to use a different metaphor in all contexts. Saying, "It's a losing battle. You've lost before you've even begun," shows some understanding and compassion. But unconsciously, it can put the two people out of sync.

And the third mismatches because she was talking about what she *feels* and this option talks about what you *see*. "I *see* what you mean. You're working hard, and there's *no end in sight*." It takes the conversation away from feelings. If she was really trying to convey her feelings, then moving the conversation away from feelings at this point would probably unconsciously come across as out of sync.

In other parts of the book, we've encouraged you to act differently—e.g., to focus on gaining clarity, help someone reframe their situation, or help someone step away from a limiting feeling. You may be noticing that in this chapter we are pointing you away from doing those things. The reason is that it pays to first build rapport. There will be time for clarity and reframing and helping afterward. In fact, we suggest that in most cases, you will be able to more quickly and more effectively understand and help someone change if you first focus on building rapport.

Rapport is not enough on its own for you to have influence. You still have to have a compelling message to reach someone. What rapport will do is give you a shot at being heard.

A Deeper Dive on Matching the Way People Talk About Feeling Versus Seeing Versus Hearing

The research about the importance of using the language of feeling versus seeing versus hearing is mixed. It's worth diving into what is and is not supported so that you can make the best use of this distinction.

In NLP, there's an idea that people have a primary representational system. The idea is that people tend to rely on one of the systems more than the others. That is, they mostly think in terms of visual experience (seeing), or auditory experience (hearing), or kinesthetic experience (feeling and movement). Those three are the most common, but smell and taste are options, too.[8]

A softer version of the claim is that what's primary depends on the context—so the same person might rely on visual (seeing) more one time, and kinesthetic (feeling and movement) more another, for example.

From a neuroscience perspective, what modality we use seems to depend on what we're trying to mentally represent more than on a tendency to use one system. If you ask anyone to imagine hearing the Beatles song "Hey Jude," chances are their brain would be active in the auditory cortex.[9] If it were active, say, in the visual cortex when they hear sounds, we would call that synesthesia.[10] That's when you experience something from one sense in another—like sounds having colors. But most of the time, for most people, you'll get the expected areas of the brain active. Ask anyone to picture the last time they were at the beach, and almost everyone can call to mind a visual mental image—the brain uses the visual cortex for visual mental images.[11] Ask someone to pay attention to what their body feels like, for instance, trying to feel their heartbeat. They're using brain regions devoted to kinesthetic (feeling or movement) processing.[12]

Psychology research also does not clearly support the idea that people have a *primary* representational system, at least in the sense of having one dominant system for processing information. For example, some readers will have heard about learning styles—e.g., that some people are visual learners, others learn best when they hear what they are learning, and others learn best by understanding with their bodies and feelings (kinesthetic learners). However, a review paper looking across the research on learning styles found that there seems to be no effect of learning styles on how well people learn.[13] That suggests people don't have a *primary* representational system in terms of how well they process information.

Nonetheless, the same research also reports that people do often have a preference for learning style—e.g., by feeling versus hearing versus seeing.[14]

So, putting the pieces together, it seems to us that the aim should not be to identify which system a person uses for processing information, but to identify which system people gravitate toward in the ways they speak or prefer to receive information. Given that, when it comes to building rapport it is probably worthwhile to try to match this kind of language. But when it comes to learning it may be different. Every learner probably benefits from learning their lessons in multiple ways—e.g., seeing, hearing, *and* feeling the lessons.

Note also that you won't always find such a preference in someone's way of describing their situation. But when you do, we encourage you to match it, or at least match it sometimes. If they have a preference then it will likely seem more familiar or natural to them to speak in those terms. Many ways of getting in sync seem to help build rapport.

Is There Ever a Time When It Makes Sense to Break Rapport?

Yes. Building trust and connection are useful in most situations, but there is a time and place for everything. At times, you need to end a conversation, for instance. It doesn't have to be someone you dislike, either. It may be a conversation with someone you like, but who won't stop talking, and you just need to keep to a schedule. Using your words or body language to mismatch—to get out of sync—can help end the conversation sooner.

Another common situation when it makes sense to break rapport is when a teacher or a boss recognizes that it is difficult to get the students or employees to do the hard things they must do, because they are overly familiar. The teacher or boss may come to realize that they don't always need to be their (the students' or employees') friend to serve them best. When the teacher or boss breaks rapport, that can jolt the students or employees out of their way of doing things. It can create a sense that the boss means business. Sometimes that is just what's needed.

While it can make sense to break rapport at times, we are not suggesting that it will be useful to go around breaking rapport all the time. For instance, the teacher or boss who never builds rapport will probably struggle to get people to engage because of a lack of trust and connection.

That said, we encourage you to experiment with breaking rapport from time to time, when you feel it would be safe enough to experiment. The reason is to help you reinforce the skills of getting in and out of sync, and the belief that you can always regain rapport.

Some people hesitate to break rapport even when they know they must challenge someone else's model of the world. They worry about damaging the relationship. Remember that you can rebuild rapport later in the conversation, or at a later date. In NLP, we often say that you can always regain rapport. Claiming this is *always* true may be an overgeneralization and probably cannot be proven, but we invite you to act as if you can. It can become a self-fulfilling prophecy.

21

MEET THEM WHERE THEY ARE BEFORE
TRYING TO GET THEM TO FOLLOW

I f you take to heart the messages in this chapter and apply them, we believe you will be able to connect with and influence other people quicker and more effectively than you may have thought possible before.

Often, we want to influence others, and frequently we need to do this quickly. For instance:

- A doctor may get only ten minutes with a patient, and want to persuade them to start a medicine or health care regimen.
- A lawyer may have only minutes to get a fact finder to trust her, or might have a fast-approaching deadline to try to arrive at a negotiated agreement.
- An executive may have only brief conversations to address tough issues with peers in other siloes of the organization.
- A partner in a romantic relationship might be in a really bad mood because of some work or family problem, and the other partner may want to help them feel better quickly.

After the last chapter, it will probably be obvious that we'll suggest the first step is to establish rapport. But what happens next?

To be fair, establishing rapport may be enough so that you can just go ahead and make your case. Building rapport helps you earn the right to be heard. For example, once the doctor and patient are in rapport, the doctor might successfully be able to get her patient to commit to some lifestyle changes that will help with diabetes management.

However, while rapport is an important first step, it is not always enough on its own. The doctor, for instance, might find that the patient resists and says, "I know I need to, but I can't do that."

The doctor has some options. The first one we'll offer is a typical approach and one that most people have tried a version of at some point. She could respond by leaning into her standard talking points that have worked many times, by saying something like "Of course you can. Lots of people make these changes and you must also. Trust me—you don't want to get full-blown diabetes." Along these lines, she might also try to motivate her patient by talking about all the terrible consequences the disease can have. But, from an NLP perspective, we would expect this approach not to work in this case. While it might work sometimes, we would anticipate it would fail much of the time. It amounts to the doctor ignoring the patient's mental model and trying to force her own mental model onto the patient.

A better approach would be to meet the patient where he is. One of the best ways to do so is to acknowledge what the patient believes to be true—that he can't make these changes. Often the simplest way to do so can be the most effective. It is to do what we call in NLP backtracking. State back what you heard using the patient's own words and phrases. We mentioned this as a tool for building rapport, too, in the last chapter. There we spoke about how it communicates—probably unconsciously—that you are in sync and similar to each other. However, backtracking can do double-duty. It is also a way of showing that you truly were listening, that you understand the patient's reality, and that you respect that it is their reality.

So, the doctor could start by saying, "You can't do that. Tell me more," or "You can't do that?" Some readers may have come across a similar recommendation in the book *Never Split the Difference* about negotiation techniques based on what's used by the FBI. In that book, they refer to it as mirroring the other side's language. We don't know whether the people who developed the FBI negotiation techniques had studied NLP. But we think it supports what we're saying that they also arrived at a similar conclusion. Our take on backtracking is that it helps you both build rapport by syncing up with the other person in how you speak, and meet them where they are by acknowledging you really understand their mental model.

To further meet the patient where he is mentally, the doctor could avoid saying certain things. Note also that the patient said, "I know I need to [make these changes]." So for the doctor to try to give him arguments about why he needs to do so actually shows she is not hearing him or accepting his model of the world. Instead, she would be better off acknowledging, "You already know you need to," and then following it up with curiosity, "so, something must be stopping you."

Remember the well-formed outcome? One of the criteria for being well-formed is that your desired outcome should be in your control. It may come as a shock to some people to hear this, but it is never in your control to change how someone else thinks, feels, or acts. No one has the power to do that. You can only make suggestions. The other person is the only one who can change how they think, feel, or act. And they are only going to change if it makes sense from their vantage point to do so. So, we recommend that you focus not on changing them, but on having the best shot at actually being heard. Rather than aiming to convince the other person of something, aim to explore what it would take for them to convince themself.

The tools for building rapport that we've discussed—mirroring and matching—already increase your odds of being listened to, but there is more you can do to have the best chances of being heard. You can meet them where they are mentally—honoring the world as it appears in their mental model. Remember that in their mental model, they behave in the best way they know how, their concerns are valid, their beliefs are reasonable (or at least their beliefs are what they accept as true), and their emotions make sense.

Their mental model is where they are starting from. You want them to get to a new way of thinking, feeling, or acting. You might find it helpful to think of your job in the communication as similar to giving directions to someone's house. Unless you know where they are starting from, you can't do it. Consider reframing your job from selling your message to giving directions from their starting point to your destination. Or you might even envision yourself going to their starting point and letting them follow you to the new destination.

NLP uses the phrase "pacing and leading" to describe meeting them where they are before trying to get them to follow. You first go at their pace—you join them and metaphorically walk alongside them in their model of the world—and then try to lead them to a different way of thinking, feeling, or acting. When you first pace them, you reinforce rapport and help them feel heard, and by being open to seeing their mental model, you increase your chances of finding the difference that makes the difference for them.

There's research both on what makes people feel heard, and on how people open up to being influenced once they do feel heard. (For those readers who prefer visual language or kinesthetic language, feeling heard means the same thing as feeling seen or feeling understood.) The research shows that people feel heard (1) when they have a chance to speak their truth; (2) when the listener pays attention, empathizes, and shows respect for them and their truth; and (3) when they experience a sense that they have some common ground with the listener. All these things contribute to feeling heard, and the more of them that happen in a conversation the better. Here, common ground means that both sides see eye-to-eye on some things, or feel that they are similar in some ways, or have what some researchers call shared reality in which they have the same experience or agree on what's true.[1]

When we recommend that you join someone where they are mentally, you can think of joining, more specifically, as doing those things that research shows make people feel heard: paying attention to them, empathizing with them, respecting what you hear, and sharing some common ground with them.

Research has shown across various studies and contexts that when people do feel heard by you, it opens them up to trusting and listening to you, and to being open to your POV or decisions. Employees in organizations, for example, who feel heard—like they had a voice and were listened to—are often willing to go along with decisions they don't like, like receiving a not-so-great performance review, or getting an assignment they don't want. Employees remain more loyal to the organization and engaged in their work after performance reviews when they feel there was a fair process, which involves feeling heard in the process.[2]

On some level, everyone knows that we can't get our way all the time. But so long as the process by which the decisions that affect us are made is experienced as fair, we're willing to accept the decision and move on amicably. Feeling like you were heard is one of the main predictors of whether people view a process as fair.

The impact of showing people we hear them on whether we can ultimately change minds can be profound. One study, for example, found that feeling heard significantly predicted how well emergency workers adapted to new processes regarding the COVID crisis.[3] Imagine if you could get people to adapt to new processes more effectively in a crisis. Wouldn't that be wonderful?

Another area where the importance of feeling heard has been well studied is law. For example, people believing they were treated fairly has been explored regarding getting them to trust authorities, be satisfied with legal outcomes, and comply with the law.[4] In this kind of research, feeling heard is an important part of whether people believe they were treated fairly.

On a day-to-day basis, using these tools shows up in situations like this: One day, Greg spoke with a disgruntled client who wanted to fire him. Being a student of NLP, Greg understood that he must first meet the client where the client was. As Greg sat across from the client, he built rapport with matching and mirroring. For instance, the client's language was predominantly visual, so Greg was careful to use words that mirrored the client's world, i.e., "I see your point," "while it appears," "the actual picture is different," etc. Greg also showed that he really heard, understood, and respected the client's mental model by repeating back the client's grievance using the client's own language patterns. That helped with both rapport and pacing. He also helped pace the client by offering empathic eye contact and using active listening. That was a way to honor where the client was mentally and join him there. In that particular situation, the client was very upset because he felt his communications were not responded to in a timely manner. He took this to mean that Greg did not respect him. After acknowledging the client's mental model, Greg honestly apologized that his behavior had caused the client to feel slighted, because we know that the meaning of communication is the effect on the listener.

Greg then worked on leading the client to a place of trust. Greg had earned the right to show the client that his case was meticulously handled at every step of the process. They further agreed that while the goal was to respond to all communication immediately, sometimes circumstances mandated as much as a twenty-four-hour delay, but under no circumstances is the delay intended as a sign of disrespect toward the client. In summary, after meeting the client where he was—which he was able to do in a matter of minutes—Greg was able to get the client to be open to listening to Greg's point of view. As a result, Greg led the client to realize that his interests were better served in staying with Greg's firm rather than going somewhere else.

At this point you might be convinced that it makes sense to try to really hear what is important to the other person, and meet them where they are mentally, before attempting to get them to do, think, or feel something else. To help you succeed at doing it, we recommend you start to notice how often we fail to do it. That will open up a world of opportunities for doing a better job at influencing others. Here are some examples.

In a small mom-and-pop start-up we've worked with, Pop made a comment to Mom about some new expenses he realized they would need to cover. Mom shot back, "You're stressing me out! Can't you see I'm in the middle of a hundred things? I don't need you to dump more shit on me right now!" Pop got defensive and tried to explain why she shouldn't feel stressed out, and why it wasn't his fault she was stressed out. Then he tried to make himself look good by claiming he was being responsible, and that she needed to be able to hear it. Tensions rose, Pop left the room, and they both were distracted and carried their bad feelings with them.

It's a totally natural, and common, reaction Pop had, isn't it? It's also the opposite of meeting Mom where she is. Rather than accepting her feelings, he discounted them. Rather than accepting that Mom was not in a position to have this conversation, Pop suggested there was something wrong with Mom.

Have you ever done something like that, where you say something, then the other person gets upset—and you then try to explain or argue why they shouldn't feel that way, and why you are actually in the right? Go ahead and call such an interaction to mind now. (For some people it will be easier to remember a time when someone did this to you—that will work, too.)

As you think about that interaction—what are some of the ways that you did not meet them where they were? (Or that they did not meet you where you were?)

What are some of the ways that you could have met them where they were? (Or that they could have met you where you were?)

Some options we see for Pop in this example to meet Mom where she is would be to say things like:

- "Sorry I stressed you out."
- "You're doing so much right now. You're carrying a lot of this business."
- "Let's talk at a better time."

How do you imagine she might react to hearing these messages?

Pop actually went back a few minutes later and tried saying things like what we've written in these three bullets. Mom then calmed down, paused her other work, and invited Pop to stay so they could talk it out. And before they got into the conversation more, she apologized for getting upset with him, and said she was just feeling overwhelmed and behind on things, and it wasn't his fault.

Notice that Pop started by apologizing. Many of us hesitate to apologize—it can feel like an admission of guilt or that we were in the wrong. But notice that Pop does not come off looking bad for apologizing. It's a fact that something he did played a part in stressing her out, and he is acknowledging that. She sees it that way and he is communicating that they agree on this piece of reality. His apology doesn't mean he had bad judgment or that he was insensitive or that he was in the wrong. Apologies can be a great way to meet someone where they are, but you don't have to apologize to do so.

Pop also showed he understood and respected other aspects of her model of the situation—in which she was doing one hundred things already, that she felt dumped on, and that right now he was not welcome. Paradoxically, meeting her there helped make it the right time to talk.

The examples so far have to do with adults having high-level conversations, but the concept applies in all kinds of contexts. For example, Josh was struggling to get his five-year-old to brush her teeth and get in bed. He was holding the toothbrush for an aggravatingly long time while she talked a mile a minute and kept pretending to fall off the bed, shouting, "Catch me!" Josh persisted in staying calm and repeatedly saying things in gentle tones, like "Sweetie, we're going to have quiet time now. We need to brush and then get in bed." It was as if she didn't notice his attempts to move bedtime along. Then Josh finally got a bright idea—just to see what would happen, he decided to join her mentally, and then try to get her to brush and get in bed. He widened his eyes and spoke super fast, saying things like, "Okay, okay, let's brush, brush, brush! Open wide, fast, open, open, open!" It was like a spell had come over her. She kept her amped-up energy and playfulness and applied it to the task of brushing her teeth, making it the easiest he could remember in a long time. "Now go spit in the sink, fast, fast, fast!" She did and ran back. "Quickly, get under the covers, get under, get under! Snuggle up. Snuggle more. Hug, hug, hug, snuggle, snuggle, snuggle!" She did. No ignoring. No resistance. No delay. And just like that, bedtime was over.

Would this particular game work every day? Probably not. But it met her where she was in that moment before asking her to do something else.

One thing we hope is coming across in our various examples is that you can meet the other person where they are and lead them elsewhere quickly, and often should. Some people may have a concern that meeting them where they are will take time and effort. We suggest the reality is just the opposite—you'll often take a lot longer and put in a lot more effort to see a change if you skip this step.

One last note—as you experiment with meeting them where they are before trying to get them to follow, remember this: a conversation is a dynamic thing. Nothing is fixed. If you turn back and see they are not following, flexibly go back and meet them whenever needed.

22

ARE THEY LIVING IT OR WATCHING THE MOVIE?

The tool we'll share in this chapter is one of the powerhouses of NLP. It very often is what leads to discovering the difference that makes the difference.

Imagine you are watching a really scary movie. You are alone and it's dark. The spooky music on the television is getting louder, and you are anticipating something bad happening. You are waiting for countless seconds when all of a sudden it does, and you almost jump out of your seat.

Now contrast this with the following. You are watching a sitcom on television. On the screen, you see an actor who is on a couch in a home theater watching a scary movie. While it is light in your living room, and there are other noises from other people in the background in your house, on the screen, the actor is alone and he's in the dark. As he is watching a movie, the music is getting louder for him. Meanwhile, you are enjoying a snack, and getting comfy by adjusting the pillows and grabbing a blanket. As you glance back at the screen, you see that the actor looks tense as he appears to be anxiously awaiting the scare that will inevitably come in the movie he's watching. The scare finally happens, and he jumps out of his seat. Do you also jump out of your seat? Probably not, at least not as much. It's less intense when you're watching someone else do it on TV than when you are experiencing it yourself.

In NLP, we call living it being associated. When we are associated, we feel like something is happening to us. We are living or reliving an experience through our own senses. We are seeing through our own eyes, hearing through our own ears, and we feel as though the consequences will be ours to suffer or enjoy. By contrast, we call watching it happen in a movie being disassociated. When we are disassociated, we think of the experience as though it were happening to someone else, and perhaps at some other time besides now. We may have an understanding of what that person is going through, but we are not really feeling all the feelings a person would have who is actually going through the experience.

Being able to shift from associated to disassociated, or vice versa, is the tool we're introducing in this chapter.

If you hang around people who use NLP a lot, you'll probably hear them say this phrase: "Go meta." For instance, "Go meta, and see what happens." Or, "Now go meta, and look at yourself in the situation." If you didn't know what it meant, it would probably sound weird. But once you know, it's a handy shorthand.

"Meta" is a term that people use a lot now—e.g., "That's so meta" to describe what they mean when someone steps out of the current situation and comments on it. Like when a company asks for feedback on its feedback process. "Whoa, that's so meta!" Or when a sports commentator comments on himself as commentator. "Man, that's so meta!" the other commentator might say in response. In NLP, we're using the word "meta" in a similar way—stepping outside the situation or experience and viewing it or commenting on it as a third party observer would. In other words, disassociating.

Research shows that making this shift—going meta—not only can play a part in decreasing the intensity of emotions, but also can help people be more rational—reinterpreting their situation, making new meaning of an experience—and move on from feeling stuck mentally and emotionally. The effects on how you think or feel of making this shift can last for weeks or months and even change your physiology and stress response.[1]

For example, one series of studies followed participants who were asked to think about a painful memory that made them feel angry or hostile[2] (e.g., a breakup or a fight where nasty things were said). Some participants were guided to associate into the experience—as if they were back in it, seeing it with their own eyes. But other participants were asked to go meta—to act as though they were a fly on the wall when the painful situation happened, observing from a distance, from a neutral third-party perspective, essentially with less skin in the game. So if Josh were doing it, he would take the perspective of the fly on the wall, and from that perspective see Josh—as he would look to an outside observer—going through that painful situation (e.g., having that fight where nasty things were said).

When the researchers asked the participants why things went down as they did, they found that the participants in the first—associated—group tended to rehash all the painful things that were said and done. They were reliving it in their minds and felt awful all over again.

When participants first took the fly on the wall perspective and then described why things went down as they did, they tended to calm down, arrive at some new understandings, and become more ready to move on.

To make this work best, the researchers pointed out that going meta and then asking "Why?" was helpful, but going meta and then asking "What happened?" didn't work. Asking "What" just got people to rehash their old gripes again. Going meta seems to make the space for finding new meaning, and then it helps to take the step of looking for new meaning once you go meta.

For instance, a person rehashing a bad experience, being associated, might say something like, "She is a total narcissist and will do anything to ruin my life." Whereas the same person reviewing the same experience as the fly on the wall, being disassociated (going meta), might say something like, "She was feeling attacked and like I did not respect her, so she was trying to put me down to feel better. I was feeling hurt, so I was not able to see that at the time."

We invite you now to think of a conversation or interaction with another person that you continue to ruminate on, one where you feel bad all over again when you do.

Now you can go meta and view the situation again, but from a distance as an impartial observer (e.g., see it from the vantage point of the fly on the wall).

As you look at those people over there—the one who looks like you and the other(s)—answer this: Why did they do and say what they did?

What, if anything, changed when you went meta and reviewed and made sense of the experience from the perspective of a neutral third-party observer?

In the examples so far, you may have noticed some mental imagery we and others have suggested to help people go meta more easily. You can conjure these up to help yourself or someone else go meta. They are:

- the impartial observer
- the fly on the wall
- the movie theater or TV

And when you do go meta, if you are observing yourself, remember to speak about yourself in the third person—he/she/they—to help you maintain the experience of perceiving some other person. You might remember the research we shared in chapter 19 that it does actually make a difference in how you experience things to switch from first-person language (I/me) to third-person language (he/she/they). As a reminder, chapter 19 was about the second-person perspective. Putting that together with what we're sharing in this chapter, you can think of three perspectives, and you are free to move—or help someone else move—from one to any of the others in order to help change how you or they experience a situation. You may find these terms to be useful for the three perspectives: self (first person), other (second person), and observer (third person).

When you can flexibly move between self, other, and observer—or guide someone else to—you can quickly and substantially challenge and expand your (or their) mental model of the situation at hand. Remember the NLP belief from chapter 7—*the person with the most flexibility exerts the most influence*. Shifting perspectives is a powerful way to be flexible.

Have you ever noticed that it is usually much easier to solve others' problems than your own? You can go meta and solve your own problems as if they were someone else's. Greg and Josh do it all the time. One of Greg's favorite ways is to watch his situation progress as a movie in which there's a character named Greg.

Right now, consider a challenge in your life that you are having difficulty resolving. Now picture a movie theater. Go and take a seat. For a moment, close your eyes as you imagine looking up at the screen and seeing yourself come to the part of the challenge that is perplexing. Remember to let the actor in the movie (who looks like you) have their own feelings. You can remain as the impartial movie watcher. Look at the actor's posture and the way they move. Hear how the actor speaks, and notice how the actor responds to what others may be saying.

From this detached point of view, answer: What are the options available to that person in the movie? What resources would benefit that person? What actions should that person take? What's a different way for that person to think about the situation they are in?

Many people find that they come up with answers that are different, or more useful, or simply that they are open to seeing more options when they look from this disassociated meta position.

So far, we've discussed going meta—the shift from associated to disassociated. That is super useful when emotions are too strong, or someone is stuck at a mental impasse. But shifts in the other direction—from disassociated to associated—can be useful, too.

Greg often has made use of that shift in his law practice, for example. Association is an extremely useful tool to help a witness recall certain details of and relate an experience. Let's contrast a short portion of a witness's direct examination by a lawyer to see how this can play out. We first show a traditional direct examination, and then how an NLP-trained lawyer might conduct one by helping his witness associate into the event.

Scenario 1—Traditional Direct Examination

LAWYER: What were you doing at the time of the crash?
WITNESS: I was sitting at the light waiting for it to change.
LAWYER: What's the next thing that happened?
WITNESS: I was hit in the back.
LAWYER: How would you describe the impact?
WITNESS: It was a pretty hard hit.
LAWYER: What happened to your body inside the car after impact?
WITNESS: I was thrown around and then hit in the face with the airbag.
LAWYER: What went through your mind when this happened?
WITNESS: I was worried if the kids were okay.

Scenario 2—Associated Direct Examination

GREG: Relax your body. Now take yourself back to the scene of the crash. You are sitting in your seat in the car, seeing what you are seeing, hearing what you are hearing, and feeling what you are feeling.

WITNESS: (breathing pattern changes—people may, for example, begin to take deep diaphragmatic breaths when they are fully associated)

GREG: Where are you?

WITNESS: I am sitting stopped at a red light at the intersection of X Street and Y Avenue.

GREG: What is the next thing that happens?

WITNESS: I hear a loud metallic bang in the back of my car. I feel this hard push and I feel my neck and back being thrown backward and forward.

GREG: Take us through what's happening as it happens.

WITNESS: Something that smells like burned rubber explodes with a *woosh*, and strikes me in the face.

GREG: What happens to your body as you are struck in the face?

WITNESS: I feel my body being thrown around the car like a bowling pin.

GREG: What are you feeling?

WITNESS: I begin to see stars from the rubber airbag hitting me in the face. I am confused. I realize that I must have been in an accident.

GREG: What else is going through your mind?

WITNESS: I am sure now that I was in a crash. I am praying that my babies in the back seat are okay.

We can probably all agree that scenario 2 is a much more compelling narrative of the events in the crash. It is very important to have the person become fully associated for him or her to recall the minute details that bolster credibility, whether it be the sounding of crunching metal or the smell of a released airbag. Also, it is very important that the lawyer's responses are in the present tense as this will keep the witness associated to the experience.

Notice that Greg did not make any suggestions to the witness about the content of the details or events of the crash, but simply the form by which the witness could remember them—from an associated perspective.

Note, however, that the crash may have been traumatic and the emotions very raw. Very strong emotions could have made it difficult for the witness to recount the events at all. If that were the case, then it would be wiser to help the witness disassociate. While the details may not be as vivid, the witness would likely find the experience more tolerable and would be able to recount more than they otherwise would have.

Another example where shifting to being more associated is helpful is when it is important to stir up emotions. For instance, a manager running a quality control division in an organization may find that her employees have not taken seriously complaints they've received from other departments. The manager has noticed that her employees generally regard the complaints from the other departments as *their* problems. Her employees continue to operate in ways that are most familiar and efficient for them, even though they have had feedback that it creates bottlenecks and stress in other departments downstream and upstream in the workflow. Everyone involved in budgeting, accounting, marketing, manufacturing, and sales is affected by her department. She needs her employees to take these complaints seriously and make some changes.

So she guides them through associating into the experience, first of a worker in one of the upstream departments, then of a worker in one of the downstream departments, and then of her own position. Her employees, as a result, can feel the stress, see the problems, and hear the frustration of those in the other positions. She is then able to get them to think about how much of a difference it would make if her department would make some changes. Finally, having stirred up those feelings in her employees of the importance of making changes, her employees take the complaints more seriously, and she engages them in experimenting with some new ways of operating.

In some of the future chapters, we'll introduce powerful tools that use association and disassociation to help you achieve goals, avoid costly mistakes, and choose your emotional state, among other things.

23

USE YOUR TIME MACHINE

You know the phrase "hindsight is 20/20"? Looking back, it's easy to see what you should have done. But somehow, it wasn't so obvious when you were back there looking forward. Most of us would cringe if we had to count the number of times we missed the mark on a goal, either because we failed to take some action or because we took the wrong action. What if you could travel in time to the future and have that 20/20 hindsight right now? You could know how things would turn out, and what you should have done instead. You could be a Monday morning quarterback, but on Sunday and during the game. Wouldn't that be nice?

Well . . . too bad—we can't travel through time . . . obviously.

However, just because we can't actually travel through time doesn't mean we can't mentally travel through time. In fact, it's rather easy to mentally time travel. The trick is in learning how to take better advantage of that skill. When you know what to do, you can get important aspects of the clarity that twenty-twenty hindsight can give.

When we say it's easy, we mean it's so easy and natural that it's probably the default for most people. So many of us live perhaps the majority of our lives in the past or future in our minds. Often, we dwell on the past—e.g., wondering, "Should I not have said that?" And frequently, we worry about the future—e.g., stressing out about whether someone will call us back. Lao Tzu said, "If you are depressed, you are living in the past. If you are anxious, you are living in the future. If you are at peace, you are living in the present." Are you at peace, and fully present, at all moments? If so, you're the exception.

Being present is usually the harder thing to do. People often study Zen or other forms of Buddhism, or practice various kinds of meditation for years in order to get better at being present. We're big fans of being present, by the way, but that's not what this chapter is about. We just mention those practices here to highlight how hard people have to work to be present, because hopefully that helps point out how natural and easy it is for us to mentally time travel. We can't seem to stop ourselves from mental time travel much of the time. In this chapter, we want to help you take advantage of that natural ability we all have—the power to *not* be present, but to mentally travel to a different time—and learn to use it more deliberately to bring about change quickly.

In earlier chapters, we've talked about shifting your perspective—for instance, by walking a mile in someone else's shoes, or by going meta. Those kinds of perspective shifts can impact the emotions, thoughts, beliefs, empathy, and physiology of the person making the shift. We find it striking how much of an impact those perspective shifts can have across so many aspects of experience. Here we're introducing another perspective shift that can be equally as impactful—seeing a situation from the vantage point of your future self or past self. Also, we'll guide you in how to do it effectively, and what pitfalls to avoid. The aim will be to mentally time travel to a distant point in time (e.g., to a time in the future when you have failed or succeeded at your goal) and then to be able to look back at the present moment from that place far off in time.

The effects of viewing a situation from a far-off point in time versus near in time have been studied extensively. Usually researchers who study that distinction refer to it either as psychological distance or as temporal discounting.[1] What the research shows is that when someone thinks about a decision or a situation or a goal as being far off in time, they have different concerns and value different things than they would if it were near in time. For example, if someone invites you to attend a conference next December and it's only January, it's normal to think big picture—e.g., "Will it be interesting?" "Will there be good opportunities to network?"

"Will it be fun to be there?" But if someone invites you to a conference in two weeks, you tend to think about the details—e.g., "Will it be a headache to change my schedule?" "Am I really going to follow up with these people I network with?" "How much fun can I really have if I'm tired from traveling and working in my hotel room to meet my deadlines?" When it's far off in time, you focus on *why* you might do it and think big picture, but when it's near, you focus on *how* you will do it and think about details.

The decisions we make tend to be different when we perceive things as far off in time compared to near, too. For example, if you offer people $1,000 now or $1,150 if they wait a year, probably many would take the $1,000 now even if they didn't need the money to cover bills right away. It's not rational from the standpoint of having more money, unless you think you're going to die before the year is up. A 15 percent increase in your money in just one year would be very good if you had invested that money. And in this choice, you can *guarantee* that kind of growth. But notice that you have to jump through some mental hoops, and reframe the decision in terms of how it compares to a normal investment if you want to justify waiting. For many people, they have to reason it out because the emotional pull is toward the money now. Somehow, the money now has more weight. Just think of what you could do with $1,000 right now! It's so easy to get into that fantasy. It has emotional charge to it. On the other hand, $1,150 in a year—for a lot of people it would probably be nice to know it's coming, but otherwise, it's a fairly abstract idea.

We even think about people (ourselves included) differently when we imagine them (or ourselves) doing something far off in time versus near.[2] Far off in time, we think about traits more—we think about how they or we tend to be in general. So if I love music, I'll probably love the idea of a concert that's scheduled far off in the future. But near in time, we might think more about how the context affects their or our behavior—traits matter less to us in the near term. Whether or not I think I'll love a concert tomorrow night will depend less on my love of music and more on my level of sleep and other obligations.

What the research boils down to is that when something is far away in time it is less tangible and more of an abstract idea. Whether we're thinking about some financial decision, some event, some goal, or ourselves in the future, this is the case. So, it's natural to focus on big-picture, broad-brush ways of thinking and feeling about something far off in time. And when something is near in time it is the opposite—we experience it as more tangible, and we think in more concrete terms. So, it feels more real and urgent, and it is natural to focus on details and practical matters. Both are useful perspectives depending on what you want to accomplish. We're not recommending one perspective over the other. But we are hoping to persuade you that you are likely to be open to different considerations and concerns, and might make different decisions, or even notice different information if you take on one versus the other perspective.

Josh regularly does exercises that take advantage of this shift with teams in organizations to help them achieve their goals, and it is usually quite an eye-opener. Before the exercise, most people experience the present moment as near in time, and the future—when they want to get to some big goal—as far off in time. As a result, the steps they can take in the near term have greater emotional weight, and they are concerned with the details and feasibility of the near term. Meanwhile, the goal is far off, so it remains somewhat abstract. They're in touch with the big-picture reasons for doing it, but the emotions around it are less intense. Their minds are full of things they "should" do to get to the goal, but if those require too much effort or conflict with things they feel they must do now, they put those off.

Here, we'll switch that around, just for a few minutes. We'll mentally act as if we were at that point in time in the future, and—to some extent—experience it as though it were near in time. That will help us get concrete about it, understand the emotional impact—good or bad—of succeeding or failing, and recognize what really needs to happen. And then we'll look back at the present moment as though it were far off in time, to help us see the big picture with more sober emotions, to recognize what actions really make most sense, regardless of what seems the easiest road to take. That kind of information tends to be remarkably valuable in getting to your goals. It gives you some of that 20/20 hindsight now.

In principle, we have access to all of this information—or at least the ability to gather it—without doing an exercise like this. You're using the same brain you were using before the exercise, after all. But taking on these unusual perspectives often is the difference that makes the difference in whether people actually discover the relevant information and give it the attention it deserves.

You can experiment with it now. Call to mind a goal you have that will be challenging—perhaps something where you're not sure exactly how you'll achieve it yet. It should be something you do really want to accomplish, however, or have as a real priority. It can be an individual or a team goal. It can be personal or work-related. It should be a goal for which there is some point in time when you would either like to, or have to, get there— e.g., "In four months' time, our team needs to roll out new operating procedures for our business unit that was recently formed by merging two others"; or, "In two years I want to have completed my first book"; or, "By the time summer comes, I'll have the body I've been wanting."

Of course, you know that you're not really going to the future. You know the difference between now and the future. We don't expect you to fully convince yourself you have traveled to the future in your mind. But we are all able to suspend disbelief to some degree. We all can get lost in thought about the future. You might think of it as being like a child, when you would imagine a fantasy world that was different from ordinary life. We're simply inviting you, for a few minutes, if you are open to experimenting, to act *as if* you were at that future point.[3]

We'll invite you to deeply associate into that future moment shortly— the moment when you seek to arrive at the goal. First, we'll help you set up what to imagine in that future moment in the most useful ways. In previous chapters, we've shared how much more you get out of the experience when you let yourself deeply associate, or step into, the experience as if it were happening now. The more you actually take on that associated perspective, the more you should see the effects. How much you associate into it is up to you.

You can also choose whether you want to imagine you have failed at your goal at that point, or succeeded. Some readers likely are surprised that we've invited them to imagine they've failed. So it's worth clarifying why. What we're doing here is not the same as positive thinking—our aim here is not to connect you with some hopeful emotion and get you pumped up. There's a time for that, of course. But that's not what this is about. Our aim is to help you expose information that can make the difference in whether you achieve your goal.

Often in business contexts, for example, we've found that people are quite drawn to imagining they've failed when doing this exercise. In fact, when they can imagine they have not just failed, but failed utterly, they tend to appreciate it most and get the most value. It helps them live up to their values of being good at risk-mitigation and being diligent. So choose, for this particular exercise, do you want to imagine you've failed or you've succeeded? You could even do it twice, first imagining failure, and then imagining success. Often people get even more useful information when they do both, one at a time.

Now, we invite you to mentally travel to that future point in time when you have either failed utterly at, or achieved true success with, your goal. Note when that time is, and say it to yourself in the present tense. Note where you are physically. Look around you, and see what you see (e.g., "It's May 20 today. I'm in my home office. The sun is just coming up out the east window. I'm looking out at a bird, and my completed manuscript is printing on the other side of the room.").

Staying in that moment you are in, hear what you hear. You can take a moment to describe what you hear, either noises or things you may say to yourself, or perhaps what others may be saying, if others are around.

While you are here in this moment (e.g., May 20, in your home office, with the sun rising and the printer printing your manuscript), feel what you feel. What is it like to be here at this point, having arrived at this outcome?

If you are open to it, you can get lost in the moment for a few minutes, seeing what you see, hearing what you hear, and feeling what you feel. What else do you notice?

From this vantage point, turn and look all the way back to that point in time where your "present" self is, back at the time of reading this book, for example. It's important that you stay in the "future" moment, now, here, in which you have failed at or succeeded at your goal, and look back to the "present," then, over there. And you can answer . . . What did you do to get from there to here?

What did you not do or avoid doing, that contributed to getting from there to here?

What caused you to end up here, starting from there?

What resources, people, and skills did you rely on, or not rely on, to get from there to here?

How did you communicate with yourself or others, or not communicate, that contributed to getting from there to here?

In what ways did you change something about yourself, or not change, to get from there to here?

You can now gently return to the present moment and associate into your current reality again, bringing back with you unconsciously or consciously whatever is useful.

What, if anything, is different now in terms of how you think, feel, or are inclined to act regarding your goal?

We've offered one example illustrating something Josh does with teams or individuals in organizations. It's natural to wonder where else this can be applied, and whether this can be done in a more conversational way.

Yes, it can be done—that is, you can use the mental time machine to gain new perspective—conversationally, and in varied contexts. For instance, anyone who must help people think about future decisions can make use of it. This could include a consultant making a sale for a long-term contract, a parent advising a teenage child on a life choice, a personal trainer aiming to get their client to change their diet and exercise, among many others.

More specifically, it can look like this: If you have worked with an accountant or financial advisor, for example, they frequently are in a position to advise you regarding decisions that will affect you far off in the future. Successful advisors can, and often do, invite you to imagine the future—e.g., your retirement. They ask questions to help both you and them get a clear understanding of, and an emotional feel for, what it will be like to have certain financial resources at that time for you in particular. That helps you associate to a certain degree into the future, and take the perspective of your future self. From that vantage point, the advisor and you can better, and more dispassionately, look at the present moment with some more psychological distance while you make financial plans.

We've given a great deal of attention to the future in this chapter. Note that traveling to the past has many useful applications, too. Studies have shown that going to the past is very similar to going to the future in your mind, in terms of the psychological mechanisms.[4] The same effects of psychological distance can be expected.

A conversational example of helping someone take a perspective from the past could look like this: Todd complains that his house isn't big enough for his growing family. Then,

- Marisa, his partner, says, "Todd. Remember when we just got married and didn't have any idea we'd be making the money we make now? We lived in that little apartment, and we thought we'd really made it. We planned out how the kids we'd have could share the second bedroom, and we loved the idea. See the house from those eyes."
- Todd: "Wow. Good point. Hmm . . . Okay, this house has loads of space and there are lots of possibilities for how to make it work. You're right. I need to chill out."

We're all mentally time traveling anyway. So everyone can do it. It pays to go the extra mile to help yourself or others step a little—or a lot—more deeply into the past or the future, to more fully take advantage of the power of that perspective.

24

CHANGE THEIR MENTAL IMAGE

One day when Josh was a young adult, at a time when he was feeling lonely, without a girlfriend, and wondering how he would make a decent living, he called up his mom to complain. He went on and on in self-pity, and talked about how he felt like there was a big gray cloud right over his head. His mom then said something kind of strange. She said, "What happens when you move that cloud far away and let the sun shine through?" Josh laughed a bit, but something was different when he pictured that. Weird! But cool. Josh relaxed a bit, felt a bit lighter, and a bit more hopeful.

Remember the central aim of NLP that we talked about back in chapter 2? It was to discover someone's mental model of the situation they are in. As you discover that mental model, you can start experimenting to find the difference that will make the difference to help them change their thoughts, feelings, or behaviors.

Well, mental models include mental images. When we think about a situation, we frequently have some visual mental image in mind. And mental images can have a powerful effect on us.

As the saying goes, a picture is worth a thousand words. When you see a picture, you instantly take in a huge amount of meaning. If we showed you a photo of a busy intersection on a chilly, damp day, for example, with cars and people and traffic lights, you could, in a split second, understand a tremendous amount. Such as, that two people together probably know each other, that there will be some difficulty as the cars and walkers try to get past one another, that a driver leaning out the window with his hand in the air is upset, that someone halfway through the intersection as the light is changing will feel rushed, and much more. There is no way that language could communicate so much in the same split second. Seeing the picture of the intersection can quickly and instantly evoke a feeling in you, too—perhaps a feeling like the background stress you sometimes feel when trying to rush on your commute home after work. Seeing the chilly, damp day may bring up some of the ways you feel on such a day.

The same holds for a picture that you see in your mind's eye. It quickly and immediately conveys a tremendous amount of information, can influence your beliefs, and can trigger feelings. And it does so nonverbally.

Research has demonstrated that seeing things in our mind's eye can have similar effects as actually perceiving things—similar brain activity, and a similar impact on us.[1] For example, constructing a visual mental image of some anxiety-provoking situation—e.g., imagine seeing yourself as you are about to go on stage to give a presentation in front of five expert judges—can affect how we feel in a similar way as actually being there.

Across various studies, it has been found that when we construct mental images of something happening in the future, it can increase the likelihood we'll act. If what we imagine is the scary aspect of something risky, we are more likely to avoid it. If what we imagine is some desirable action—like voting—we're more likely to do the desirable action. If what we imagine has to do with the ways we will find our path to some goal, we are more likely to get to that goal.[2]

Mental imagery has been shown in research to have the power to evoke emotions, and to help people regulate their emotions, too. And the findings suggest that seeing mental images in our mind's eye has an influence on us apart from just how language affects us.[3]

In NLP, we take mental images seriously as a part of someone's mental model. We pay attention when someone describes what they may see in their mind's eye, and then get curious about what happens if they change what they see in their mind's eye. For instance, one of the most common changes to try is to explore what happens if you move a mental image closer (making it larger) or farther away (making it smaller).

Research shows that when people imagine some mental image move closer or farther away, it changes how they feel about whatever it is they have in mind. It tends to become less intense when they imagine seeing it far away and smaller, and more intense when they imagine seeing it closer and larger.[4] So, if they are picturing something negative or unpleasant—like an image of a person they dislike—they feel worse when seeing the image of that person move closer and larger in their mind's eye; and they feel less bad when seeing the image of that person move farther away and smaller in their mind's eye. Anecdotally, we also know of people with trauma and phobias who have benefited from doing this. In trauma, there's often a mental image that keeps coming to mind—a flashback of the triggering event. And in phobias, there is sometimes a distorted mental image—for instance, a person with a fear of dogs may have an image of a dog jumping to attack them. Moving these images far away and making the mental images small in their mind's eye seems to help them calm their emotions and get some perspective quickly.

This kind of finding fits with a much more richly studied effect, where things that are psychologically near—like it happened today, nearby, or to someone like me—are experienced differently than things that are psychologically distant—like it happened a long time ago, somewhere far away, or to someone not like me.[5] For instance, what's near has been shown to be more intense emotionally—an embarrassing memory is more likely to be experienced as psychologically near, and a more neutral memory as psychologically distant.[6]

There's less research on positive emotions, but the equivalent would be something like this: if it were something positive a person had in mind—like an image of their recent trip to the Andes—they would feel better when they see the image of their trip move closer and get larger in their mind's eye; and they would feel less good when they see the image of their trip move farther away and get smaller in their mind's eye.

So far, we've been talking about the modality of vision. In NLP, we use the term "submodalities" to refer to the different features of a modality. The submodalities of vision include things like:

- distance
- size

- color
- brightness
- blur
- location (e.g., left, right, above, below, in front, and behind)

Some of you may find it helpful to think of the camera app on your phone. When you press the edit button, you get a list of features you can alter—zoom in or out, crop, adjust the color, brightness, contrast, and so on.

What Josh's mom did was to suggest he shift the distance, color, and brightness, among other things, of his mental image. Instead of a gray cloud closely over his head, he pictured a gray cloud far off in the distance, and a bright golden ray of sunlight coming through from above where the cloud had previously been.

Try it now. Picture something that is bothering you.

What happens when you take the mental image and move it so that it is far away and small, or even disappears in the distance because it shrank away?

Does it bother you to the same degree after doing that?

Even eight-year-olds can do this. Josh's son tried it out when he read an early version of this chapter to him. He pictured some ice cream instead of something that was bothering him.

JOSH: What happens when you bring that picture of the ice cream in your mind up close and make it large?

EIGHT-YEAR-OLD: I want to eat it more.

JOSH: What happens when you move that picture of the ice cream in your mind far away and small?

EIGHT-YEAR-OLD: I don't want to eat it as much.

Josh did not have an agenda to try to get him to eat less ice cream, by the way, and ice cream had not been part of any discussions recently. These were his son's spontaneous responses—it's just what his son noticed happening in his own experience.

Note that once in a while you won't get the specific effect that someone prefers to bring a positive thing closer, or move a negative thing far away. For instance, if someone is trying to avoid eating ice cream, seeing it close and large in their mind could be a negative experience, not a more positive one. What matters is the meaning of the image to the person. At times, also, there may not be any effect of changing the image. But quite often, it's reasonable to expect there will be some effect. Remember, there's no failure, only feedback. When you experiment with changing your own or someone else's mental image, aim to explore with curiosity how, if at all, a particular submodality shift has an effect. For example, perhaps brightness or location could matter, but not distance so much. We find that if you keep exploring you will typically find a difference that makes a difference.

To introduce the concept of submodality shifts, we gave you examples that had to do with just one perceptual modality—vision. That was just so we could keep things simpler while we introduced the idea. But you can do something similar with things you hear in your mind's ear, or even with feelings. The submodalities of hearing would be things like:

- volume
- pitch
- tone
- location

The submodalities of feeling would be things like:

- temperature
- pressure
- size (e.g., how much of your body it covers)
- location (e.g., what part of your body you feel it in)

This is how it can play out in a real-life situation. Laura—a seasoned consultant—had gotten hired to do consulting for a small firm. However, the CEO of the small firm really struggled with giving people autonomy. He (the CEO) set up a test. Anyone who was going to interface with clients would have to prove to him that they would present the company and the IP exactly as he would. Some people who had not been able to pass the test did not work there much longer. As it was, the CEO was still heavily involved in almost all client interactions. Only a couple of people had some degree of autonomy at this point. It was Laura's turn to be tested. As you can imagine, she was seriously stressed out. It was a setup for failure, and it was seriously throwing her off her game. She had been successful at similar roles at other companies in the past. But now, she kept messing up when she practiced.

What would happen is that every time she tried to prepare, she would get distracted and anxious because she would imagine his reaction. She would hear his voice in her mind saying, "Laura," and it would make her cringe because she knew he only said her name when he was about to express disappointment and criticize. And the whole time she prepared, she could just see this guy's face in her mind showing disappointment, right in front of her.

With the help of an NLP coach, Laura made a plan. During her prep, if she thought of the CEO, and, during the test, if he spoke to her, she would do the following:

- turn the volume way down on this guy's voice, so it was barely audible
- turn the pitch way up, like a squeaky mouse
- see the guy with a clown nose on, waving his arms like a monkey
- put the mental image of him far away, and make it small

Suddenly, Laura was free to ignore her intrusive thoughts and worries about how the CEO would react. That freed Laura to focus on using her own good judgment. It was as if she didn't hear a word the CEO said during the whole test. It turned out Laura performed better on the test than anyone before her and became one of the few who was given some freedom to interact with clients as she saw fit.

We're not suggesting you always find a way to make your CEO into a ridiculous tiny, quiet, squeaky, monkey-arm-waving clown in your mind who you can ignore. But in this case, that was actually the best way to serve him, the company, and Laura. It was a case where the CEO was getting in his own way.

Another example that combines different shifts is this one. An entrepreneur we know goes through a financial "dark night of the soul" every few years when his business affairs inevitably go through a cyclical downturn. Even though each time is not his first rodeo, he *sees* utter failure. In his mind's eye, he sees an image of himself ruined financially, embarrassed, having lost his family home, and bankrupt. He sees, in his mind, the FOR SALE sign outside the family home. He pictures his wife having to sell her jewelry to pay the outstanding bills. He sees in his mind's eye an image in which he feels the humiliation of running out of money and refusing his children's needs. He pictures shuttering the business, and imagines faces of derision and scorn with insincere sympathy from family and friends. This doomsday scenario has no sounds, but always has a feeling. He feels it as a sinking sensation in the location of his sternum.

He understands that, as NLPers often say, the map is not the territory— that is, that his mental model (his map) in which he imagines financial ruin isn't necessarily true (may not be an accurate depiction of the territory). He's learned to make changes to what he sees, hears, and feels in his mind. Visually, he dims what he sees in his mind's eye—reducing the brightness—and moves it far away. He then brings a new mental image in to where the old one was in his mind's eye—it is a picture of success. He adds an auditory piece, and hears himself saying loudly, "Everything before this worked out for me, and so will this." While this mantra is playing in the background, he does one more step. He moves the feeling up from his sternum to his heart. The new stuff that he sees, hears, and feels usually moves him from anxiety to excited anticipation, and fairly quickly.

Here are a few more submodality shifts you can experiment with right now:

a. Is there something in your life where, when you think of it, you get a knot in the pit of your stomach?
   ○ If so, what happens when you move that sensation up to the center of your chest, and make it warmer?
   ○ If the feeling is becoming nice, what happens when you make it bigger, so it fills more of your body?
b. Imagine hearing someone you admire saying something meaningful to you (e.g., in *Star Wars* when Luke hears, "Use the force,

Luke," in his mind in the trusted and soothing voice of Obi-Wan Kenobi).

○ What happens when you make it very quiet and/or muffled?

○ What happens when you make it louder and/or clearer?

c. Think of some situation that sucks. Some people may get a feeling when they do this, for instance, as if a heavy weight were on their shoulders; others might hear something, like their own voice in their head saying, "I'm such an idiot!"; others might have a visual mental image, like of a person who is difficult; and others may have some combination, perhaps.

○ Experiment with some changes. Have fun exploring what happens with a curious and open mind. If you don't like the effects of some change, you can change it back.

○ What did you notice when you experimented?

Constructing or influencing someone's mental image as an effective means of influence is nothing new. Authors help us create rich mental images so that we feel transported into a novel. Sales pitches invite us to visualize ourselves needing or using the product. And research supports their efforts. Research on marketing, for example, shows that getting people to form mental imagery of some vacation destination makes tourism messaging more persuasive.[7] And, when trying to persuade someone of something—like that a certain location is safe—how vivid their mental imagery is regarding the implications of the message predicts how much they are persuaded by it.[8]

In this chapter, we're just adding some important nuance—that you can do more than focus on the content of the imagery, but also the form. We're also highlighting that not all thinking is done in words. To understand someone's mental model, pay attention to how they mentally represent their situation visually, auditorily, kinesthetically, or in terms of other sensory modalities. This is a way of going beyond words, or working so efficiently that words are unnecessary.

25

CHOOSE YOUR STATE AND
HELP OTHERS CHOOSE THEIRS

When writing this book, Josh went to ask his wife for help. She said, "You know what . . . I think I need to move my body right now. I'm not in a good state to help. I'm antsy and distracted." Earlier in her life, she would have pushed through, taken a deep sigh, and, fighting herself internally, would have tried to stay put and talk. But she had learned by this point that she could be of far greater service if she were to show up for this conversation in a better state.

When there's an interaction between you and another person, the state you each are in can make a big difference in how things go. If either person is distracted, irritated, annoyed, or feels defensive, it probably won't be a very productive interaction, will it? But if at least one of you is mentally present, calm, patient, or open-minded, it is far more likely to be time well spent.

How do *you* perform when you're not in a good state? Think of an actual important context for you as you reflect (e.g., presenting in a key meeting when you feel like an imposter, dealing with a behavior issue when you are angry and depleted, or trying to build your business when you are filled with fear and doubt).

How do you perform when you are in a good state? For example, presenting in a key meeting when you are confident, dealing with a behavior issue when you are calm and refreshed, or trying to build your business when you are filled with courage and hope.

Did you notice any differences in your two answers?

We find that most people we ask have had many firsthand experiences in which their state made a difference. But we also find that most people don't know that this represents an incredible opportunity.

Before going further, we should note something. You may have noticed that the examples we gave of a "good" state were things that generally feel good; and our examples of "bad" states were things that mostly feel bad. We thought they would make for examples that were easier to start with. But what's a "good" state depends on the context. Things that feel bad can be right in the right moment. For example, being anxious before an exam can get a college student to focus on studying. If they weren't anxious, they might be more likely to party instead.

In NLP, we take the attitude that there's a positive intention behind everything we do. That means we're saying there's a positive intention behind being in a mental or emotional state that feels bad. States that feel bad still do something useful for us. So instead of "good," think "useful"; and instead of "bad," think "not useful."

In this chapter, our aim is to help you recognize that (a) you can actually choose your state to a much greater degree than many—perhaps most—people are aware of, and (b) when you choose, it is best to consider not what would feel nicest, but what would be most useful for your context.

Research has shown that the state we're in affects us in a number of ways, some obvious and some unexpected, and that states that feel bad can very much be useful. On the more obvious side, when people have relatively more positive emotions at work, for instance, they are more likely to go the extra mile for the company or team they are part of, to cooperate, and to share resources.[1] That probably comes as no surprise—many people assume that feeling good is a good thing.

Perhaps more surprising, however, is that people can be more effective decision-makers and planners in a negative state. People in a negative state—like feeling anxious—are more likely to be vigilant, and put in the effort needed for deep analysis.[2] Downside planning, or playing the devil's advocate, doesn't usually feel good, but it helps us identify things that need attention. Also, it has been shown that having negative feelings—like feeling sad—can make you more persuasive as a communicator.[3] Negative emotions also have been demonstrated to help people avoid being deceived—in eye-witness testimony experiments, people in positive moods were more easily misled, but those in negative moods were not so easily misled.[4]

Our point is not to provide a list of all the demonstrated effects of each state. Instead, it is to show that the different states we have can, and often probably do, serve a purpose.

That said, it's not always obvious at first what purpose a state serves. A person who fears public speaking, for example, may think that their fear serves no value at all, and view it purely as self-sabotage. But fear is useful, for instance, for focusing your attention and getting you energized for a big event. It may be that the fear is doing more harm than good. But the positive intention remains. And this is often a critical clue to figuring out what state would serve you best. Our approach in NLP is to find a more adaptive way to get the benefit that the fear is useful for, but without all the self-sabotage. In other words, it would be to find a more adaptive way to get focused and energized for the big event.

There's a question you can ask to help figure out what would be more adaptive. It is a question that is very commonly used by psychotherapists and coaches. The question is: "How is that serving you?" We invite you to start thinking about your mental-emotional states in terms of how they do, or can, serve you. For example, an executive tells his coach that when he gets treated disrespectfully in a meeting by coworkers, he gets really angry and can't collaborate anymore. The coach might inquire, "How does getting angry like that serve you?" The executive getting coached might, at first, say it serves no good purpose at all. But as he reflects a bit more, he will usually identify how it serves him, and respond with something like "It's how I make sure I don't get pushed around." The coach and executive would then work on finding better ways to ensure he does not get pushed around, where he can be less angry and collaborate more effectively, even when he doesn't like how someone treated him.

You may find it valuable to reflect right now on how some of your states serve you. Think of a time when you were anxious or stressed or scared. How did that serve you?

Think of a time when you were curious, open-minded, or flexible. How did that serve you?

Recall a time when you were serious or passionate. How did that serve you?

Think of a time when you were playful or excited. How did that serve you?

Now, let's go back to a time when you were in a state that was not useful—it really got in the way somehow. You could go back to the example from the start of the chapter, or pick something new. (The examples we offered at the start of the chapter were: presenting in a key meeting when you feel like an imposter, dealing with a behavior issue when you are angry and depleted, and trying to build your business when you are filled with fear and doubt.)

How did that "bad" state serve you? What was the positive intention behind being in that mental-emotional state? For example, you might be filled with fear and doubt about your business prospects because you don't want to be poor, or become a failure, or look like a fool. The positive intention is to have money, avoid failing, or not look like a fool. But the fear and doubt aren't getting the job done.

Looking back on that time, with the benefit of hindsight and some psychological distance now, what would be a more adaptive way for you to get that positive intention with less of the unwanted side effects? For example, it could be that you retain some fear and doubt but turn down the volume so it's just in the background; or it could be that you replace it with cool reason; or perhaps courage would serve you better. Reflect on what would work for you. You don't have to know how to get into that more useful state yet.

Our aim so far in this chapter has been to highlight how valuable it can be to get into the right—most useful—mental or emotional state for whatever task you are engaging in. This brings up the question "How do you get into the right state for the challenges you actually face?"

How Can You Get Into the Right State?

There are many techniques for doing so. We'll offer one really good one in this chapter. NLP includes many more, as do many other schools of thought and practices beyond NLP—for instance, twenty minutes of light jogging can transform your state for the rest of the day, so that you can think clearly, prioritize well, and reduce anxiety.[5] Josh wrote more about that in his last book, *Two Awesome Hours*, if you want to dig into it. But the technique we'll offer here is something you can do while reading this book, and you can use it anytime.

This tool for choosing your state is to recall a moment from your past when you were in the desired state. This is such a reliable method that a number of studies use it as the method by which the experimenters get participants to experience a desired target state. For instance, researchers have to first get study participants to feel a certain emotion before they can test what happens when people feel that emotion. Having participants recall an emotional memory is a really good way to get them to feel the emotion.

If you've been reflecting on some of the questions we've posed in this chapter, you've already been doing this to a degree. You're capable of experiencing any state you've ever experienced. It's already within you. The trick is just in learning ways to access those states more easily. Memories are a fantastic tool for doing so.

You can put it to use right now. As you reflect on the coming days, weeks, or months, is there some important event or task coming up for which you'd really like to perform well?

What mental-emotional state would you like to be in for that event or task? Here are a few examples that may help you choose:

- confident
- playful
- a little nervous
- fired up
- present

- calm
- non-attached
- optimistic
- reserved
- relaxed
- serious
- indignant
- passionate
- curious
- thoughtful
- in touch with the big picture
- self-referenced
- clear
- like an artist creating a masterpiece

For instance, at times when Josh is running a training, he wants to be *curious* about how his messages and activities are landing, and *not attached* to things working a specific way. Other times, he wants to *feel playful*, because he knows the journey ahead will be full of discovery and his playfulness can set the tone for the whole group. However, if he is presenting to a team and giving them bad news, he wants to be *serious* and possibly a touch *sad*, so he can meet them where they are and best work together. The state that will be right will depend on the person and the context. This is your opportunity to think about what would be most useful for you. In that light, what state would you like to be in for the event or task you have in mind?

When, in your experience, have you been in that state? For example, if you picked "playful," when have you felt playful in the past? It does not need to be in the same environment. For instance, Josh could recall a time when he was playful with his kids at the park.

You can step back into that memory now. There may be something that you see, or hear, in your mind as you do so. You can notice what it feels like. You may wish to pause for a moment as you allow yourself to connect more deeply with what being in that memory was like.

Let yourself stay in that experience for a time, or even amplify it if appropriate, for ten or twenty seconds at least.

For those of you who took a moment to step back into a memory just now, that state you just experienced is a resource. You can make use of it, when you choose to, to help you succeed. In many cases, all you will need to do to access that resource is to pause and remember that you would like to do so. For instance, right before teaching a class, Josh pauses and reminds himself what state he would like to be in—e.g., playful—and he will give himself a minute to reconnect with that state.

That said, there is more we can do to make it easier to access your chosen resource state. We can add a memory cue. There's a scene in the movie *Ratatouille* in which a food critic takes a bite of our hero's signature dish (our hero is an aspiring chef), and it instantly transports the critic back to his memories and experiences of being a child, eating his own mother's cooking. A scent, a taste, a place, a person, an image, a sound, a voice, a touch, a movement, a word—they can all be cues that transport us back to an earlier time. What happened was that at some point the cue got associated with the memory.

Just like Dr. Ivan Pavlov's dogs that were trained to salivate when they heard a bell, regardless of the accompanying smell of food, we are trained, consciously or unconsciously, to respond to outside triggers or cues. For example, most of us still have a visceral reaction when we hear certain songs. When Bon Jovi's "You Give Love a Bad Name" comes on the radio Greg is almost always nostalgically transported to his teenage years and the associated feelings of angst, hope, and excitement.

You can take advantage of existing cues, or you can create memory cues on purpose. When you do, you can use the cue as a way to bring back the memory more easily. It's not hard to create a memory cue. Learning to associate a cue with a memory is one of the more well-documented phenomena in neuroscience and psychology research. For many decades, scientists have known that even pigeons and snails can learn to associate a cue with something else.

Associating a cue with a memory takes advantage of one of the most central and basic laws of nervous systems, known as Hebb's Law—commonly paraphrased as: neurons that fire together wire together. Let's say you go to a new restaurant and try their food. It turns out to be really good. While you're eating you see the restaurant's name and logo on the menu, on the door, on the matchbooks, all over the place. Your neurons that have to do with enjoying the food are active at about the same time as your neurons that have to do with seeing the restaurant's logo and name. In your brain, neurons that have to do with enjoying the food and neurons that have to do with seeing the name and logo that are close enough to connect form stronger physical connections—they wire together—because they were active at about the same time—they fired together. A week later you see the name of the restaurant and the logo on a billboard on the way home from work, and instantly you start experiencing a trace of those good feelings you had at the restaurant again and wondering if you can go back soon. The logo and name became cues to help you recall the experience of being at the restaurant.

Many cues become resident in our minds, regardless of whether we want them. We suspect most readers can easily picture the Nike swoosh, and know the phrase "Just do it." Those are cues that lead you to think about Nike, and feel whatever feelings you have about Nike. If you've ever had a catchy jingle stuck in your head for a product, that's another example.[6] However, you don't have to just accept what cues get linked to memories. You can make your own cues, and choose what memories they link to.

Once we decide that a cue is worthy, the key is to set up the cue in a way that's easy to access when you need it, and the cue triggers the rest.

So, how do you set up a good—easy-to-access—memory cue? That will depend on what memory you want to connect the cue to. For instance, many people have a memory of getting a feeling of calm or peacefulness when they were at the beach. Many people also have an easy time picturing being at the beach—picturing either a specific memory, or just mental images based on their memories of being there. Usually, it is easy for someone with such a memory or experience to pause and picture the beach. Picturing the beach in their mind is a lot easier than trying to just feel calm and peaceful. But seeing that image of the beach in their mind is a great cue for those people. Closing their eyes and picturing the beach can help bring them back fairly quickly to that memory and experience. The more they have practiced and strengthened the association between the visual mental image and the feeling of calm, the better it will work as a cue.

But that doesn't mean that a visual mental image of the beach is always the best or easiest-to-access cue. Someone else might find it easy to hear the sound of the waves in their mind's ear. For them, imagining the sound of the waves would be a great cue.

Research suggests that cues based on any of the senses should be just as effective at bringing back the target memory.[7] So, what cue is best really is a question of what is easy for you to access for your specific context.

Greg has a fun one he uses from time to time. There are moments when he loses his cool with his kids, and starts to get really angry. That just makes things worse most of the time, of course, and he knows that nothing constructive is accomplished while in an unconstructive state. So he gives himself a wet willy. For people who did not spend a portion of their childhood in the US, or who may not have come across it, a wet willy is when a kid licks the tip of his finger and sticks it in his friend's ear to startle and annoy his friend. It's cold and wet and gross. When Greg does this to himself, he immediately snaps out of losing his temper and laughs at himself. The cue Greg created is kinesthetic—a thing he does and feels with his body. It's easy for him to access—to think of and do when he needs to. And he's associated it strongly with the desired state—laughing at himself.

What Greg does there actually accomplishes two things. One is what we talked about—reminding him to laugh at himself. The other is what we call a pattern interrupt. The wet willy jolts him out of following the same old pattern, the same old mental routine he's in. Sometimes, just interrupting a non-resourceful state is all you need to do to get to a more useful state. In the documentary *I Am Not Your Guru*, Tony Robbins talks about how he will do whatever he feels it takes—acting weird, swearing, etc.—to interrupt the pattern and snap people out of their non-resourceful states or ways of thinking.

Here's another example of a useful cue. One executive who Josh coached had made a lot of progress on earning the trust and commitment of the people in his business units while they worked together. An important part of this executive's progress was from learning to step into the perspectives of the people he led. To help him do so during the rush of the day, he developed an anchor. Josh only learned about the anchor after the executive had used it many times, when he said to Josh, "I hear your voice [in those moments]." In the executive's mind, in those key moments when he needed to, he heard Josh's voice saying to take their perspective. Hearing Josh's voice saying a few key words and in a certain tone, in his mind, was his cue for getting into the right mental state.

A different senior organizational leader who Josh coached had often found herself presenting at high-stakes meetings with a number of high-powered individuals in the room. Public speaking, however, used to make her very uncomfortable. One of the tools she developed to help her quickly shift her mental and emotional state to something more useful, and refocus on her message, was a subtle pinch from one hand to the other. She could do this without anyone noticing. There was nothing special about the pinch on its own. It worked because it was a cue she had strongly associated with her desired mental and emotional state, and she had practiced entering that desired state when she needed to. The pinch served as a small but critical step to help her access the state more easily. The pinch became a great memory cue.

Anchoring

In NLP, we refer to these cues as anchors. An anchor for a boat helps it stay connected to a certain spot in the water. Instead of anchoring a boat to a spot on the water, we're anchoring a memory or experience to a certain cue. The anchor helps you find your way back to the experience or memory more easily.

For instance, Greg had a tough negotiation coming up. For this negotiation, he knew he was in the right, but he also did not have much leverage. So, he knew that he may not obtain the result he sought at this stage. However, he thought his best bet would be to get the other side to negotiate against themselves as much as possible. As long as he could stay calm and curious, keep asking questions, and keep backtracking—

reflecting back to them what he was hearing—he could probably make progress. He's found, as have many negotiators, that people sometimes negotiate both for and against themselves when you can do this, and often reveal a portion of their strategy that they may not have otherwise revealed. But it was hard to stay calm and curious in this case, and he knew he could get easily triggered by some of their more incendiary claims.

So Greg's desired state was *calm and curious*. Greg likes to meditate and has memories of getting to a deep place of being calm and curious while meditating. Greg found that putting his thumbs and pointer fingers together was something he could do during the negotiation without being noticed by anyone, and it could serve as a good anchor. Something about it reminds him of how he sits when meditating. Putting his thumbs and pointer fingers together like that is not something he does a lot at other times, and it is not strongly associated with anything else for him.

To "install," as we say, the anchor, Greg deeply associated into the experience of being calm and curious by accessing his memories of meditation. This was on a different day, before the negotiation. While deeply associated into that experience, he put his thumbs and pointer fingers together. In this way, he created a connection between that hand gesture and the state of being calm and curious.

You can think of your own situation now. Call to mind some event or task coming up that is important to you.

What would be a useful state for you to be in for that event or task?

What do you think could be an anchor that you could associate to the useful state, that you can use as a memory cue to help you access the state later when you want to? Often the simplest ones are: (1) a visual mental image—like picturing a place, a person, or a symbol; (2) something you hear in your mind—like a word or phrase, perhaps in the voice of a specific person, or a sound; or (3) a movement or action—like putting your hand on your heart, touching your ear, or pinching your hand.

The anchor should be something that is not strongly connected to some different state at this point in your life. For example, if you already pinch your hand every time you get nervous then it is already associated with getting nervous. It won't become a great anchor for feeling confident. Or, if you already feel a sense of jealousy that your brother lives by the beach but you don't, when you picture the beach, it might already be associated with jealousy. It won't be a great anchor for feeling peaceful, for example.

For some of you, you may find that the anchor you've chosen already works—it already helps you access that useful state.

Whether or not it already works, you can strengthen the anchor. Some readers may want assistance with this. If so, we have a recording at nlpdifference.com where Josh will guide you through the process. It is easier to do this with someone else guiding. However, for those readers who feel ready to try it on their own, the steps are these:

1. Associate deeply into the remembered experience, so you get into the desired state.
2. Activate the anchor while deeply associated into the remembered experience (i.e., if the anchor is an image, see it; if it's a sound or word, hear it; if it's a movement, do it).
3. Stop activating the anchor.
4. Break the state by distracting yourself.
5. Repeat steps 1–4 to strengthen the connection between the anchor and state.
6. Test to see if you've created a useful anchor. "Fire the anchor," as we say in NLP, and just note what happens. Does it help you access the state more easily? If not, repeat steps 1–4.

You can think of it like installing new buttons. We all have buttons that people can push. This is about installing new buttons that do things we'd rather have them do. So a parent might get their buttons pushed when their teenager rolls their eyes at them. But now, the parent can press their own new button—e.g., maybe they've created an anchor of picturing their kid as a baby. Pressing that button—picturing their kid as a baby—helps them get in touch with a sense of wisdom and patience.

Ultimately, there's no magic here. All we're doing in this chapter is giving you a scaffolding to make it easier to do something you already can do. Everyone is capable of remembering a prior experience. Doing so can be a quick and powerful way to get into a more useful or desirable state.

Memory cues can help you access your memories more easily. With simple associative learning, you can associate new cues—anchors—to your memories and desired states. The stronger the association, the better the anchors work.

Like a scaffolding, anchors are often temporary. They are just tools we can consciously use until we get so good at getting into the desired state, or helping others to, that we don't really need the anchor. Over time, for instance, Greg has had less and less need to consciously get into a calm and curious state for certain negotiations. It's becoming more automatic now. The less he touches his fingers as an anchor, the less doing so has any effect. The effect of the anchor will fade with disuse—neurons that don't fire together don't wire together.

Guiding Others to More Useful States

We've introduced these ideas largely with examples of getting *yourself* into a useful state, but we all have the ability, even in day-to-day interactions, to help others access more resourceful states, too. For instance, a financial advisor might find it helpful to get a client to step into a mental state in which they are in touch with what it may feel like in retirement. That financial advisor can even make use of anchors they've learned about in their relationship with the client—e.g., by referencing the name of a special place, such as the client's beach house on the outer banks of North Carolina where they hope to retire to. Perhaps the client is worried about short-term noise in the market. Referencing that beach house can help the client recapture the right resourceful state for the conversation about long-term investing.

Alternatively, a teacher might periodically need to get their students into a state of being quiet and attentive. A teacher might have a hand gesture they teach the kids to associate with getting into this state. When the kids see that hand gesture and copy it, it quickly gets all the kids into a mode of pausing and listening.

Or a leader in an organization may need to get their team to go the extra mile before a deadline. It may be useful to get them into a state of feeling energized about having a meaningful contribution. Over time, this leader has frequently used the phrase "our time to shine" to motivate this state. In the minds of the team members, the phrase has come to be associated with a number of tough but meaningful experiences in which they all worked hard together. Using that phrase serves as an anchor and helps the team rally more quickly.

Another way to guide others to a resourceful state is to get into that state yourself. It's contagious. For example, research shows that when people feel a certain emotion, others they interact with are likely to take on some of that.[8] A pessimistic, or apathetic, or overly anxious leader can really drag down the whole team just by being in the room with them. Whereas an optimistic, caring, and determined leader can lift up the whole team by showing up.

Often, you can achieve a useful shift in people's mental or emotional state just by suggesting that you all take a moment to recenter. After all, most people are showing up to meetings distracted by other obligations, "fires" they had to put out, or stress.

Still another option is to reframe the situation. For instance, Josh might get super worried about being late to the airport, and his wife could reframe the situation for him by saying, "Hey, the whole point of this vacation is to relax and not take everything so seriously. Let's start now. I mean, you can't control the traffic, and what's the worst that will happen if we're late? We'll get on a later flight and have time for dinner." This will put Josh in a more resourceful state for anything they want to talk about on the way to the airport.

But remember that just because it is resourceful or useful does not always mean it feels good. Politicians and nonprofits will often try to stir up anger or a sense of injustice in order to get people to take action on behalf of a cause they believe in.

And one more we'll offer you is to use the pattern interrupt. For instance, you could suggest a change of scenery, you could find something to laugh about, or you could do something unexpected. Any of those could snap the other person or people out of whatever state they were in.

This is not an exhaustive list. Our point in highlighting these alternatives is to show how many options are available to us all and really are within reach for most people in most contexts.

To help make this your own, we invite you now to think about some important event or task coming up that involves another person or other people.

What do you think would be a useful state for them to be in for this event or task?

What ideas do you have about how you might help bring about a useful state in them?

It's an interesting thing to think about, isn't it? And, we find, it's often something people haven't given much attention to before. But it can be the difference that makes the difference.

26

DON'T BELIEVE EVERYTHING YOU BELIEVE

How do you get someone—yourself or others—to change a belief when it at first feels like too big of a change?

For instance, you may want:

- the senior management in your organization to believe you should get funding for your area of the business when others have a better case on paper.
- a family member who has always dismissed the idea to believe they really should and can stop smoking.
- yourself to believe something more empowering—like that you can enjoy and excel at public speaking, which your job demands—even if it now feels like an impossibility for you.

Sometimes we may seek to change a particular belief, but the new belief just feels like a leap too far for the person we hope to influence.

However, such beliefs can change. This example from Greg's upbringing shows how it can happen. Greg was born and raised in the former Soviet Union, and emigrated to the United States in 1979 at the ripe age of eleven. All children in the former USSR were indoctrinated into atheism from a very early age. So upon arrival to the US, Greg's "truth" was very much that there was no God. When confronted with the proposition that

God is a part of everyday life, he refused to entertain that possibility as it clashed directly with his model of reality.

But with time, Greg began to doubt atheism, as he was exposed to religious teaching, spirituality, and ideas about the order and perfection of creation. He became open to believing as he saw, learned, and experienced events that were difficult for him to explain using his previous model of reality. He eventually came to have a new "truth," which was not atheism.

Unfortunately, the process took close to twenty years, and you did not buy this book for the twenty-year plan. However, in this story are the seeds of what we can make use of for quick belief change.

(1) Greg started out definitively atheist. Then (2) Greg had the experience of becoming open to doubting atheism. Then (3) he had the experience of being open to believing something else. And only after that (4) did he have a belief in a higher power. Rather than leaping all the way from definitively atheist to definitively not-atheist, he took smaller steps.

It's no big surprise that breaking something into small steps can be helpful. What may come as more of a surprise is that you can break belief change into small steps.

At least two popular and research-backed approaches to helping people change within psychotherapy highlight the importance of recognizing that when people struggle with change, it is important to break the change down into steps. One of those approaches goes by the name of the trans-theoretical model. (Don't worry—we won't quiz you on the name.) In that approach, the therapist looks for whether the person changing is at an early stage in their process—e.g., not aware of a need or desire to change; or thinking about it and wanting it, but no commitment. Or whether they are at a later stage in the process—e.g., congruently committed to behaving differently. When the therapist understands the stage the patient is at, the therapist can know what work needs to be done. For instance, at an early stage it may be more important to help the patient become open to changing. But at a later stage, it may be more important to help them make concrete plans to change their behavior. Matching the mental work with the stage matters for whether they make progress. Try to jump ahead and patients may push back or give up.[1]

The other approach we're referring to is called motivational interviewing.

In that approach, when someone says they want a change, but also resists changing, the therapist does not try to convince them to change or make concrete plans to change, but instead meets them where they are. The therapist invites the patient to start exploring what could motivate them to change. The therapist, moreover, does not presume to have all the answers, but guides the patient to discover what would motivate them to move to the next appropriate step for them. Motivational interviewing has been shown, across various contexts, to help people make the changes they need to make in therapy.[2]

In this chapter, we're not teaching therapy, and those approaches pertained to behavior changes that a patient may be working on. Here, we're just talking about a belief change. However, we think the evidence about the value of those approaches helps make the points that you can and should break down a belief change that seems too big into smaller steps; and when you do, there's reason to believe it will serve you better in the end.

Nonetheless, that insight alone usually won't be enough. Even if you like the idea of breaking that belief change down into smaller steps, what would those steps even be? The solution that NLP offers is to focus on the form, not on the content, and let the person whose belief will change fill in the content. This is similar to the approach from motivational interviewing, in which the therapist does not try to guess what specifically would best motivate the patient, but instead helps them come up with those arguments, stories, personal experiences, experiments, and so on that they think might motivate them.

Over the years, as psychotherapy has developed and been researched, there have been various calls for therapists to step away from needing to be the experts on content, and instead to focus on form. For instance, if someone is struggling with a difficult relationship, the therapist can serve the patient better if she does not get into the weeds of he said/she said and giving advice about what to specifically say or do, but instead stays focused on guiding the patient through the processes of discovering useful goals, attending to their needs, learning about their triggers, tolerating or regulating their feelings, and so on. The therapist maintains a high-level view of the processes to go through and the general form of what the patient should try to experience or accomplish, and in this way guides a more useful and efficient process for change.[3]

The form we're offering you here is this:

Step 0: (We called it zero because it is the beginning, so you won't have to actively take this step. But we mention it to remind you this is where the person starts—pace and then lead.) They believe the old belief. Meet them where they are. Acknowledge and respect their mental model.

Step 1: *They become open to doubting.* You don't have to know what they would believe when they are open to doubting. Just help them connect with their ability to be open to doubt, and then let them explore how that can apply to the target belief.

Step 2: *They become open to believing.* You don't have to know what they would believe when they are open to believing. Just help them connect with their ability to be open to believing something new, and then let them explore how that can apply to the target belief.

Step 3: *They believe a new belief.* Just help them connect with their ability to believe something new that they once did not believe, and then let them explore how that can apply to the target belief.

Specifically working on getting someone to be open to doubting, or open to believing, is an important part of the work in research-backed cognitive therapy and substance abuse work, as well.

In cognitive therapy, a patient and therapist work, in part, on changing the patient's thoughts. Within that process, the therapist may periodically ask the patient to indicate how confident they are in their old thoughts or in their new thoughts. For instance, the patient may be working on getting over a fear of social events. They may have identified that an old and limiting thought was "I am unlikable and unwanted." And they may have come up with a more useful new thought to replace it, such as "The people I want to connect with will like me when they get to know me." As time progresses, across one or more sessions, the therapist can ask the patient to rate their confidence in these beliefs. For example, 80 percent confident that "I am unlikable and unwanted" essentially means they are open to doubting the old belief; 80 percent confident that "People I want to connect with will like me when they get to know me" effectively means they are open to believing the new belief. The specific percentages are not our point here—

but just that there is some percentage where they don't fully believe and are open to considering an alternative. In cognitive therapy, the therapist can test for that kind of shift as a form of progress. The therapist then may continue to nudge the person to change that percentage. That is, the change is not just assumed to be all or nothing. Cognitive therapy approaches that include these evolving shifts in how much confidence the patient has in their old and new beliefs have been highly effective for a broad range of challenges and changes people seek in their lives.[4]

Likewise, in alcoholism treatment, experts have highlighted that the most important work is often to move people from believing they need alcohol, to doubting it, to believing that they should or they can stop drinking. Focusing on that process of belief change at first can be more fruitful than trying to jump all the way to changing the drinking behavior.[5]

In the contexts we face day to day, we can often bring people from an old belief to being open to doubting that belief. That is a step many people can and are willing to take, at least for a time. From being open to doubt to being open to believing a new belief is another step many people are capable of taking and willing to explore. And from being open to believing to believing the new belief is another step that is often within reach for many people and something they are willing to consider. To help you bring someone along these steps, we're drawing elements from a couple of tools from NLP. One of those tools is called chaining. From chaining, we're borrowing the idea of creating a chain of safe, achievable, ecological steps from the present state to the desired state. The other tool is an approach to belief change called the belief change cycle that highlights specific types of experiences people go through in the process of changing their beliefs.

Pulling from these two tools, we can create a series of steps like this—for ourselves or others—because every person has experience from their own life to draw on in which they:

- used to believe something they no longer believe.
- were open to doubt.
- were open to believing.
- believed something they previously had not believed.

In NLP, we view each of those life experiences as a resource. You can reflect for a moment and identify some of those resources for yourself right now.

What is something you used to believe that you no longer believe? For example, "I used to hate public speaking. And I believed I was terrible at it. I thought it was something that could not be learned. Then I saw other people move from fearing it to liking it and get much better at it, so I thought maybe it could be learned. I took a class, and discovered that I could get better, too. Now I am comfortable with it, I know it can be learned, and I believe I am good at it."

What is something you used to believe that you became open to doubting? (It could be that you use the same answer as the previous question, but just focus on an earlier part of the process, or it could be something else, such as something you currently are just beginning to question that you used to believe.)

What is something you do not yet believe, but you are open to considering?

What is something that you previously did not believe, but you now do believe?

With those answers, you now have resources from your own experience to help you connect with letting go of a belief, being open to doubt, being open to believing, and taking on a new belief.

We'll take advantage of lessons from previous chapters to offer you a deep way to take someone through these steps. And then we'll include a more conversational approach for day-to-day contexts.

The deep way is this. You can try it out now with step 1. What is some belief that would be useful for you to let go of? For instance, maybe you don't believe you can ever repair your relationship with your brother. Or perhaps you believe you will never be able to change the way you eat in the ways you know you should. Or possibly you may believe that you can't get ahead in your career even if you take the right steps. Success might feel more like a nice fantasy than a real possibility.

STEP 1: *When have you been open to doubting something you used to believe?* For example, perhaps you used to believe you could never get a tattoo, and now you are not so sure it's off-limits. Note that it doesn't matter if your example pertains to the same context as the belief you want to change. What matters is just that it is an experience you had of being open to doubting.

- ○ Go ahead and spend twenty or thirty seconds associating into that experience of being open to doubting. Step back into that time in your mind as if you were there. See what you see, hear what you hear, and feel what you feel in that moment now of being open to doubting.
- ○ Explore changing some of the submodalities to see what enables you to connect more deeply with that experience of being open to doubting (e.g., if you have a visual mental image in mind connected with that experience, what happens when you make that mental image more vivid or close in your mind's eye?).
- ○ Give yourself an anchor—a memory cue—to make it easier to recall this experience (e.g., perhaps hearing the words "open to doubting" in your mind's ear will work as an anchor; or perhaps you can imagine a symbol to serve as this anchor that you see, hear, or feel).

Now use that anchor to help you connect to the experience of being open to doubting. As you experience being open to doubting, apply it to the old belief you want to let go of—e.g., to the belief that you can't repair your relationship with your brother. Let that form the basis of a new way of considering the old belief. What happens when you consider being open to doubting your old belief now, in this way?

Sometimes, going through that one step is enough, or at least enough for now. However, if you'd like to go further right now, you can answer the questions for step 2 also.

STEP 2: *When have you been open to believing something new?* For example, perhaps you used to believe you were an imposter in your work, but now you are beginning to suspect that you really do know a thing or two.

- ○ Associate into that experience from your history, of being open to believing.
- ○ Explore submodalities to connect more deeply with being open to believing.
- ○ Anchor the experience of being open to believing.

Now apply the experience of being open to believing to the new belief you want. Use the anchor to help you. What happens when you consider being open to believing the new belief now, in this way?

A more conversational, day-to-day example of this tool can look like this:

Nora, an operations leader at a big cosmetics company, has recently taken over management of a factory that has historically underperformed. Attempts were even made to shut the facility down. Since taking over she has found that it has fallen into disrepair and is asking for $1 million to renovate and get it up to speed. The senior leadership in the company only has so much to spend to upgrade and maintain the various factories, and many of them don't want to allocate money to hers because they don't believe the factory will ever perform well enough. They think the money would be better spent upgrading factories with a better track record. Nora gets her chance to make her pitch, and says the following:

"Right now, we struggle to meet demand in the region. That's the only reason this facility hasn't been shut down yet. Over time, it's been clear that the organization can get by in this region, but barely. It would cost a lot to bring this facility up to speed, and given its track record, there's a risk the investment won't pay off well enough. There are limited funds for facility upgrades, and our strongest regions need funds to stay on top. I get it. However, I also know that you've all had experiences where you were sure of something and then discovered it wasn't so. We all remember the brands we tried to import from other regions of the globe that we don't sell anymore, for instance. At a certain point, you became open to the idea that maybe you didn't have the whole picture. Later, you came to think something else might be the better way forward. And ultimately, you changed course, and put your convictions and your budgets behind the new approach.

"I'm not asking you to give me the funding I'm seeking yet. For now, I'm asking you to be open to doubting the idea that it's best for the organization to focus the funds elsewhere. I invite you today, and as you tour my facility in the future, to stay open to the idea that with the right management, personnel, and systems in place, having this facility in top shape can help us grow our footprint in the region substantially, and reduce strain on other regions at the same time."

Nora helped them all connect with the experiences of letting go of an old belief they used to hold, becoming open to doubt, becoming open to believing, and adopting a new belief. She then focused her efforts on getting them open to doubting their convictions that the money belonged elsewhere. And she invited them to start getting open to believing there could be a path in which funding really did belong in her facility.

As another example, in a different domain, here's a fun—and quick— way that Josh's dad once used this tool with him. Josh asked his dad for advice on how to manage all of his work. His dad gave him some good advice. But although Josh thought the advice sounded fine, he didn't believe it would work for him. So his dad said, "That's okay in this case. You don't have to believe this will work for it to work." And just like that, Josh became open to believing it could work.

If someone says, "I'm not ready to make that decision. I'm just not convinced," you can follow up with something like this: "In that case, could you be open to being convinced for the next twenty minutes, while we talk? At that point, if you're not convinced, no need to stay open to it anymore."

It's often not in your control to move someone all the way to taking on a new belief that feels like a leap for them. In those cases, focus on getting them open to doubting the old belief, or open to believing the new one.

27

LET THEM DO THE WORK

Unfortunately lost to history is Mark Twain's little-known story *Chronicles of Huck and Tom: Midlife Crisis and Fence-Painting*. It was the 1870s, and our favorite troublemakers, Huck and Tom, were then pushing forty and running a fence-painting company together. It seemed so exciting when they got started, to paint fences all day, every day of their working lives, but it eventually lost its charm. "Tom," Huck said, "we need to get other people to paint these fences. My hands are getting cramped. And I miss the days of river adventures and cave explorations. We need to find some suckers—I mean employees—to help us paint."

"Sure, buddy," Tom answered.

So Huck put up an ad to hire some painters. But they all wanted too much money. Huck lamented, "I can't get anyone to want to paint for us!"

With a twinkle in his eye, Tom said as he smiled, "No sweat. I got this."

Tom posted something on YouTheater showing himself having tons of fun painting. (YouTheater was all the rage at the time. Imagine TikTok but with live theater and snail-mail comments. The way it worked was that Tom just kept repeating the same twenty-second live play all day long at the downtown theater. People could comment by mailing letters to the editor of the local paper. To DM—direct message—someone, you would walk up and talk to them. It was amazing technology, ahead of its time. But all the VC money was in lightbulbs and telegraphs, so it didn't last.)

In the comments, everyone was asking how they could try what Tom was doing. Then Tom posted, "First 10 people to slide into my DMs GET TO PAINT FOR FREE!"

The next day when he showed up for work, Huck's mouth dropped open. "But . . ." he sputtered. "I couldn't pay them enough to do it, and you have them begging to do it for free!"

Sauntering over like a wise, much older man imparting a great life lesson, Tom put an arm around his little buddy Huck and explained, "Listen, Huckleberry. You can never make someone do something. They gotta want to do it. They have to convince themselves. I just nudged them in the right direction and helped them consider how much they wanted to do it."

We've obviously made up this story, but Huck's blunder is 100 percent real. Often, we think, like Huck, that the burden of changing how someone else thinks, feels, or acts falls on us. But here is the kicker—people only really change when they convince themselves to do it. You may be noticing this is a recurring theme in the book. In this chapter, we offer you a powerful tool for helping people convince themselves. In many cases, this can also require less work on your part than if you were to try to convince them.

Do you remember the meta model from chapters 12 through 16? We shared a bunch of tools for getting very specific about someone's mental model. Well, now we're going to suggest you do just the opposite, and get vague instead of specific. There's a time and a place for everything.

Sometimes people have barriers to even trying on an idea. For instance, you might be trying to persuade a business leader to listen more to their employees. You have great logical arguments, and anecdotes from your own experience to offer, but they have already decided it would take too much time. They tell you that the cost outweighs the benefits and who knows if they'd end up doing anything differently, anyway? Essentially, they say, "Thanks, but no thanks. Nice idea, but it won't work for me." However, you suspect they haven't really considered it deeply in the way you have.

At such a time, saying something like this can help: "I wonder . . . in what ways will you achieve your goals quicker when you take the time to listen to your employees?"

Put yourself in the shoes of a business leader for a moment, and see what happens when you consider the ways you will achieve your goals quicker when you take the time to listen to your employees.

We'd bet that most of you fairly quickly can imagine quite a few ways you could achieve your goals quicker by taking the time to listen to your employees. The employees might help you avoid an obstacle or costly mistake; or some of the employees might drag their feet if they're not bought in, and listening will help you get their buy-in.

Notice that in posing this question to the business leader, you've said nothing about why listening to the employees will help them achieve their goals. There was no attempt to persuade with arguments. The question merely suggested it was a good idea and let the business leader fill in the pieces, in whatever way worked best for them.

The question "In what ways will you achieve your goals quicker when you take the time to listen to your employees?" makes it easier for them to convince themselves. It bypasses the mental firewall that the business leader has to your advice, and points their brain toward really considering the idea.

This question is built on a language pattern that comes from hypnotherapy.

At first, that might be off-putting for some people. Hypnosis? "Surely Josh and Greg are not going to suggest we go around hypnotizing people and making them run around like a chicken," you may be thinking. We think that would be crazy, and not so useful. We're not going to suggest that. What we are going to suggest is that we can all benefit by learning a thing or two about how hypnotherapists are able to help people make changes to their thoughts, feelings, and behaviors.

Ultimately, you might find it helpful to think of hypnotherapy as the art of suggestion. Rather than directly confronting someone, relying only on logical arguments, or diving straight into problem-solving with them, in hypnotherapy, you make suggestions that point the other person toward finding their own solutions.

We also won't be asking you to put anyone into a trance to make use of this tool in day-to-day contexts. Research has shown that you don't need to have someone in a trance for the suggestions that hypnotherapists use to be helpful.[1] While a trance may be useful in some therapeutic contexts, our point is that these suggestions can be useful in everyday situations, too.

Specifically, these suggestions can be useful in helping you get someone to thoughtfully consider an idea. It's not possible to control someone else's thoughts or behaviors, as we've highlighted throughout the book. After considering your suggestion, they may very well dismiss it. In fact, they will dismiss it if it is not ecological or useful for them. That is not in your control. Instead, what we're offering in this chapter is about helping the other person get out of their own way—getting them to the point where they don't dismiss your ideas prematurely, without really considering the value.

It turns out that the use of hypnotic suggestion has actually been researched in various ways over the years, and appears to be an effective tool for many people to achieve a wide range of different kinds of meaningful positive changes (e.g., regarding pain, smoking, anxiety, PTSD, and depression).[2] However, perhaps because of things like stage hypnosis in magic shows, hypnotherapy—which is not the same as stage hypnosis—had a bum rap for a time. But it's regarded as a legitimate endeavor now, accepted in many clinical and research circles. The US federal government funds research on it. Some of the mechanisms by which hypnotic suggestion works are being studied, too, even at the level of brain activity. Findings suggest that it may influence what people focus on or their ability to focus. It may help them manage their emotional reactions and get in touch with or control what's going on in their bodies. And it may free them from thinking about themselves as much as they might otherwise.[3]

Under normal circumstances in the brain, there's an area that is active during something called cognitive control. Cognitive control includes things like inhibiting yourself from doing or saying something you shouldn't, or choosing where to focus. There's another nearby region that's active whenever we need to monitor and react to internal conflict—like trying to choose where to put your attention when your kid in the back seat just screamed, but you're trying not to miss your exit from a crowded highway. These two brain regions, involved in cognitive control and monitoring conflict, usually work together. That makes sense. Your ability to inhibit your reaction to your kid is important in that moment, so you can choose to focus on getting off the highway safely, and then attend to your kid.

In hypnosis, the conflict monitoring area and the cognitive control area can decouple[4]—that is, the two areas become more independent. Bad for driving, but perhaps good for keeping an open mind. No one can say for certain how to interpret those brain findings, but it sure does seem to fit with the idea that hypnotherapy is helpful in getting people to be open to considering ideas that might at first appear to conflict with their other beliefs.

There are many language patterns useful for the art of suggestion—too many to include in this book and do them justice. In NLP, they are generally grouped together and called the Milton Model, as they were collected from modeling Milton Erickson, MD, often considered the father of hypnotherapy in the United States as he worked with his patients. In this chapter, we'll share one of these language patterns that we believe holds tremendous potential as a communication tool, and can be incorporated into many everyday contexts.

That language pattern is the use of presuppositions. That's when you presuppose something to be true.

So, let's come back to that sentence from before. "I wonder . . . in what ways will you achieve your goals quicker when you take the time to listen to your employees?"

The question presupposes you can and will achieve your goals—and do so quicker—when you listen to your employees. It also presupposes that there are multiple ways of doing so. All that is left for you to do as the listener is to fill in the specific examples. Typically, upon hearing this question, the brain is already off to the races solving this problem. Note that you're not asking the listener to presuppose these things. If you did, they would evaluate each step in the logic, because that is where you'd be pointing their attention. That might sound more like this:

"Do you believe listening to your employees can and will help you achieve your goals?"

"Will you accept the idea that you can and will achieve those goals quicker than you otherwise would when you listen to your employees?"

"Do you agree that although it takes time to listen to your employees, there may be something you learn that makes the overall process take less time?"

"Do you believe that it is therefore worth taking extra time to listen to your employees?"

Instead of asking them to believe these things, you're just presupposing these things and thus inviting their brains to jump into the thought process at that point as if you and they were already well down this path.

The efficacy of research on hypnotic suggestions implies that most people will jump into the thought process already well down this path. That said, there's no mind control here. It can certainly happen that someone will say something like "Well, that would never happen. It would take forever. I can't take any more time to listen to them now." In other words, they are still free to decline your invitation. They might even get annoyed with you for pressing the point. Remember, there's no failure, only feedback. In almost all cases, we suspect that's an outcome you could manage, so the downside would be small. The upside can be the difference that makes the difference in whether you get someone to change their thoughts, feelings, or behaviors.

Notice how this was a vague question, too. That's part of how these suggestions work. We did not try to drill down into who, specifically, they should listen to, and how, specifically, they should listen, or what their goals were, or whether they are well-formed outcomes. We left it totally open—presupposed that they had goals, that they could listen, and that there were solutions that met the criteria of "better" and "quicker"—and let them do the work of filling in the specifics.

Here are a few more examples from different walks of life.

Bedtime with School-age Kids

KID: Daddy, I can't sleep.

DAD: [some options below]

"I don't know if you realize that it's okay now to let the day go." (Presupposes it's okay to let the day go now. This is different from if the dad had just said, "It's okay to let the day go." That's an assertion or a plea. It implicitly invites the kid to evaluate the truth of the assertion. That's different from presupposing it.)

"You can remember that there is nothing you have to do tonight as you continue to relax your body." (Presupposes there is nothing the kid has to do tonight, and that they are already in the process of relaxing their body and are capable of continuing to do so.)

"You might be surprised by how quickly you fall asleep now." (Presupposes that they will be falling asleep quickly, and that this is actually happening now, whether or not they were aware of it.)

A Lawyer Trying to Guide a Client to Settle

Suppose you are a lawyer representing a client who rejects a fair settlement offer and unreasonably insists on going to trial. But you can tell they are clouded in their judgment by anger or another limiting emotion. From your experience and the specifics of the case, you have good reason to believe your client will be far more satisfied if they avoid trial, get some meaningful level of justice and compensation through that means, and move on with their life much more quickly and painlessly.

You can try explaining this to them. You can come up with every argument till Sunday, spend a lot of time at it, wear yourself down doing it, and potentially erode the attorney-client relationship. But they are ready to dismiss it all. "I know you mean well, but this is important to me," and things like that, they reply.

Or you can try letting them do the work. Help them get past some of their logical brain, mental filters, and their need to prop up their ego so they can really consider their situation. You can say something like:

> *"How good will you feel a month from now when you've settled all this in a way that works for you?" (Presupposes this can all be done in a month, that settling this will result in feeling better, and that it is possible to settle in a way that works for them.)*

> *"I don't know if you realize how close you are to finding a solution that works for you, and being able to move on with your life." (Presupposes they can move on with their life soon, and that they are not only capable of, but already close to, finding a solution that works for them.)*

You may find it helpful to experiment with some presuppositions for some situation of your own. Think of a presentation that you'll be giving soon. If you don't have one coming up, think of one you will have to, or hope to, give at some point.

How does it help you to remember that there's a good reason it's you presenting?

How does it benefit the audience that you're the one presenting?

Each of these questions presupposes the truth of certain ideas, and implicitly invites you to step into the thought process already presupposing them.

The first question presupposes that there is a good reason, that you already know it on some level, that you are capable of remembering that, and that it will help when you do.

The second question presupposes that it will benefit the audience, and that you're capable of knowing how it does.

Some people find it helpful to have some more concrete guidance on what they should presuppose and how to do it.

What should you presuppose? Whether you are aiming to motivate, influence, help, or lead someone, you can use your language to presuppose certain useful things that are necessarily true. For instance, presuppose they are creative, capable of improving, have positive intentions, and/or can find solutions where they previously did not see any.

How can you do it? Here are a couple of helpful tips:

Start your sentence as you would when sharing a fact—e.g., "Did you know that . . . ?" "I don't know if you realize . . ." "You may remember . . ."

Start your sentence with a question about what will happen when X is true—e.g., "How will you feel when . . . ?" "What will it be like to . . . ?" "How will it help to . . . ?"

Putting the what and how together, you might say a sentence like this: "I don't know if you realize you had a positive intention in avoiding the issue." Or "How will it help you to find other ways to achieve that positive intention?"

People show up to conversations with many mental filters about what's possible, how they'll feel if this or that happens, what has to happen, what they think about others, and so on. Their egos get in the way of listening with an open mind. Their prior beliefs get in the way, too. Even when they mean well, they're often only paying partial attention. They might nod along, but in their mind they're not really deeply focusing on the point. They're not deeply considering how it might apply to them. Ironically, it can be best to step away from trying to be convincing in those moments. Instead, let them do the work. Leverage the art of suggestion, staying vague on the content, and point the person you wish to influence in the right direction, with presuppositions.

Some readers may be thinking at this point, "How do I know when to get specific, so I can try to understand their model of the world? . . . And when to get vague to make use of suggestions, with presuppositions, like in this chapter?" They seem like opposite approaches. The short answer is this—and it's a useful way of approaching everything in this book: start by trying to understand the person's mental model. When you are not clear about something about their mental model that seems important, try to get specific. If you find yourself, at some point, wanting to do more to help them along the path of deeply considering an idea, try offering suggestions like those we've discussed here. Keep exploring, in search of the difference that makes the difference for that person in their unique context.

28

A NOTE ON COMBINING THE TOOLS

FROM THIS BOOK

lthough we've introduced each NLP concept or tool in separate chapters, nobody said you have to use them separately. We suspect that many readers came to this conclusion on their own already, but it may help to see some examples.

For instance, it could make sense to do something like this in almost any context:

1. First establish rapport,
2. then identify a well-formed outcome.
3. To better identify a well-formed outcome, you can ask meta model questions.

If you were helping someone navigate working with others on a long-term goal, it could make sense to:

1. Help the person take the perspective of some important other people involved—walk a mile in their shoes.
2. Take a future perspective.
3. Identify and tap into resourceful states.

If someone keeps getting triggered by another person pushing their buttons, it could make sense to:

1. Meet them where they are before trying to get them to change their reactions—pace and lead.
2. Help them identify the positive intention behind their reactions so they can find better ways to arrive at that positive intention.
3. Help them go meta—like watching a movie, instead of living it—and from that perspective, guide them to interpret the situation that used to trigger them.
4. Help them plan a better reaction—guide them by presupposing they are able to plan a better reaction in the way you speak.
5. Help them associate into the future perspective, and test out the new reaction.

When you take an NLP practitioner or master practitioner training, in addition to all the NLP concepts and tools like those in this book and more, you'll find that people in the field have created longer techniques that combine multiple concepts and tools, usually in a sequence of steps. Some of these longer techniques have been given names. One of them might be presented in a class as good for managing stress, another for handling conflict, another for forgiving and moving on, another for behaving differently to things that used to trigger you, and so on. Practicing with these longer techniques is a great way for learners to master the skills.

Researchers have actually also begun to do clinical trials looking at the efficacy of longer techniques like those you might see in an NLP practitioner or master practitioner training, as applied to some clinically important outcome. For example, there is an approach to treating PTSD that is called the Reconsolidation of Traumatic Memories Protocol (the RTM Protocol). That title is a mouthful, but what it refers to is changing how you experience, and react to, your memories. The RTM Protocol is derived from NLP. It has also been adapted to facilitate scientific research into best practices and for studying clinical outcomes. The steps are very similar to the steps in some of the longer techniques you'd find in an NLP practitioner or master practitioner training. For example, RTM includes going meta (disassociation) from the traumatic memory in powerful ways, and changing the submodalities of the mental imagery of the traumatic memory—such as seeing the event as if it were in a movie playing on a screen, and in black-and-white, among other shifts. When it works, the protocol helps people engage with the memory of their trauma without experiencing the same emotional suffering.

In studies, this protocol has outperformed other therapies for the treatment of PTSD.[1] For instance, a group of UK veterans who were diagnosed with PTSD were either randomly assigned to this protocol or to a CBT (cognitive behavioral therapy) protocol. When assessed at twenty weeks, 16 percent of the CBT veterans no longer had PTSD, while 48 percent of the RTM veterans no longer had PTSD.[2]

Teaching people to treat PTSD in a clinical setting is beyond the scope of this book, and not our aim here either. Instead, we mention this research as evidence of the potential impact of these concepts and tools when combined.

We know that some of our readers are eager to experiment and to combine the various concepts and tools from this book for their personal or work needs. In that case, let this brief chapter serve as a motivation for you to do so. However, we also know that some of our readers would like to keep things simple, to focus on one concept or tool at a time while they are starting to apply some of this to their day-to-day lives. Both are good ways to go.

CONCLUSION

ongratulations! You did it. You finished the book—well, almost finished. Greg and Josh are proud that you picked up our book and pow-
ered through to the end. We are excited about the opportunities that
you will uncover by simply using the concepts and tools in this book.
Before we give you our final thoughts, we thought it would be helpful, to
use Greg's vernacular, to summarize the evidence.

You now know how to make and achieve a well-formed outcome or
goal. Let's pretend that the goal of reading this book was to accomplish a
specific outcome. Initially, we shared with you how to set a well-formed
outcome. Remember back in chapter 1, we shared the five questions to ask
to turbo-boost your results.

With your goal in mind, you asked yourself these questions:

1. Is it focused on what I want, instead of on what I don't want?
2. Will getting my goal cause other problems for me?
3. Is it within my control?
4. Can I clearly define success?
5. When and where, specifically, do I want it?

In section 1, we discussed eight beliefs that can make you limitless.
Together these beliefs form the mindset that enables people to master the

tools of NLP. Many people consider these beliefs to be useful guidelines to follow for a life well-lived. We learned:

- How we experience the world is not the same as reality (chapter 2).

  The way we or anyone else views the world is not the absolute truth, but rather a model of the world—distorted in some ways, missing information here and there—and if we want to understand their thoughts, feelings, or actions we need to understand and appreciate their mental model of the world. We started with this belief because the whole endeavor of NLP can be boiled down to understanding someone's mental model. Once you understand their mental model, you are much better equipped to find the difference that makes the difference for each person and each context. When you find that difference, change can happen fast, and be profound and lasting.

- Ask, "Why not me?" (chapter 3).

  "I can't" is in most instances an incorrect limiting belief. With some extreme exceptions, as long as anyone before us has done it, so can we—because we can learn from their mental model. Presume this and you will find opportunities wherever you find people before you who have succeeded.

- All I need is already within me (chapter 4).

  Each one of us has everything we need inside of us already to reach the next step of our journey.

- There's no failure, only feedback (chapter 5).

  Every time we act we get a result, and no matter what the result may be, it is never failure, but feedback about how we can course-correct.

- How my message landed matters more than what I meant (chapter 6).

  No matter what we meant when we said it, what matters more is what the other person heard. Whether seeking to guide someone else to change or to change ourselves, we depend on others in important ways in almost all circumstances. So success often depends on what we manage to communicate. Make it your responsibility to understand how your message landed, and you will approach every interaction in a more adaptive way.

- If at first I don't succeed, I must try *something else* (chapter 7).

  The more flexible we become, the more likely we are to achieve our desired results.

- Assume good intentions (chapter 8).

  People always have positive intentions for their behaviors, and are not acting just to spite us or to sabotage themselves when they act badly. Speak to the positive intention behind their behavior, and you can find breakthroughs and move beyond conflict more quickly.

- If I knew then what I knew then . . . I'd do it all the same, necessarily (chapter 9).

  People act to the best of their abilities at the time they act.

  This belief can help you get past blame, and instead move quickly toward finding the difference that makes the difference.

We strongly encourage everyone to upgrade their brain software to adopt these beliefs. To build on the programming metaphor in neurolinguistic programming, let these foundational beliefs form your operating system—the background against which other functions will work.

Deeply adopting these beliefs can be quite a change for some people. Many of us have had weeks, months, or even years in our lives when we've woken up in the morning, day-in-and-day-out, believing limiting, and at times even horrible, things about ourselves. Such as that we're not worthy, or not capable, or fundamentally flawed. Probably everyone has had the experience of limiting themselves more than they would like to through their beliefs. What if we stopped limiting ourselves in those ways? Would our lives improve? Would life be easier, and more exciting? Would we achieve more of what is important to us? The research on self-fulfilling prophecies that we cited in section 1 of this book certainly suggests this would all happen. But we will also answer these questions with another question—how could that not be the case?

In section 2, we shared tools to help you quickly and effectively come to understand someone else's mental model of the world. Because once you do, you are much better equipped to experiment to find the difference that makes the difference for them to be able to change. The tools were:

- Be curious (chapter 10).

     When you become genuinely curious, you become a more flexible and effective communicator.

And we followed that with guidance on what, specifically, to be curious about, so that you can most quickly and effectively understand someone's mental model.

- Just the facts (chapter 11).

     What someone says or does and what we take it to mean are not the same. Learn to separate facts from interpretation. Get curious about how else the facts could be interpreted.
- Don't should on yourself (chapter 12)!

     People often "should" themselves into bad situations when they really shouldn't. We can serve them by leading them into making their "shoulds" into something more adaptive, like "will do," "get to do," or "won't do," without all the emotional baggage of "should." Get curious about the mode someone is operating with (e.g., "should"), and whether a change to that mode of operating will help.
- Something's missing here (chapter 13).

     By paying attention when others are speaking, we can notice what's not said—and therefore not clear—in their speech patterns, and ask appropriate clarifying questions to get to the heart of any issue. Get curious about what's ambiguous, or not stated clearly.
- Who, specifically (chapter 14)?

     "They" or "people" may really just refer to one or a small number of people—so the problem is much more manageable than it may at first seem. It's not always clear who someone is referring to when they speak—to you as the listener, but also often to them as the speaker. When someone shares opinions, beliefs, or judgments with you as though they were fact, or as though they were true for all people, get curious about whether they have specific people in mind, or according to whom those opinions, beliefs, or judgments belong.

- How, specifically (chapter 15)?

  There are many ways in which people can be unclear about how something happens. When they are unclear in their speech, it often means there is something valuable to learn. Get curious about how, specifically, they go about doing what they've stated. For instance, if they say, "We have a value of integrity," ask, "How, specifically, do you value integrity when people operate with, or without, it?" Or someone might say they know what others think. If so, you can ask, "How, specifically, do you know that they think that?" Getting curious about how, specifically, things happen can often help someone move from being stuck to taking appropriate actions.

- Do they really do that all the time (chapter 16)?

  People often overgeneralize—"always" is not always always, "never" is not usually never, and "everyone" is seldom everyone. Problems become more manageable when we help people avoid overgeneralizing. Get curious about whether people are overgeneralizing and help them get more accurate. Doing so frequently makes intractable problems more manageable, and helps people move from overreaction to appropriate reaction.

- Watch their eyes for clues (chapter 17).

  The eyes can help you guess what someone is focused on (e.g., a lot of looking down can mean they are focused on their feelings and doing a lot of self-talk, while if they are looking up a lot, they may be picturing something). Get curious when you notice eye gaze direction about what type of processing they are doing (e.g., picturing an image, or feeling a feeling).

- Who's driving (chapter 18)?

  We become more capable in all walks of life when we learn balance between giving others authority, and turning inward to trust our own authority. Get curious about whether someone is relying too much on their own authority or giving others too much authority, and explore whether shifting that balance would be adaptive for their specific situation.

- Walk a mile in their shoes, in your mind (chapter 19).

    In order to understand another's perspective quickly and profoundly, it's amazing what you can discover when you learn to mentally walk a mile in their shoes. Get curious about what it is like to see the world through their eyes, and you can discover how to find breakthroughs in connecting with them. You can, when desired, also model them by doing so, and build your own skillset as you learn about how they do what they do.

Make no mistake about it. Although section 2 is called "How to Understand Someone's Mind," it applies to us as well. Putting aside the egoic considerations, we are all human, and pretty much subject to the same wiring. By learning how to understand others, we are learning how to understand ourselves. We are subject to the same kinds of limitations as others. We generalize, distort, and delete important facts in our mental models that show up in our speech patterns. These show up both in how we communicate to ourselves and others. If you want to change yourself, start by understanding your mental model of the situation you are in. If you want to help someone else change, start by understanding their mental model of the situation they are in. It will help you and them think about what the differences may be that could make the difference.

Then in section 3, we offered tools on how to change someone's mind (yours or theirs). The tools were:

- How to get along with people (chapter 20).

    Before we can influence others, we must earn the right to influence. We shared how central rapport is to trust and a sense of connection, and to people becoming truly open to hearing one another. We also shared specific ways to strengthen rapport through matching overall posture, nonverbal movements and use of voice, and ways people describe their experience.
- Meet them where they are before trying to get them to follow (chapter 21).

Once rapport is established we can meet others where they live mentally, and then pace and lead them to a beneficial place. This also serves the purpose of helping us earn the right to influence. It can make people feel heard and understood. This helps people feel that you care, you know their specific needs, and you are being fair and reasonable with them. When you take the time to meet them where they are, they often are willing to reciprocate, and become more open to where you would like to lead them.

- Are they living it or watching the movie (chapter 22)?

  We learned how to make experiences more intense or less intense, and how to change the meaning we make of our experiences by moving from first to third person ("going meta," also called "disassociating"), and vice versa.

- Use your time machine (chapter 23).

  You can use your internal time machine (or guide anyone else to do the same) and see any situation as your own past or future self might see it, which can quickly and powerfully change how you interpret the situation, how effectively you plan for it, and how you feel about it.

- Change their mental image (chapter 24).

  Mental imagery both reflects and affects our thoughts, feelings, and behaviors. You can guide someone to change what they see in their mind's eye, hear in their mind's ear, or feel in their body. It can be a surprisingly quick and effective nonverbal way for people to manage the situation they are in, or find a way to move on.

- Choose your state and help others choose theirs (chapter 25).

  We shared why and how to guide ourselves and others to useful states, and how to anchor these states for easy recall at any time.

- Don't believe everything you believe (chapter 26).

  When we want to believe something but it feels like a leap too far, it is possible to break that belief change into bite-size steps by guiding the person who is changing through the *form* of belief change, rather than trying to convince them of the *content*.

- Let them do the work (chapter 27).

  We introduced how to use hypnotic suggestions to help

someone get out of their own way, and rather than dismiss new ideas prematurely, to really consider new possibilities. Through using presuppositions we showed how you can set someone up to discover how they can lead themself out of non-resourceful states in ways that work for them.

- Last, in chapter 28, we invited you to become curious about, and experiment with, combining the tools we've presented.

There are exercises or reflection questions embedded in the chapters to help you get these concepts "into the muscle." These exercises and questions are also amalgamated in Appendix A for easy reference, along with space to jot down your thoughts or answers. We strongly encourage you to do these exercises if you haven't. If you have, and are so motivated, we encourage you to do them again, applied to different challenges. The more exercises you do, the more you will incorporate the learning into your everyday ways of being—both consciously and unconsciously. That said, the book was designed to be of value when read in various ways. It may help to think of it like a cookbook of culinary masterpieces. Some of you will read it for ideas, and may put it on the shelf for a while before glancing through it again from time to time. Others will come back and try certain recipes, and then make them your own. And still others will keep it at hand to create or enhance many meals that will delight. We wrote this book because we believe that NLP is a jewel that has remained hidden from too many people, but that can profoundly improve the lives of everyone who is willing to take a brave step into a new direction. After all, since countless people have improved their lives through NLP, so can you. And we all have the resources we need to take our next step.

Josh and Greg sincerely hope that this book is the difference that makes the difference in your life.

AUTHORS' NOTE

We are hopeful that this book makes a positive impact in your life. Please remember that this is not the end, but rather the beginning of a wonderful journey. If you liked what you found here, NLP has much more to offer. You can visit nlpdifference.com for a list of additional resources as well as trainings available to our readers. Across those trainings, we have mapped the tools and concepts in this book to different lines of work—for lawyers, financial advisors, managers, etc.—with concrete examples and exercises to help you arrive at what you can actually say and do in various contexts.

Finally, if you want to contact Josh or Greg for any reason, they can be reached at josh@nlpdifference.com and greg@nlpdifference.com.

ACKNOWLEDGMENTS

Josh would like to thank the many teachers and students of NLP he has had in his life, who have helped him learn so much about NLP—in particular, his parents, Susan and Don Davis; Steven Leeds; Rachel Hott; Trudy Steinfeld; Rob Schwartz; Robert Dilts; and Judith Delozier. Josh also wishes to thank his wife, Daniela, for every kind of support he needed every step of the way. It's hard to imagine having written this without her. And thank you to Greg for being a model of great collaboration, and for making sure our senses of humor showed up in these pages. The whole is better than the sum of the parts.

Greg would like to express his deepest gratitude to the incredible role models who have shaped his journey and inspired this work. Tony Robbins set him on the path of more—more potential, more growth, and more purpose. His influence has been a guiding light in Greg's personal and professional life. Mary and Ed of Princeton NLP provided the foundation of his NLP training. Their teaching and guidance have equipped him with the tools to transform the way he thinks, communicates, and leads. Dr. Srikumar Rao helped him see through the illusion and embrace the deeper truths of life. His wisdom has been invaluable in shifting Greg's mindset toward one of greater peace and understanding. And Big Poppa Don Keenan showed him what it truly means to be a trial lawyer. His mentorship has taught Greg not only how to fight for justice but also how to be a better advocate, leader, and person. To all the remarkable teachers, mentors, and guides whose paths he's had the privilege to cross, thank you. Greg is not an original, but rather an original retread—a reflection of their wisdom, insights, and lessons. Every conversation, experience, and teaching he's absorbed along the way is woven into the fabric of who he is. This book stands as a testament to their influence, and he is profoundly grateful to have walked a part of the journey with each of them.

We also wish to thank our editor, Joel Fotinos, for helping us write in a way that we hope made the book become a meaningful conversation with you, the reader. We thank Emily Anderson and the production staff for ensuring a beautiful product. We thank our agent, Giles Anderson, for seeing the potential in this project and finding the right team to bring it to life. And we thank you, reader, for taking these lessons beyond the pages in wonderful ways.

APPENDIX A

1. Do You Know Where You're Going?

What's something you'd like to change or improve at? _____

_____

_____

_____

Is your goal, as you have it in your mind, focused on a negative thing you
are moving away from or a positive thing you are moving toward? _____

_____

_____

_____

If it is focused on what you're moving away from, what is the positive thing
you're moving toward? _____

_____

_____

_____

As you think about your goal, will the work you put in toward it cause
other problems? _____

_____

_____

_____

Here's another way to think about the problems that may arise: If you get your desired outcome, what will happen next? Are you okay with that?

_____

_____

_____

_____

Is your goal entirely within your control? What is within your control that would move you in the right direction? _____

_____

_____

_____

If you're not sure how to find an outcome in your control, set a learning goal. What is a learning goal that would move you in the right direction?

_____

_____

_____

_____

With your goal, do you have a clear idea of what success would look like? Could you clearly know whether you have achieved it? What would success look like? What would have to be the case for you to clearly know you achieved it? _____

_____

_____

_____

What is the context when you want your outcome? Specify when and where you'll behave differently than you used to, and specify how you'll behave differently. _____

_____

_____

_____

What is your new well-formed outcome? _____

_____

_____

_____

Section 1. The Right Mindset: Eight Beliefs That Will Make You Limitless

2. How We Experience the World Is Not the Same as Reality
Exercise 1: What Is Your Mental Model of the World?

Exercise 1A: Mental Model of Resistance

What's the environment like when you try to do that thing you're resisting, and how does that affect you? For example, "It's always after work, and the kids have constant needs, so I'm tired and can't focus." _____

_____

_____

_____

How do you behave when you think about or try to do that thing you're resisting? For example, "I procrastinate by going on social media. I need to be more disciplined." _____

_____

_____

_____

What abilities do you lack pertaining to that thing you're resisting? For example, "I have no patience." _____

_____

_____

_____

How does it serve you to resist doing that thing you're resisting? For example, "I won't have to face my fears of inadequacy." _____

_____

_____

_____

What do you think of yourself when you resist doing that thing? For example, "I'm a failure. I'm a waste of space." _____

_____

_____

_____

What's your place in the world, or value to others, when you resist doing that thing? For example, "I'm nobody special, fairly insignificant." _____

_____

_____

_____

Exercise 1B: Mental Model of Achievement

What's the environment like when you try to do that thing you're wholly embracing, and how does that affect you? For example, "It's during the day, when I am fresh mentally and don't have distractions, so I can focus."

_____

_____

_____

_____

How do you behave when you think about or try to do that thing you're wholly embracing? For example, "I take a deep breath and smile, and gather all the materials I need." _____

_____

_____

_____

What useful abilities do you have pertaining to that thing you're wholly embracing? For example, "I'm very good at getting to the heart of what's important." _____

_____

_____

_____

How does it serve you to wholly embrace that thing you're wholly embracing? For example, "It gives me an outlet for creativity, and makes me feel productive." _____

_____

_____

_____

What do you think of yourself when you embrace doing that thing? For example, "I'm a Jedi." _____

_____

_____

_____

What's your place in the world, or value to others, when you embrace doing that thing? For example, "People are inspired by how I work, and thankful for what I can do." _____

_____

_____

_____

Exercise 1C: Compare the Models

Is there anything different in the two cases—the one where you resist something, and the one where you embrace something? _____

_____

_____

_____

Is there anything you'd like to borrow from the one where you embrace something and use it to enhance or expand your mental model for the one where you've been resisting it?

For example, building on the examples we offered, you could change how your environment affects you; take a deep breath and smile; make use of your ability to get to the heart of the matter; use the goal as an outlet for creativity; use the goal to expand your Jedi self-image; consider how others will thank you for working on this goal. _____

_____

_____

_____

3. Why Not Me?

Exercise 1: Try on the Belief

If you believed that the change you seek were really, fully possible for you because if someone else has done it, you can, too . . .

How would you think and behave differently from what you've been doing?

_____

_____

_____

How would you interpret the meaning of your efforts and "failures"? _____

_____

_____

Would you seek and study role models? Who, specifically? _____

_____

_____

How would you react to others' success? _____

_____

_____

What else is different when you approach situations with this belief? _____

_____

_____

Would there be anything wrong with approaching every situation with this belief? _____

_____

_____

_____

Exercise 2: Be Like Neo

Pick a skill you'd like to build. How would you describe the skill? _____

_____

_____

Who does it well? It could be someone you know personally, or have never met, living or dead. _____

_____

_____

_____

Do you already know anything about their mental model for this skill? For example, how they think, feel, and what they believe? _____

_____

_____

_____

What do you imagine is different about their mental model and yours for this skill? _____

_____

_____

_____

How can you learn more about their mental model for this skill? For example, interview them, read a biography, observe them. _____

_____

_____

_____

4. All I Need Is Already Within Me

Right now, we invite you to do a little experiment. Your aim will be to notice what happens—to discover whether there is a useful difference for you. Think about a challenge or goal about which you have some doubts, feel overwhelmed, or even feel a little hopeless.

Now reflect on these questions, which should help you focus on the resources you have now to take the right next steps:

What are the first few steps? _____

_____

_____

_____

What's stopping you from taking your next step? _____

_____

_____

_____

How do you need to develop yourself so you can take that step? _____

_____

_____

_____

What would happen if you were to believe that you have the resources to develop yourself in that way? _____

_____

_____

Is there some aspect of this goal or challenge you are not so good at yet? Is there a class you can take? A book you can read? A YouTube video you can look up? _____

_____

_____

_____

Who else (whether or not you know them personally) has made progress on this kind of goal or challenge? _____

_____

_____

_____

What resources would be useful in making progress? A resource could be internal—e.g., curiosity, confidence, energy, or perhaps a belief that _how someone sees the world is not the same as reality_, or, _if it's possible for someone in the world it's possible for me_. A resource could also be external— e.g., a person who could offer advice. _____

_____

_____

_____

What does it feel like when you believe that all you need is already within you now? _____

_____

_____

_____

5. There's No Failure, Only Feedback

Consider some moment of self-doubt you've had. For example, maybe you felt like you said the wrong thing and embarrassed yourself, and then doubted whether others liked or respected you. _____

_____

_____

_____

What if there was no such thing as failure? What if that was simply useful feedback? In what ways would that shift your attitude, thoughts, and feelings about that situation? _____

_____

_____

_____

Right now, think of something that did not go as you would have liked. Tell yourself, "There's no failure, only feedback." Notice what changes when you do. _____

_____

_____

_____

You can take a moment now and call to mind a time when you coursecorrected and moved on. You're capable of this, aren't you? _____

_____

_____

_____

6. How My Message Landed Matters More than What I Meant

Many readers will find it helpful to take a moment at this point to think about how to put these ideas into practice. You can start by calling to mind a difficult or important conversation. It could be one that happened recently and isn't resolved, is ongoing, or is coming up. For example, perhaps there is some feedback you'd like to give someone and you don't know whether they'll take it well.

What message would you like for this person (or people) to get? _____

_____

_____

_____

What is one way they could take it wrong or get upset as a result? _____

_____

_____

_____

Picture yourself in that conversation—in your mind's eye, imagine seeing them or hearing them get upset or take it wrong.

Now imagine trying to find out what you have communicated. What happens when you get curious about what the situation looks like from their side? _____

_____

_____

_____

What would you do or say if you understood their perspective and took responsibility for having communicated what they thought you communicated? _____

_____

_____

_____

How will you be more likely to get the conversation to a good outcome when you take this approach? _____

_____

_____

_____

7. If at First I Don't Succeed, I Must Try *Something Else*

To be flexible in pursuit of a goal, try this: Call to mind a goal you're working on. It could be the goal from chapter 1, or something else (e.g., "I want to create a digital version of my classes to sell").

Now think through these steps:

Step 1: Clarify your ultimate need.

What is the reason you want to achieve your goal? In other words, why is it important to you? Another way of asking is, what's the ultimate need you're trying to serve? For example, "I want to find a way to generate some passive income." _____

_____

_____

STEP 2: ACCEPT YOUR SITUATION.
What's one problem or challenge to getting your goal? For example, "My partner thinks we should go in a different direction." _____

_____

_____

STEP 3: FLEX.
Holding that ultimate need in mind, what other ideas do you already have about how to get there? Some people might say, "I don't know." Well, in that case, answer this instead: If you did know, what do you think might be some ways to get there? For example, passive income can come from subscriptions, rent, licenses, or other digital assets besides digital classes.

_____

_____

_____

_____

8. Assume Good Intentions

Try this right now. Remember a recent time when your partner, one of your kids, or someone close to you said something to you in an annoyed or angry tone.

At this moment, you can step back from that memory and think about what the positive intention was behind it. What was the positive intention?

_____

_____

_____

_____

Ask yourself, "Why was that important to them to say or do?" as many times as it takes to get the answer. Perhaps they shouted at you to hurry up or you'd be late to an event. Why did they do it? Was it to make sure you got somewhere on time? Was it to feel stress-free? Was it because they wanted to share some special time with you, and wanted to be in a good mood for it? Likely they made it hard to be stress-free and enjoy the special time. But the intent was there. _____

_____

_____

_____

How does it affect you to see that positive intention? _____

_____

_____

_____

Next time they do something similar, and you remember that positive intention, what will you do or say differently? _____

_____

_____

_____

9. If I Knew Then What I Knew Then

EXERCISE I

You can try on this reframe right now yourself. Think of something from the past where you wish you had done things differently. _____

_____

_____

_____

What changes when you remember, "If I knew then what I knew then, I'd do it exactly the same"? _____

_____

_____

_____

What happens when you take this to heart: "Given my model of the world back then, I behaved in the best way I knew how, and made the best choices I knew how"? _____

_____

_____

_____

Exercise 2

Which of the eight foundational NLP beliefs have you found yourself thinking about the most, or putting to use? _____

_____

_____

_____

If you put a belief to use, what was different from how things used to be?

_____

_____

_____

Have you told anyone else about any of these beliefs? If so, why? _____

_____

_____

_____

Pick one or more belief that has resonated for you.
How would you describe it to someone else? _____

_____

_____

_____

Why is it valuable to believe this? How does it benefit you? How does it change your thoughts, feelings, or behaviors in a useful way? _____

_____

_____

_____

Section 2. How to Understand Someone's Mind

10. Be Curious About Their Mental Model

EXERCISE I

People limit themselves by believing they have the answers or by falling in love with their own ideas in all kinds of situations. Here are a few that may help some readers recognize it in their own behavior (you may wish to provide examples for each of these now):

Have you ever found yourself waiting for someone to finish making their point so you could then make yours? _____

Have you ever gone into a situation thinking you know what the problem is, and then focused your energy on showing you were right? _____

Have you ever been involved in an argument and been determined to win no matter what was said? _____

Have you ever been in love with your creative idea and focused your attention on getting your idea included in the final product? _____

These are not bad things to do or to want, per se. Everything has a time and a place. But these are experiences where we have the opposite of the kind of curiosity that's needed to make NLP really work.

To bring this home a bit more, right now you can pick one of those situations we mentioned above where you may have gotten attached to your own idea. Think about an example from your own life. For example, when you may have just waited for someone to finish talking so you could make your point.

Imagine how things would have gone had you gotten curious about what the others involved were saying or putting forward. Really curious—like you wanted to actually understand what made sense about their point of view.

What might you have learned? _____

_____

_____

_____

How do you think it would have affected them if you had been curious in that way? _____

_____

_____

_____

How would it have opened them up to listening more to your point, or to thoughtfully considering your ideas? _____

_____

_____

_____

Exercise 2

You may find it helpful right now to think about a situation in your own life involving another person that you might approach with deeper curiosity. Is there some breakthrough you are seeking with someone in a work or personal context—e.g., changing employee behavior, moving a sales lead forward, getting your kid to do their homework, asking your partner for more intimacy, etc.? _____

_____

_____

_____

You can do a little mental prep now that should serve you in the aim of staying curious about the other person's mental model whenever you do engage with them. We'll go through each of the four steps we outlined in the chapter.

STEP 1: *Learn to recognize what you don't understand.*
With that situation in mind, what are some things you don't fully understand? _____

_____

_____

_____

STEP 2: *Ask questions.*

What questions would help you understand better? _____

_____

_____

_____

STEP 3: *Be open to any answer.*

Imagine how they might answer. What happens when you accept that
what they said is true for them, and serves them in some positive
way? _____

_____

_____

_____

STEP 4: *Update your thinking to incorporate what you've just learned.*

Mentally try on what you came up with in step 3. How would you
operate if your mental model were more like theirs? What new questions does this bring up for you, if any? _____

_____

_____

_____

11. Just the Facts

EXERCISE 1

Try this little thought experiment. Have you ever been speaking to
someone about something personal and they sat back and crossed their
arms, as if to show they were in judgment, or did not seem very open
toward you?

How else could you interpret them sitting back and crossing their arms?

_____

_____

Have you ever felt a little cold and crossed your arms to keep warm while talking to someone?

The thing is—you never really know the reason why the arms are crossed. What NLP invites you to do is to suspend judgment until you find out why the arms are crossed.

EXERCISE 2

Here's a quick game you can play to get better at separating facts (sensory information) from interpretation.

a. Picture yourself asking a question at a busy store, and the salesperson rolls their eyes.
→ Pretty rude, right?

How else could their eye movement be interpreted? _____

_____

_____

b. Imagine you're working hard to get things done on time so you and your partner can go join friends for a dinner reservation. Your partner calls out, "You need to stop doing that. It's 6:40! We're going to be late."
→ Do they think you're stupid or just incompetent? You feel it's unfair to be judged as being bad about timing, and you shout back about how they are the one making you late.
　　How else could their comments be interpreted? _____

_____

_____

c. Imagine you are presenting or leading a meeting. You notice that one of the most senior and relevant people in the audience is looking at her phone more and more, and not paying attention to you. Eventually, she even starts talking to others quietly and referring to the phone. → She does not care at all about your presentation, does she? Obviously, she realized this was a waste of her time pretty quickly, and moved on. It's clear that this whole presentation was a disaster.

How else could her behavior be interpreted? _____

_____

_____

_____

d. Now think of something someone did that bothered you at some point.

How else could you interpret what they said or did? _____

_____

_____

_____

12. Don't Should on Yourself!

Exercise 1

Think about something on your agenda for this week for which you're thinking, "I have to do this."

Now consider . . . what would have to be different for you to think, "I get to do it"? What happens when you switch your mode of operating from "have to" to "get to"? _____

_____

_____

_____

Exercise 2

You can experiment with these questions right now as you think about the ways you talk to yourself. Think of a situation in your own life where, although you want to do something, you feel that you can't. A slight variation on this is that you want to do it and feel that you really should do it, but you just keep not doing it.

With that situation in mind, now ask yourself, "What's stopping me?" ___

_____

_____

_____

As you answered that question, did you start to notice any useful thoughts or ideas about things you might do differently? _____

_____

_____

_____

EXERCISE 3

What should or shouldn't you be doing in your life right now? Let's move beyond that feeling of should or shouldn't.

If it's a "should," what's stopping you? And what would happen if you didn't do it? _____

_____

_____

_____

If it's a "shouldn't," what would happen if you did do it? _____

_____

_____

_____

13. Something's Missing Here

EXERCISE 1

You may find it helpful to do a little practice right now. Here are five phrases many people are likely to hear sometime this week. Get curious about what's missing, and consider how you could ask follow-up questions to gain clarity.

1. "I just can't."
2. "We need to do better."
3. "Whose responsibility is it?"

4. "I get that you're upset. Tell me why."
5. "I've got a big day tomorrow. I need everyone's help."

ANSWER KEY: (1) "Can't do what?"; (2) "Do better at what?"; (3) "What are they responsible for?"; (4) "Why what? Do you mean why this happened or why I'm upset or something else?"; (5) "Help with what?" There are other good ways of asking similar questions. These are just examples.

EXERCISE 2

Over the course of the next day, see if you can find at least one example of a deletion where the missing information might make a difference. Look for it in a conversation or an email. When you spot a deletion, get curious, and ask a follow-up question or two.

After you've done the above: What was the deletion, how did you ask for clarity, and what happened when you did gain clarity? _____

_____

_____

_____

14. Who, Specifically?

It may help to try this out on yourself right now. We all engage in self-talk, and we're frequently not so nice to ourselves. Yes, research shows it's not just you—we all do it. We're referring to the ways we silently speak to ourselves in our mind's ear (and occasionally out loud, too). Here are some really common ways people talk to themselves that can be limiting. Do any of these sound like something you've said to yourself?:

- "You can't show up looking like that."
- "Nobody will want to talk to you."
- "People won't take you seriously."
- "You can't do that—it would be so embarrassing."
- "Everyone will look at you like you're crazy."

If none of those sound like the way you've talked to yourself, you can think of a time when you worried about what was proper or what other people would think in whatever way you spoke to yourself.

With that situation in mind, notice what happens when you ask yourself these questions: "Who, specifically?" And "According to whom?" For example, "Who, specifically, thinks you can't show up like that?" "Who, specifically, will not want to talk to you?" "It would be embarrassing—according to whom?" Get specific in your answers about actual people.

_____

_____

_____

_____

15. How, Specifically?

You may find it helpful to ask yourself this question ("How, specifically?") now to get a firsthand sense of how it works. Do you need to reach a decision about something, but you struggle to do so? You can pause and call to mind an example of something like that now (e.g., "I need to make a decision about what health care plan to sign up for").

"Decision" is a verb that's been turned into a noun. It's not a tangible thing. Turn it back into a verb with this question and notice what, if anything, happens. How, specifically, are you deciding? _____

_____

_____

Here's another one to try. Do you have some problem with a relationship you are in? It could be a personal relationship with a partner, friend, or relative; or a professional relationship, like with a difficult colleague or client. You can take a moment and think of an example now.

"Relationship" is a verb that has been turned into a noun, into a fixed thing. But it's not a fixed thing. Let's turn it back into a verb and see what happens. How, specifically, have you been relating to this person, or failing to relate? How, specifically, would you like to relate to this person?

_____

_____

_____

_____

16. Do They Really Do That All the Time?

You can experiment right now by applying this to the way you speak to yourself in your mind. Are you someone who has ever said to yourself, "It's never enough" or "Nothing's ever enough"?

Now ask yourself, "Never? Was there really never even one time when I or others felt that what I did was enough?" _____

_____

_____

_____

You can also think about some pet peeve of yours. Is there a person who always does that annoying thing (your pet peeve)? For example, they always leave the kitchen a mess; or they always take all the credit; or they only ever think about what they want, not what you want; or they always treat you disrespectfully, etc.

Now ask yourself, "Always? Every time? There was never even one time when that was not entirely true?"_____

_____

_____

_____

What happens when you openly and honestly explore these questions?

_____

_____

_____

_____

17. Watch Their Eyes for Clues

Picture, in your mind, the last place you went on vacation. Give yourself a moment to remember it, and once you do, go ahead and picture it in more detail.

Did you gaze up some of the time while picturing it? _____

_____

_____

_____

Now, try this one. How do you feel right now? Take a moment to connect with how you are feeling physically and/or emotionally. What's going on in your body?

Did you look down for a decent part of the time that you were considering how you felt? _____

_____

_____

_____

And one more. How does the Beatles song "I Want to Hold Your Hand" go? Just go ahead and hear it in your head.

Were your eyes roughly in the middle (not up or down) and did they go to the side somewhat? Not the whole time, but for a good chunk of time?

_____

_____

_____

_____

18. Who's Driving?

EXERCISE 1

You can experiment with this shift toward being self-referenced now, if you like. Call to mind a situation in which you are very concerned with what others may think. For example, you're hosting a party and you are stressed about what the guests will think of your house; you're embarrassed about something you said and are worried people thought poorly of you; you are going to lead a meeting or present or do a sales pitch and you are preoccupied with how it will be received; you're going on a date; you're providing care, etc.

Now ask yourself, "What do *I want* to get out of this?" For example, "What do I want from this party—is it to have fun with friends?" Remember the well-formed outcome from chapter 1, and pick things you want to get that are within your control. _____

_____

_____

And ask yourself, "What do *I think* about this?" For example, "What do I think of my house—would I be happy if I came to a party here with my friends?" _____

_____

_____

_____

EXERCISE 2

You can try out becoming more other-referenced in your own experience now. Do you ever find yourself blaming others or getting mad at them (in your mind or out loud) for things they did or did not do? _____

If so, that's a situation in which you were probably too self-referenced. In your mind now, see that situation from some distance, as though you were a fly on the wall. Remember the NLP belief *every behavior has a positive intention.* Looking at the situation now, what happens when you consider the positive intention of the person you blamed or got mad at? Why did they do what they did? _____

_____

_____

_____

EXERCISE 3

Is there a situation in which you have not stayed within your boundaries? Perhaps by taking on more work than you know you can handle? Perhaps by giving too much of your energy to someone or some task, and feeling too drained to take care of other important things? Perhaps by pushing yourself to keep up with others when it didn't feel right?

If there is a situation like that for you, you have probably been too other-referenced (being the passenger), letting others' needs and wants drive your behavior. What would happen in that situation if you did honor your boundaries? _____

_____

_____

_____

What's stopping you from honoring your boundaries? _____

_____

_____

What would be an ideal way for you to engage in a situation like that, whether or not you believe it is possible yet? _____

_____

_____

_____

How would maintaining your boundaries help you attend to others' needs more effectively than if you didn't maintain your boundaries? _____

_____

_____

_____

19. Walk a Mile in Their Shoes, in Your Mind

Think of a person who you have been struggling to communicate or collaborate with. It could be someone with whom you have a work relationship or a personal relationship. For example, if you are the head of a department in an organization, is there a head of another department who you often butt heads with? If you are in consulting or sales, is there a client whose behavior is hard to predict? If you are in a romantic relationship, does your partner sometimes get upset with you unexpectedly, or demand things of you that seem unfair? _____

_____

_____

_____

How do you see that person in your mind's eye right now? Picture them.

_____

_____

_____

_____

Take a close look at that picture of them. What is their posture—how are they standing or sitting? What facial expressions are they making? What are they doing with their eyes? Notice everything you can about their body—head, neck, shoulders, torso, arms, hands, legs, feet. _____

_____

_____

_____

Take on their posture and facial expressions to the degree you're able to right now.

Now, in your mind's eye, look back at yourself. (For example, if Greg were doing this and taking on his wife's perspective, he would take on the posture of his wife, and—in his mind's eye—look back at Greg.) Describe the person you see. For example, "He [Greg] is tall. He looks tired around his eyes, and his hands and legs are fidgety. He looks distracted. His shoulders and neck look tense. He's looking away while we're talking, not at me." Give this some time—as if you were the other person, looking back at someone else, describe the person you see. _____

_____

_____

_____

Now, answer these questions as if you were the other person, using I/me pronouns:

- What do you see, hear, and feel? _____

  _____

  _____

- What's important to you? _____

  _____

_____

_____

- What do you believe? _____

_____

_____

_____

- What are you capable of? _____

_____

_____

_____

- How do you think of yourself/what's your identity? _____

_____

_____

_____

Now, look back at yourself one more time in your mind's eye. (For example, if Greg is taking his wife's perspective, then he would see Greg in his mind's eye, as though looking from his wife's eyes.) Answer these questions using he/she/they pronouns:

- What do you wish he/she/they understood? _____

_____

_____

_____

- What would you like to say to, or ask of, him/her/them? _____

_____

_____

_____

- What do you wish he/she/they would (or would not) think, feel, or do?

_____

_____

_____

_____

- What would you like to say to him/her/them? Go ahead and say it, either out loud or in your head silently. _____

_____

_____

_____

Now let that all go, and step back into your own perspective. What, if anything, did you discover that could be useful? _____

_____

_____

_____

Section 3. How to Change Someone's Mind (Yours or Theirs)

20. How to Get Along with People

EXERCISE 1

From your own experience, think of a person who you don't trust, or who you don't think understands you, or who you feel is disrespectful toward you.

Now recall a time (or imagine one, if nothing comes to mind from memory) when they tried to persuade you to do something you didn't want to do (e.g., to volunteer for a committee, to accept their political beliefs, to buy something, or to agree to some arrangement).

How open were you to being influenced by them? _____

_____

_____

_____

EXERCISE 2

Have you ever had a conversation where you were in sync with someone? It will help to think of a specific example.

Did you feel like they understood you and you understood them? Did you feel at ease with them? Did you feel some level of trust? Were you open to their ideas? _____

_____

_____

_____

EXERCISE 3

Have you ever had a conversation where you were out of sync with the other person? Think of a specific example of being out of sync.

Did you feel like they understood you and you understood them? Did you feel at ease with them? How much were you ready to trust them and accept their ideas? _____

_____

_____

_____

EXERCISE 4

Imagine you're having a conversation with a single mom you know who works full-time and has three young children. In the conversation with you, she vents, "I feel like I can't even come up for air. Everybody needs something all the time. I'm drowning in it all. It's just too much."

How could you respond so that you join her in using her ways of describing things? _____

_____

_____

See if you can come up with a response to the single mom that mismatches her. _____

_____

_____

21. Meet Them Where They Are Before Trying to Get Them to Follow

Have you ever done something where you say something, then the other person gets upset—and you then try to explain or argue why they shouldn't feel that way, and why you are actually in the right? Go ahead and call such an interaction to mind now. (For some people it will be easier to remember a time when someone did this to you—that will work, too.)

As you think about that interaction, what are some of the ways that you did not meet them where they were? (Or that they did not meet you where you were?) _____

_____

_____

_____

What are some of the ways that you could have met them where they were? (Or that they could have met you where you were?) _____

_____

_____

_____

22. Are They Living It or Watching the Movie?

EXERCISE 1

We invite you now to think of a conversation or interaction with another person that you continue to ruminate on, and feel bad all over again when you do.

Now you can go meta, and view the situation again, but from a distance, as an impartial observer (e.g., see it from the vantage point of the fly on the wall). _____

_____

_____

_____

As you look at those people over there—the one who looks like you and the other(s)—answer this: Why did they do and say what they did? _____

_____

_____

_____

What, if anything, changed when you went meta, and reviewed and made sense of the experience from the perspective of a neutral third-party observer? _____

_____

_____

_____

Exercise 2

Right now, consider a challenge in your life that you are having difficulty resolving. Now picture a movie theater. Go and take a seat. For a moment, close your eyes as you imagine looking up at the screen and seeing yourself come to the part of the challenge that is perplexing. Remember to let the actor in the movie (who looks like you) have their own feelings. You can remain as the impartial movie watcher. Look at the actor's posture and the way they move. Hear how the actor speaks, and notice how the actor responds to what others may be saying.

From this detached point of view, answer . . .

- What are the options available to that person in the movie? _____

  _____

  _____

- What resources would benefit that person? _____

  _____

  _____

- What actions should that person take? _____

  _____

  _____

- What's a different way for that person to think about the situation they are in? _____

_____

_____

_____

23. Use Your Time Machine

You can experiment with it now. Call to mind a goal you have that will be challenging—perhaps something where you're not sure exactly how you'll achieve it yet. It should be something you do really want to accomplish, however, or have as a real priority. It can be an individual or a team goal. It can be personal or work-related. It should be a goal for which there is some point in time when you would either like to, or have to, get there—e.g., "In four months' time our team needs to roll out new operating procedures for our business unit that was recently formed by merging two others"; or "In two years I want to have completed my first book"; or "By the time summer comes, I'll have the body I've been wanting."

We'll invite you to deeply associate into that future moment shortly—the moment when you seek to arrive at the goal. First, we'll help you set up what to imagine in that future moment in the most useful ways. In previous chapters, we've shared how much more you get out of the experience when you let yourself deeply associate, or step into, the experience as if it were happening now. The more you actually take on that associated perspective, the more you should see the effects. How much you associate into it is up to you.

You can also choose whether you want to imagine you have failed at your goal at that point, or succeeded. Often, people get even more useful information when they do both, one at a time.

Now, we invite you to mentally travel to that future point in time when you have either failed utterly at, or achieved true success with, your goal. Note when that time is, and say it to yourself in the present tense. Note where you are physically. Look around you, and see what you see (e.g., "It's May 20 today. I'm in my home office. The sun is just coming up out the east window. I'm looking out at a bird, and my completed manuscript is printing on the other side of the room."). _____

_____

_____

_____

Staying in that moment you are in, hear what you hear. You can take a moment to describe what you hear, either noises, or things you may say to yourself, or perhaps what others may be saying, if others are around.

_____

_____

_____

_____

While you are here in this moment (e.g., May 20, in your home office, with the sun rising and the printer printing your manuscript), feel what you feel. What is it like to be here at this point, having arrived at this outcome? _____

_____

_____

_____

If you are open to it, you can get lost in the moment for a few minutes, seeing what you see, hearing what you hear, and feeling what you feel. What else do you notice? _____

_____

_____

_____

From this vantage point, turn and look all the way back to that point in time where your "present" self is, back at the time of reading this book, for example. It's important that you stay in the "future" moment, now, here, in which you have failed at or succeeded at your goal, and look back to the "present," then, over there. And you can answer: What did you do to get from there to here? _____

_____

_____

_____

What did you not do or avoid doing that contributed to getting from there to here? _____

_____

_____

_____

What caused you to end up here, starting from there? _____

_____

_____

_____

What resources, people, and skills did you rely on, or not rely on, to get
from there to here? _____

_____

_____

_____

How did you communicate with yourself or others, or not communicate,
that contributed to getting from there to here? _____

_____

_____

_____

In what ways did you change something about yourself, or not change, to
get from there to here? _____

_____

_____

_____

You can now gently return to the present moment and associate into
your current reality again, bringing back with you, unconsciously or consciously, whatever is useful.

What, if anything, is different now in terms of how you think, feel, or are
inclined to act, regarding your goal? _____

_____

_____

_____

24. Change Their Mental Image

EXERCISE 1
Try it now. Picture something that is bothering you.

What happens when you take the mental image and move it so that it is far away and small, or even disappears in the distance because it shrank away?

_____

_____

_____

_____

Does it bother you to the same degree after doing that? _____

_____

_____

_____

EXERCISE 2

Is there something in your life where, when you think of it, you get a knot in the pit of your stomach? _____

_____

_____

_____

If so, what happens when you move that sensation up to the center of your chest, and make it warmer? _____

_____

_____

_____

If the feeling is becoming nice, what happens when you make it bigger, so it fills more of your body? _____

_____

_____

_____

EXERCISE 3

Imagine hearing someone you admire saying something meaningful to you—e.g., in *Star Wars* when Luke hears, "Use the force, Luke," in his mind in the trusted and soothing voice of Obi-Wan Kenobi.

What happens when you make it very quiet and/or muffled? _____

_____

_____

_____

What happens when you make it louder and/or clearer? _____

_____

_____

_____

EXERCISE 4

Think of some situation that sucks. Some people may get a feeling when they do this—for instance, as if a heavy weight were on their shoulders; others might hear something—like their own voice in their head saying, "I'm such an idiot!"; others might have a visual mental image—like of a person who is difficult; and others may have some combination, perhaps.

Experiment with some changes. Have fun exploring what happens with a curious and open mind. If you don't like the effects of some change, you can change it back.

What did you notice when you experimented? _____

_____

_____

_____

25. Choose Your State and Help Others Choose Theirs

EXERCISE 1

How do *you* perform when you're not in a good state? Think of an actual important context for you as you reflect (e.g., presenting in a key meeting when you feel like an imposter, dealing with a behavior issue when you are angry and depleted, or trying to build your business when you are filled with fear and doubt). _____

_____

_____

_____

How do you perform when you are in a good state? For example, presenting in a key meeting when you are confident, dealing with a behavior issue when you are calm and refreshed, or trying to build your business when you are filled with courage and hope. _____

_____

_____

_____

Did you notice any differences in your two answers? _____

_____

_____

_____

Exercise 2

You may find it valuable to reflect right now on how some of your states serve you. Think of a time when you were anxious or stressed or scared. How did that serve you? _____

_____

_____

_____

Think of a time when you were curious, open-minded, or flexible. How did that serve you? _____

_____

_____

_____

Recall a time when you were serious or passionate. How did that serve you? _____

_____

_____

_____

Think of a time when you were playful or excited. How did that serve you?

_____

_____

_____

_____

Exercise 3

Now, let's go back to a time when you were in a state that was not useful—it really got in the way somehow. You could go back to the example from the start of the chapter, or pick something new.

How did that "bad" state serve you? What was the positive intention behind being in that mental-emotional state? For example, you might be filled with fear and doubt about your business prospects because you don't want to be poor, or become a failure, or look like a fool. The positive intention is to have money, avoid failing, or not look like a fool. But the fear and doubt aren't getting the job done. _____

_____

_____

_____

Looking back on that time, with the benefit of hindsight and some psychological distance now, what would be a more adaptive way for you to get that positive intention with less of the unwanted side effects? For example, it could be that you retain some fear and doubt but turn down the volume so it's just in the background; or it could be that you replace it with cool reason; or perhaps courage would serve you better. Reflect on what would work for you. You don't have to know how to get into that more useful state yet. _____

_____

_____

_____

Exercise 4

As you reflect on the coming days, weeks, or months, is there some important event or task coming up for which you'd really like to perform well?

_____

_____

_____

What mental-emotional state would you like to be in for that event or task?

_____

_____

_____

When, in your experience, have you been in that state? For example, if you picked "playful," when have you felt playful in the past? It does not need to be in the same environment. For instance, Josh could recall a time when he was playful with his kids at the park, even though he wants now to be playful while presenting to a class. _____

_____

_____

You can step back into that memory now. There may be something that you see in your mind's eye, or hear, as you do so. You can notice what it feels like. You may wish to pause for a moment as you allow yourself to connect more deeply with what being in that memory was like.

_____

_____

_____

_____

Let yourself stay in that experience for a time, or even amplify it if appropriate, for ten or twenty seconds at least.

What do you think could be an anchor that you could associate to the useful state, that you can use as a memory cue to help you access the state later when you want to? _____

_____

_____

(If you would like help associating that anchor strongly to the memory and state you've chosen, you can visit www.nlpdifference.com for a recording to guide you through that process.)

EXERCISE 5
We invite you now to think about some important event or task coming up that involves another person or other people.

What do you think would be a useful state for them to be in for this event or task? _____

_____

_____

_____

What ideas do you have about how you might help bring about a useful state in them? _____

_____

_____

_____

26. Don't Believe Everything You Believe

Exercise 1

We can create a chain like this—for ourselves or others—because every person has experience from their own life to draw on in which they:

- used to believe something they no longer believe
- were open to doubt
- were open to believing
- believed something they previously had not believed

In NLP, we view each of those life experiences as a resource. You can reflect for a moment and identify some of those resources for yourself right now.

What is something you used to believe that you no longer believe? For example, "I used to hate public speaking. And I believed I was terrible at it. I thought it was something that could not be learned. Then I saw other people move from fearing it to liking it and get much better at it, so I thought maybe it could be learned. I took a class, and discovered that I could get better, too. Now I am comfortable with it, I know it can be learned, and I believe I am good at it." _____

_____

_____

_____

What is something you used to believe that you became open to doubting?
(It could be that you use the same answer as the previous question but just
focus on an earlier part of the process, or it could be something else, such as
something you currently are just beginning to question that you used to believe.) _____

_____

_____

_____

What is something you do not yet believe, but you are open to considering?

_____

_____

_____

_____

What is something that you previously did not believe, but you now do believe? _____

_____

_____

_____

With those answers, you now have resources from your own experience to
help you connect with letting go of a belief, being open to doubt, being
open to believing, and taking on a new belief. What, if anything, do you
notice about how you were able to go about making those changes? _____

_____

_____

_____

EXERCISE 2: THE DEEP WAY

What is some belief that would be useful for you to let go of? For instance,
maybe you don't believe you can ever repair your relationship with your
brother. Or perhaps you believe you will never be able to change the way
you eat in the ways you know you should. Or possibly you may believe

that you can't get ahead in your career even if you take the right steps. Success might feel more like a nice fantasy than a real possibility.

_____

_____

_____

_____

When have you been open to doubting something you used to believe?

_____

_____

_____

_____

- Go ahead and spend twenty or thirty seconds associating into that experience of being open to doubting. Step back into that time in your mind, as if you were there. See what you see, hear what you hear, and feel what you feel in that moment now of being open to doubting.

  _____

  _____

  _____

  _____

- Explore changing some of the submodalities to see what enables you to connect more deeply with that experience of being open to doubting (e.g., if you have a visual mental image in mind connected with that experience, what happens when you make that mental image more vivid or close in your mind's eye?). _____

  _____

  _____

  _____

- Give yourself an anchor—a memory cue—to make it easier to recall this experience (e.g., perhaps hearing the words "open to doubting" in your mind's ear will work as an anchor; or perhaps you can imagine a symbol to serve as this anchor that you see, hear, or feel). _____

  _____

_____

_____

Now use that anchor to help you connect to the experience of being open to doubting. As you experience being open to doubting, apply it to the old belief you want to let go of—e.g., to the belief that you can't repair your relationship with your brother. Let that form the basis of a new way of considering the old belief. What happens when you consider being open to doubting your old belief now in this way? _____

_____

_____

_____

27. Let Them Do the Work

Exercise 1
Sometimes people have barriers to even trying on an idea. For instance, you might be trying to persuade a business leader to listen more to their employees. At such a time, saying something like this can help: "I wonder . . . in what ways will you achieve your goals quicker when you take the time to listen to your employees?"

Put yourself in the shoes of the business leader for a moment, and see what happens when you consider the ways you will achieve your goals quicker when you take the time to listen to your employees. _____

_____

_____

_____

Exercise 2
You may find it helpful to experiment with some presuppositions for some situation of your own. Think of a presentation that you'll be giving soon. If you don't have one coming up, think of one you will have to, or hope to, give at some point.

How does it help you to remember that there's a good reason it's you presenting? _____

_____

_____

How does it benefit the audience that you're the one presenting?

_____

_____

_____

_____

APPENDIX B

Below is a guided set of steps and questions to interview someone, and to help you learn and adopt aspects of someone's mental model.

1. Identify a person who has a capability or quality that you would like to study, from whom you can request an interview.
2. Invite them for an interview or conversation. If you're unsure how to do so, some language you might use, for example, could be: "I really admire how you" and then explain what capability or quality you admire, followed by "Would you mind if we found some time to chat so I can ask you about how you do that?"
3. Before the interview:
   a. Remind yourself that your aim is to discover more about their mental model. Aim to learn what mental model enables someone to have their capability or quality.
   b. Remember that there's no failure, only feedback.
   c. Recall that your aim in the interview is to discover whether there is something from their mental model that you can use to enrich or expand your own, so that you can better take on this capability or quality in ways that are ecological for you. Your aim does not have to be to be like them.

4. In the interview you can ask questions such as these:

    a. Do you know how you do it? If so, tell me how you go about doing it.

    b. Is there anything that would stop you from doing it?

    c. Are there contexts in which you do it and contexts in which you don't? What are they?

    d. What's important to you about doing this?

    e. What do you believe with respect to doing this?

    f. How do you see yourself (your identity) when you do this?

        As you hear the answers to each question, consider whether you understand. Try on what you hear and explore how or whether it is working for you in your context. If not, ask for clarity. Use the cartography questions (at the end of chapter 16 there is a summary of them) to gain clarity when something is not totally clear.

        If you imagine that something would stop you from doing what they do, ask whether that issue or limitation comes up for them also, and if so, what they do about it.

5. Thank them and ask them if they have any questions for you.

6. After the interview is done, associate into a future scenario in which you would like to take on some of what you have learned. Explore what happens when you imagine yourself engaging in that future scenario with your updated mental model, and with this new or enhanced capability or quality. As you do so, remember there's no failure, only feedback. Consider after doing this, how would you like to keep growing and evolving now?

7. Reflect on what you may have learned that you would like to make use of.

GLOSSARY

ANCHORING: A process for making it easier to recall and reconnect with an inner resource or mental/emotional state. The process involves establishing what's called an anchor, which is like a memory cue. You build an association between the anchor and a desired inner resource or state. Anchors are often visual, like when you picture a place in your mind; auditory, like when you hear a word or phrase in your mind; or kinesthetic, like when you touch your wrist with your other hand. Once the anchor is established, then enacting the anchor helps bring you back to that inner resource or state.

ASSOCIATION: The act of being immersed (associated) into an experience, as though it were happening to you in real time, and as though you were seeing, hearing, feeling, and otherwise experiencing a situation from the first-person perspective.

BACKTRACKING: When communicating with someone else, backtracking refers to offering back to them what you are hearing—to either build rapport or help you gain greater clarity. Backtracking should include using key aspects of the specific language someone uses, rather than paraphrasing. They choose their words for a reason, and this is a way of respecting their model of the world while listening deeply.

CAUSE AND EFFECT: A language pattern in which someone implies that one thing causes another, regardless of whether such a causal link is true or even possible.

CHAINING: Breaking down a change that is too big for someone to make into safe, ecological, and achievable steps, and then linking each step together as in a chain, in order to create a bridge from their present state to their desired outcome.

DELETION: A language pattern in which someone leaves out important information.

DISASSOCIATION: The act of not being associated into an experience. Instead, when disassociated, you experience a situation as though you were observing it happening to another person, perhaps in another time besides the present. Whatever you see, hear, feel, or otherwise experience belongs to you as the observer. If the situation involves people (yourself or others), as the disassociated observer, you let them have their feelings and thoughts, and observe as if you were outside the situation.

ECOLOGICAL: Forming part of a balanced system. You may have a desired outcome, but if pursuing it or attaining it would cause other unacceptable problems for you, then it is not ecological.

EYE-ACCESSING CUES: When people think, they often shift their gaze. There is a theory that the direction of gaze pertains to information they are attempting to access. For example, up may indicate they are accessing visual information, and down may indicate they are accessing feelings-related information. The eye-gaze direction could then serve as a cue regarding what type of information the person may be accessing.

FAILURE FRAME: Whenever we attempt to do something, it is possible that it will not work as we have intended. A failure frame is a way of interpreting this outcome as failure—e.g., that the attempt failed, that you failed, or that you are a failure.

FEEDBACK FRAME: Whenever we attempt to do something, it is possible that it will not work as we have intended. A feedback frame is a way of interpreting this outcome as information that can be used to course-correct.

FIRST-PERSON PERSPECTIVE: The perspective from your own eyes, ears, and other senses. Sometimes, this is referred to as perceiving from the perspective of the self. This is one of multiple perspectives that you can take on in your mind. Alternative perspectives that are not first person, for example, are imagining how others who you interact with perceive you, or how an objective observer might perceive you.

HYPNOTIC SUGGESTIONS: Statements or questions that serve as indirect invitations for someone to consider an idea thoughtfully and deeply. Suggestions involve language patterns that tend to be less confrontational than others—less about proving a point or winning an argument. For many people, offering them hypnotic suggestions can open doors to quick and meaningful communication and change.

INTERPRETATION VERSUS SENSORY-BASED INFORMATION: Sensory-based information is the set of facts that can be detected with the eyes, ears, and other sense organs. Interpretation is what you take that sensory-based information to mean. The facts and the interpretation are not the same. Remember that, and you can gain a lot of understanding quickly. For instance, if Josh is talking to Greg, and Greg gets distracted on his phone, Josh might think, *He's getting bored and annoyed we're still talking about this.* The facts are just that he picked up the phone and looked at it for a while. The interpretation is what Josh thought. But there are many other ways to interpret those facts.

LACK OF REFERENTIAL INDEX: A language pattern in which someone is unclear about who (or what), specifically, they are referring to.

LANGUAGE PATTERNS: Ways of using language that you may encounter from time to time—for example, regarding how someone generalizes or leaves out information. You can learn to recognize such language patterns and that can offer you clues into someone's model of the world as well as suggest useful ways for you to respond to them.

LIMITING BELIEF: A belief that keeps a person from behaving in some adaptive or useful ways. Such a belief can hold them back from achieving a desired outcome.

LOST PERFORMATIVE: A language pattern in which someone leaves out information about who, specifically, was responsible for an action or opinion.

MATCHING/MISMATCHING: Matching is joining someone—being in sync with someone—in their verbal or nonverbal ways of communicating. Mismatching is being out of sync with someone in their verbal or nonverbal ways of communicating.

MENTAL MODEL: The way in which a person experiences reality. Rather than capturing all possible information, in our minds we form a model of any situation we encounter. What we capture in a mental model is based in part on what is useful, and on what mental filters we arrive with from prior experience. It is a good idea to assume that your mental model is always incomplete and inaccurate in some ways. Nonetheless, among other things, the mental model suggests to us what is true, what is possible, and what the rules of engagement are for a situation.

META MODEL: A collection of language patterns that suggest useful information about a speaker's mental model. It is common to follow up after noticing one of the language patterns in ways specific to that pattern to gain clarity and facilitate positive change.

META POSITION (AND "GOING META"): A position from which you have the perspective of an impartial observer who is disassociated from the experience of the person or people you are observing. The terms "going meta" or "go meta" or "step into the meta position" refer to stepping, metaphorically, into a third-person observer perspective in your mind, disassociated from the first-person (self) or second-person (other) perspectives of the people involved in a situation. So if Josh were thinking about a conversation he had had with Greg, and Josh were to go meta, he would observe both Josh and Greg from the perspective of an impartial observer.

MILTON MODEL: A collection of language patterns and tools built by studying the communication of Dr. Milton Erikson as he worked with patients. The language patterns and tools are associated with Eriksonian Hypnotherapy and hypnotic suggestion.

MIND READING: A language pattern in which someone says things that imply they know the thoughts or feelings of another person.

MIRRORING: Joining someone—being in sync with someone—in their verbal or nonverbal ways of communicating. We use the words *mirroring* and *matching* to refer to the same idea. (See also **MATCHING**.)

MODAL OPERATORS OF NECESSITY AND MODAL OPERATORS OF POSSIBILITY: Language patterns in which someone uses words or phrases that suggest they have a relationship with a certain task or goal that may be limiting them. For example, "should" and "have to" are modal operators of necessity; "can't" is a modal operator of possibility.

MODELING: Learning someone's mental model for a situation, skill, or ability.

NOMINALIZATION: A language pattern in which someone changes a verb into a noun, thus taking a process and treating it as if it were a thing.

OTHER-REFERENCED: Using as a reference point for decisions or judgments the needs, interests, feelings, and values of another person. For example, when you defer to the judgment of others you are other-referenced.

PACING AND LEADING: Pacing and leading involves first joining someone in terms of their mental model and matching or mirroring them (pacing). This helps you build rapport and earn the right to influence. After pacing, you then can more easily lead them to a different way of thinking, feeling, or behaving.

PATTERN INTERRUPT: Something that stops a nonresourceful thought process, way of behaving, or mental/emotional state.

PERSPECTIVE GETTING: Finding out what someone else thinks or feels by asking them questions, listening to them speak, or reading what they have written, and taking seriously what you learn, with an open and curious mind. The goal should be to learn about, not judge, their experience.

PERSPECTIVE TAKING: Imagining what someone else thinks or feels. This can be valuable for building compassion, but what you imagine is likely to be less accurate than what you would learn with perspective getting.

POSITIVE INTENTION: The adaptive function or positive desired outcome motivating someone's thoughts, feelings, or behaviors—even if those thoughts, feelings, or behaviors are not positive or adaptive.

PRESUPPOSITIONS: The use of presuppositions is a language pattern in which certain things are presumed to be true. Using presuppositions can help someone explore thoughtfully what would come next were those things to be true.

RAPPORT: A connection between people in which they trust and often like each other. They tend to feel a mutual understanding, are comfortable with open communication, and may feel like the connection is easy or like they "click" with each other.

REFRAMING: Creating new meaning for a set of facts by changing the context in which you consider those facts.

REPRESENTATIONAL SYSTEM (VAK): When you think, you often have visual mental images, hear yourself saying something in your mind (self-talk), or have feelings. Those are important parts of how you represent reality in your mental models. When you have visual mental images, you're using the visual representational system. When it is something you hear, like self-talk, you're using the auditory representational system. And when it is something you feel, or has to do with bodily movement, you're using the kinesthetic representational system. You can use the acronym VAK as a guide regarding what to look for when trying to understand how someone represents reality—look for evidence of their visual, auditory, and kinesthetic mental representations. Those three are probably the most common, but people think in terms of other representational systems, too—like gustatory or olfactory.

SECOND-PERSON PERSPECTIVE: The perspective from someone else in an interaction who is interacting with you. If Josh were speaking with Greg, and Josh took on the second-person perspective, Josh would be imagining Greg's perspective as he interacts with Josh. This is not the same as third-person perspective, which is how an outside observer would see both Greg and Josh in the interaction.

SELF-REFERENCED: Using your own needs, interests, feelings, and values as a reference point for decisions or judgments. For example, you are self-referenced when you don't worry about what others think.

STATE (OR MENTAL-EMOTIONAL STATE): An attitude of mind and body. Examples include confident, peaceful, present, concerned, curious, worried, and so on.

SUBMODALITIES: The components of the modalities of subjective experience. Subjective experience often includes visual, auditory, and kinesthetic (VAK) aspects—you could describe them as different modalities of subjective experience. For example, upon entering a room, you might see how the furniture is laid out, hear the air conditioner, and feel the temperature. The submodalities are components of each of those modalities. For visual, they would include properties like brightness, color, and distance. For auditory, they would include properties like volume, location, and pitch. For kinesthetic, they would include properties like roughness, stillness, and warmth.

THIRD-PERSON PERSPECTIVE (SEE META POSITION): The perspective from an outside observer. If Josh were speaking with Greg, and Josh took on the third-person perspective, Josh would be imagining seeing Greg and Josh interact as though from the outside. He would not be taking on the perspective of either Josh or Greg.

UNIVERSAL QUANTIFIERS: A language pattern in which someone implies that something is without exception (e.g., "Nobody ever cares"). Often this pattern reflects an overgeneralization.

UNSPECIFIED VERBS: A language pattern in which someone is unclear about how, specifically, an action or process occurs.

WELL-FORMED OUTCOME: A desired outcome that meets the following five criteria: (1) it's focused on what you want rather than on what you don't want; (2) it's ecological; (3) it's within your control; (4) you can clearly define/measure its success; and (5) you can specify the context—when and where—you want it.

NOTES

Introduction

1. Gregory Bateson was an influential anthropologist. He is often credited with introducing the concept of searching for "a difference which makes a difference," as a definition of information. That search has been perhaps the core endeavor of NLP since its origins, especially with respect to understanding someone's subjective experience of the situation they find themself in. The title of our book was inspired by this idea.

2. Bandler and Grinder (1975). *Patterns of the Hypnotic Techniques of Milton H. Erickson, M.D., Volume 1.*

3. Virginia Satir's description and quote are from the back cover of Bandler, R., & Grinder, J. (1975). *The Structure Magic, vol.1: A Book About Language and Therapy.* Science and Behavior Books, Inc.

1: Do You Know Where You're Going?

1. Berkman, E. T. & Lieberman, M. D., "Approaching the Bad and Avoiding the Good: Lateral Prefrontal Cortical Asymmetry Distinguishes between Action and Valence." *Journal of Cognitive Neuroscience*, 22, no. 9 (2010): 1970–1979.

2. Brockner, J. & Higgins, E. T., "Regulatory Focus Theory: Implications for the Study of Emotions at Work." *Organizational Behavior and Human Decision Processes*, 86, no. 1 (2001): 35–66; Higgins, E. T., "Promotion and Prevention Experiences: Relating Emotions to Nonemotional Motivational States." *Handbook of Affect and Social Cognition*, ed. J. P. Forgas (Lawrence Erlbaum Associates Publishers, 2001), 186–211.

3. Bateson, G., *Steps to an Ecology of Mind: Collected Essays in Anthropology, Psychiatry, Evolution, and Epistemology* (University of Chicago Press, 2000).

4. Davis, D. I., *Alcoholism Treatment: An Integrative Family and Individual Approach* (Gardner Press, 1987).

5. Zimmerman, B. J., & Kitsantas, A., "Developmental Phases in Self-Regulation: Shifting from Process Goals to Outcome Goals." *Journal of Educational Psychology*, 89, no. 1 (1997): 29.

6. Seijts, G. H., & Latham, G. P., "Learning versus Performance Goals: When Should Each Be Used?" *Academy of Management Perspectives*, 19, no. 1 (2005): 124–131; Dweck, Carol, *Mindset: The New Psychology of Success* (Random House: 2006).

7. Garrison, J., Erdeniz, B., & Done, J., "Prediction Error in Reinforcement Learning: A Meta-analysis of Neuroimaging Studies." *Neuroscience & Biobehavioral Reviews*, 37, no. 7 (2013): 1297–1310; Schultz, W., "Dopamine Reward Prediction Error Coding." *Dialogues in Clinical Neuroscience* (2022).

8. Gollwitzer, P. M., & Sheeran, P., "Implementation Intentions and Goal Achievement: A Meta-analysis of Effects and Processes." *Advances in Experimental Social Psychology*, 38 (2006): 69–119.

9. Some readers may be wondering how these five well-formed-outcome criteria align with the popular five criteria that form part of SMART goals. We see SMART goals as a smart way to set goals, and we think the well-formed outcome from NLP offers some useful things that SMART goals don't cover. There is certainly some overlap in the two models, but they are not the same. S—specific, M—measurable, A—achievable, R—relevant, and T—time-bound. The biggest distinction probably has to do with the second question—"Will achieving your goal cause you other problems?" (Or, in NLP language, "Is the goal ecological?") That is perhaps touched on with the "relevant" criterion, but not deeply addressed. Another distinction we see is that the well-formed outcome encourages people to state their goal in the positive, in terms of what they are moving toward. That is not called out in the SMART goal approach.

2: How We Experience the World Is Not the Same as Reality

1. Marois, R., & Ivanoff, J., "Capacity Limits of Information Processing in the Brain." *Trends in Cognitive Sciences*, 9, no. 6 (2005): 296–305.

2. Press, C., Kok, P., & Yon, D., "The Perceptual Prediction Paradox." *Trends in Cognitive Sciences*, 24, no. 1 (2020): 13–24.

3. Higgins, E. T., & Rholes, W. S., "'Saying Is Believing': Effects of Message Modification on Memory and Liking for the Person Described." *Journal of Experimental Social Psychology*, 14, no. 4 (1978): 363–378.

4. Witt, J. K., "Action Potential Influences Spatial Perception: Evidence for Genuine Top-down Effects on Perception." *Psychonomic Bulletin & Review*, 24 (2017): 999–1021.

5. Cope, T. E., Sohoglu, E., Sedley, W., Patterson, K., Jones, P. S., Wiggins, J., . . . & Rowe, J. B., "Evidence for Causal Top-down Frontal Contributions to Predictive Processes in Speech Perception." *Nature Communications*, 8, no. 1 (2017): 2154.

6. These six factors come from an approach to discovering someone's mental model that was created by Robert Dilts called modeling with logical levels. Each of the six factors is a level:

environment, behavior, capabilities, beliefs, identity, and larger purpose in relation to others. Special thanks to Susan Davis for expanding on the original model, with relation to others.

7. Beck, A. T., & Dozois, D. J., "Cognitive Therapy: Current Status and Future Directions." *Annual Review of Medicine*, 62 (2011): 397–409.

8. In NLP, it is common for people to use the phrase "the map is not the territory" to capture this idea. We offer that metaphor here in case it is helpful. Suppose you are driving in a new city and don't know much about it. You look at the map to try to understand where you can go. The map is good for some things, like finding a gas station and getting across town, but terrible for other things, like figuring out how to get a feel for the culture, or find a good meal. The map represents everything you know about the new city. But once you start walking around, you enrich what you know. In your mind, you expand your map of how to navigate and take advantage of the city. The map in your mind is what dictates your moves. But the map is not and never will be as rich as the real city. In NLP, we aim to keep expanding and enriching this map.

3: Why Not Me?

1. Nussbaum, A. D., & Dweck, C. S., "Defensiveness versus Remediation: Self-theories and Modes of Self-esteem Maintenance." *Personality and Social Psychology Bulletin*, 34, no. 5 (2008): 599–612.

2. Hoyt, C. L., Burnette, J. L., & Innella, A. N., "I Can Do That: The Impact of Implicit Theories on Leadership Role Model Effectiveness." *Personality and Social Psychology Bulletin*, 38, no. 2 (2012): 257–268.

3. Dweck, C. S. *Mindset: The New Psychology of Success* (Random House, 2006).

4. Downey, G., & Feldman, S. I., "Implications of Rejection Sensitivity for Intimate Relationships." *Journal of Personality and Social Psychology*, 70, no. 6 (1996): 1327; Bandura, A., "Self-Efficacy Mechanism in Human Agency." *American Psychologist*, 37, no. 2 (1982): 122; Brown, L. A., Wiley, J. F., Wolitzky-Taylor, K., Roy-Byrne, P., Sherbourne, C., Stein, M. B., . . . & Craske, M. G., "Changes in Self-efficacy and Outcome Expectancy as Predictors of Anxiety Outcomes from the CALM Study." *Depression and Anxiety*, 31, no. 8 (2014): 678–689.

4: All I Need Is Already Within Me

1. The term "neurolinguistic programming" invokes a computer programming metaphor. It is not uncommon in NLP circles for people to use that metaphor. Some people, for example, may find it helpful to talk about installing new programs to replace old ones, or to edit or debug their neurolinguistic programs. They may find it helpful to talk about coding, or changing the code. The programming metaphor suggests that with the right inputs, we will operate similarly as we have in the past, while the old program runs. It also implies that we can change our programming and thus change how we operate.

2. Schwarzer, R., & Luszczynska, A., "Self-efficacy." Eds. Ruch, W., Bakker, A.B., Tay, L., & Gander, F., *Handbook of Positive Psychology Assessment* (2023): 207–217; Seligman, M. E., "Learned Helplessness." *Annual Review of Medicine*, 23, no. 1 (1972): 407–412.

3. Cascio, C. N., O'Donnell, M. B., Tinney, F. J., Lieberman, M. D., Taylor, S. E., Strecher, V. J., & Falk, E. B., "Self-affirmation Activates Brain Systems Associated with Self-related Processing and Reward and Is Reinforced by Future Orientation." *Social Cognitive and Affective Neuroscience*, 11, no. 4 (2016): 621–629.

4. Some people prefer one of these versions of the belief: *People already have all of the resources they need in order to effect a change,* or *Each of us has the resources to meet our next developmental challenge.* You can choose which version works best for you.

5: There's No Failure, Only Feedback

1. Ochsner, K. N., Ray, R. D., Cooper, J. C., Robertson, E. R., Chopra, S., Gabrieli, J. D., & Gross, J. J., "For Better or for Worse: Neural Systems Supporting the Cognitive Down- and Up-regulation of Negative Emotion." *Neuroimage*, 23, no. 2 (2004): 483–499; Denny, B. T., Inhoff, M. C., Zerubavel, N., Davachi, L., & Ochsner, K. N., "Getting over It: Long-lasting Effects of Emotion Regulation on Amygdala Response." *Psychological Science*, 26, no. 9 (2015): 1377–1388.

2. Mangels, J. A., Butterfield, B., Lamb, J., Good, C., & Dweck, C. S., "Why Do Beliefs about Intelligence Influence Learning Success?: A Social Cognitive Neuroscience Model." *Social Cognitive and Affective Neuroscience*, 1, no. 2 (2006): 75–86.

6: How My Message Landed Matters More than What I Meant

1. Tversky, A., & Kahneman, D. "Judgment under Uncertainty: Heuristics and Biases." *Science,* 185, no. 4157 (1974): 1124–1131; Kahneman, D., & Tversky, A., "Prospect Theory: An Analysis of Decision under Risk." *Econometrica*, 47, no. 2 (1979): 263–292.

2. Kappes, A., Harvey, A. H., Lohrenz, T., Montague, P. R., & Sharot, T., "Confirmation Bias in the Utilization of Others' Opinion Strength." *Nature Neuroscience*, 23, no. 1 (2020): 130–137.

3. Korteling, J. E., & Toet, A., "Cognitive Biases." *Encyclopedia of Behavioral Neuroscience* (2022): 610–619.

7: If at First I Don't Succeed, I Must Try *Something Else*

1. Bond, F. W., Flaxman, P. E., & Lloyd, J., *Mindfulness and Meditation in the Workplace: An Acceptance and Commitment Therapy Approach* (Oxford University Press, 2016).

2. Gloster, A. T., Walder, N., Levin, M. E., Twohig, M. P., & Karekla, M., "The Empirical Status of Acceptance and Commitment Therapy: A Review of Meta-analyses." *Journal of Contextual Behavioral Science*, 18 (2020): 181–192.

3. Some readers might wonder whether being committed to a value or goal, and being flexible in how you get there, is the same as believing the ends justify the means. We do not see them as the same. You can highly value taking a good path to your goal, whether or not you embrace this kind of flexibility.

8: Assume Good Intentions

1. Kellogg, S., "Dialogical Encounters: Contemporary Perspectives on Chairwork." *Psychotherapy: Theory, Research, Practice, Training*, 41, no. 3 (2004): 310.

2. Williams, J. C., & Lynn, S. J., "Acceptance: An Historical and Conceptual Review." *Imagination, Cognition and Personality*, 30, no. 1 (2010): 5–56.

3. Carson, S. H., & Langer, E. J., "Mindfulness and Self-acceptance." *Journal of Rational-emotive and Cognitive-behavior Therapy*, 24 (2006): 29–43.

9: If I Knew Then What I Knew Then

1. Farber, B. A., & Doolin, E. M., "Positive Regard." *Psychotherapy*, 48, no. 1 (2011): 58.

2. Dilts and DeLozier have written a comprehensive encyclopedia of NLP. They outline all the presuppositions of NLP, among much more. It is an extraordinary resource for those who are deeply invested in NLP. Dilts, B. & DeLozier, J., *Encyclopedia of Systemic Neuro-Linguistic Programming and NLP New Coding.* (NLP University Press: 2000).

10: Be Curious About Their Mental Model

1. Eyal, T., Steffel, M., & Epley, N., "Perspective Mistaking: Accurately Understanding the Mind of Another Requires Getting Perspective, Not Taking Perspective." *Journal of Personality and Social Psychology*, 114, no. 4 (2018): 547.

11: Just the Facts

1. Loftus, E. F., "Memory Distortion and False Memory Creation." *Journal of the American Academy of Psychiatry and the Law Online*, 24, no. 3 (1996): 281–295; Loftus, E. F., Miller, D. G., & Burns, H. J., "Semantic Integration of Verbal Information Into a Visual Memory." *Journal of Experimental Psychology: Human Learning and Memory*, 4, no. 1 (1978): 19–31.

2. Kaplan, R. L., Van Damme, I., Levine, L. J., & Loftus, E. F., "Emotion and False Memory." *Emotion Review*, 8, no. 1 (2016): 8–13.

3. Ramirez, S., Liu, X., Lin, P. A., Suh, J., Pignatelli, M., Redondo, R. L., . . . & Tonegawa, S., "Creating a False Memory in the Hippocampus." *Science*, 341, no. 6144 (2013): 387–391.

4. Costandi, M., "Evidence-based Justice: Corrupted Memory." *Nature*, 500, no. 7462 (2013): 268–270.

5. Riener, C., "New Approaches and Debates on Top-down Perceptual Processing." *Teaching of Psychology*, 46, no. 3 (2019): 267–272.

6. Higgins, E. T. "Knowledge Activation: Accessibility, Applicability, and Salience." In E. T. Higgins & A. W. Kruglanski (Eds.), *Social Psychology: Handbook of Basic Principles*, 133–168 (The Guilford Press, 1996).

12: Don't Should on Yourself!

1. Neenan, M., "Tackling Procrastination: An REBT Perspective for Coaches." *Journal of Rational-Emotive & Cognitive-Behavior Therapy*, 26 (2008): 53–62.

2. Field, T. A., Beeson, E. T., & Jones, L. K., "The New ABCs: A Practitioner's Guide to Neuroscience-informed Cognitive Behavior Therapy." *Journal of Mental Health Counseling*, 37, no. 3 (2015): 206–220.

3. Ochsner, K. N., Ray, R. D., Cooper, J. C., Robertson, E. R., Chopra, S., Gabrieli, J. D., & Gross, J. J., "For Better or for Worse: Neural Systems Supporting the Cognitive Down- and Up-regulation of Negative Emotion." *Neuroimage*, 23, no. 2 (2004): 483–499.

4. The third cartography question we've offered—"Why is that necessary/impossible?"—is not likely to appear in other NLP trainings, to our knowledge, regarding the topic of modal operators. We have included it because we believe it can help to understand someone's mental model. The other two cartography questions, however, are commonly taught. They not only can help to reveal someone's mental model, but they can also help someone to challenge and expand their mental model in adaptive ways.

13: Something's Missing Here

1. Covin, R., Dozois, D. J., Ogniewicz, A., & Seeds, P. M., "Measuring Cognitive Errors: Initial Development of the Cognitive Distortions Scale (CDS)." *International Journal of Cognitive Therapy*, 4, no. 3 (2011): 297–322.

2. Burns, D. D. *The Feeling Good Handbook: The Groundbreaking Program with Powerful New Techniques and Step-by-Step Exercises to Overcome Depression, Conquer Anxiety, and Enjoy Greater Intimacy* (Plume, 1999); Burns, D. D., *Feeling Good: The New Mood Therapy* (William Morrow and Company, 1980).

3. Pinker, S., *The Stuff of Thought: Language as a Window into Human Nature* (Penguin, 2007).

14: Who, Specifically?

1. The lack of referential index pattern can refer to a "what" that is unclear at times, and not always a "who." We've focused just on the instances of this pattern in which the "who" is unclear in this chapter to help the reader learn to spot language patterns that can be usefully followed up with the cartography question "Who, specifically?"

2. Smith, J. R., & Louis, W. R., "Do as We Say and as We Do: The Interplay of Descriptive and Injunctive Group Norms in the Attitude–Behaviour Relationship." *British Journal of Social Psychology*, 47, no. 4 (2008): 647–666.

3. Pryor, C., Perfors, A., & Howe, P. D., "Conformity to the Descriptive Norms of People with Opposing Political or Social Beliefs." *PloS one*, 14, no. 7 (2019): e0219464.

4. Kross, E., *Chatter: The Voice in Our Head, Why It Matters, and How to Harness It* (Crown: 2021).

15: How, Specifically?

1. Vigliocco, G., Vinson, D. P., Druks, J., Barber, H., & Cappa, S. F., "Nouns and Verbs in the Brain: A Review of Behavioural, Electrophysiological, Neuropsychological, and Imaging Studies." *Neuroscience & Biobehavioral Reviews*, 35, no. 3 (2011): 407–426.

2. Ibid.

16: Do They Really Do That All the Time?

1. Beck, A. T., *Cognitive Therapy and the Emotional Disorders* (Penguin, 1979).

2. Eckhardt, C. I., & Kassinove, H., "Articulated Cognitive Distortions and Cognitive Deficiencies in Maritally Violent Men." *Journal of Cognitive Psychotherapy*, 12, no. 3 (1998): 231–250.

3. Kuru, E., Safak, Y., Özdemir, İ., Tulacı, R. G., Özdel, K., Özkula, N. G., & Örsel, S., "Cognitive Distortions in Patients with Social Anxiety Disorder: Comparison of a Clinical Group and Healthy Controls." *The European Journal of Psychiatry*, 32, no. 2 (2018): 97–104.

4. Gramlich, J. "Fewer Than 1 Percent of Federal Criminal Defendants Were Acquitted in 2022," Pew Research Center, June 14, 2023, https://www.pewresearch.org/short-reads/2023/06/14/fewer-than-1-of-defendants-in-federal-criminal-cases-were-acquitted-in-2022/.

17: Watch Their Eyes for Clues

1. Ehrlichman, H., & Micic, D., "Why Do People Move Their Eyes When They Think? Current Directions in Psychological Science," 21, no. 2 (2012): 96–100, https://doi.org/10.1177/0963721412436810.

2. In NLP, we use the terms "visual" for things you see in your mind's eye, "auditory" for things you hear in your mind's ear, and "kinesthetic" for things that have to do with feeling the body (like body awareness, touch, and movement). If you see those terms elsewhere, we are referring to the same things. We've used the more common language—seeing, hearing, feeling—in this chapter to simplify. But the terms visual, auditory, and kinesthetic are useful in other areas, so we'll come back to them in other parts of the book.

3. E.g., Buckner, M., Meara, N. M., Reese, E. J., & Reese, M., "Eye Movement as an Indicator of Sensory Components in Thought." *Journal of Counseling Psychology*, 34, no. 3 (1987): 283.

   Some of the research literature on NLP eye patterns is also reviewed in Ahmad (2013), who also did not find support for a one-to-one mapping in which the predictions were always true: Ahmad, K. Z., "Lying Eyes: The Truth about NLP Eye Patterns and Their Relationship with Academic Performance in Business and Management Studies (MBA)." *International Journal of Business and Management*, 8, no. 23 (2013): 67.

4. Krajbich, I., Mitsumasu, A., Polania, R., Ruff, C. C., & Fehr, E., "A Causal Role for the Right Frontal Eye Fields in Value Comparison." *elife*, 10 (2021): e67477.

5. Valiente-Gómez, A., Moreno-Alcázar, A., Treen, D., Cedrón, C., Colom, F., Perez, V., & Amann, B. L., "EMDR beyond PTSD: A Systematic Literature Review." *Frontiers in Psychology*, 8 (2017): 1668; Seidler, G. H., & Wagner, F. E., "Comparing the Efficacy of EMDR and Trauma-focused Cognitive Behavioral Therapy in the Treatment of PTSD: A Meta-analytic Study." *Psychological Medicine*, 36, no. 11 (2006): 1515–1522.

6. Laeng, B., Bloem, I. M., D'Ascenzo, S., & Tommasi, L., "Scrutinizing Visual Images: The Role of Gaze in Mental Imagery and Memory." *Cognition*, 131, no. 2 (2014): 263–283.

18: Who's Driving?

1. Hashimoto, T., Takeuchi, H., Taki, Y., Sekiguchi, A., Nouchi, R., Kotozaki, Y., . . . & Kawashima, R., "Neuroanatomical Correlates of the Sense of Control: Gray and White Matter Volumes Associated with an Internal Locus of Control." *Neuroimage*, 119 (2015): 146–151; Ng, T. W., Sorensen, K. L., & Eby, L. T., "Locus of Control at Work: A Meta-analysis." *Journal of Organizational Behavior: The International Journal of Industrial, Occupational and Organizational Psychology and Behavior*, 27, no. 8 (2006): 1057–1087; Wallston, S. B., & Wallston, K. A., "Locus of Control and Health: A Review of the Literature." *Health Education Monographs*, 6, no. 1 (1978): 107–117; Rotter, J. B., "Generalized Expectancies for Internal Versus External Control of Reinforcement." *Psychological Monographs: General and Applied*, 80, no. 1 (1966): 1–28; Cascio, M. I., Magnano, P., Elastico, S., Costantino, V., Zapparrata, V., & Battiato, A., "The Relationship Among Self-Efficacy Beliefs, External Locus of Control and Work Stress in Public Setting Schoolteachers." *Open Journal of Social Sciences*, 2, no. 11 (2014): 149–156; Wiech, K., Kalisch, R., Weiskopf, N., Pleger, B., Stephan, K. E., & Dolan, R. J., "Anterolateral Prefrontal Cortex Mediates the Analgesic Effect of Expected and Perceived Control Over Pain." *Journal of Neuroscience*, 26, no. 44 (2006): 11501–11509.

2. For further evidence that self- and other-referenced approaches are both useful, psychological research shows there are even contexts in which we are more resilient to stressors when we believe that someone else is in charge—e.g., Reknes, I., Visockaite, G., Liefooghe, A., Lovakov, A., & Einarsen, S. V., "Locus of Control Moderates the Relationship Between Exposure to Bullying Behaviors and Psychological Strain." *Frontiers in Psychology*, 10 (2019): 1323.

3. Nett, R. J., Witte, T. K., Holzbauer, S. M., Elchos, B. L., Campagnolo, E. R., Musgrave, K. J., . . . & Funk, R. H., "Risk Factors for Suicide, Attitudes toward Mental Illness, and Practice-related Stressors among US Veterinarians." *Journal of the American Veterinary Medical Association*, 247, no. 8 (2015): 945–955.

4. Best, C. O., Perret, J. L., Hewson, J., Khosa, D. K., Conlon, P. D., & Jones-Bitton, A., "A Survey of Veterinarian Mental Health and Resilience in Ontario, Canada." *The Canadian Veterinary Journal*, 61, no. 2 (2020): 166.

5. West, C. P., Dyrbye, L. N., Erwin, P. J., & Shanafelt, T. D., "Interventions to Prevent and Reduce Physician Burnout: A Systematic Review and Meta-analysis." *The Lancet*, 388. No. 10057 (2016): 2272–2281.

19: Walk a Mile in Their Shoes, in Your Mind

1. Note that Dilts and DeLozier share that this shift to second person perspective is "utilized in practically every process" in NLP. Dilts, B. & DeLozier, J., *Encyclopedia of Systemic Neuro-Linguistic Programming and NLP New Coding* (NLP University Press, 2000) p. 1180.

2. Yee, N., & Bailenson, J. N., "Walk a Mile in Digital Shoes: The Impact of Embodied Perspective-taking on the Reduction of Negative Stereotyping in Immersive Virtual Environments." *Proceedings of PRESENCE*, 24 (2006): 26.

3. Herrera, F., Bailenson, J., Weisz, E., Ogle, E., & Zaki, J., "Building Long-term Empathy: A Large-scale Comparison of Traditional and Virtual Reality Perspective-taking." *PloS one*, 13, no. 10 (2018): e0204494.

4. Davis, J. I., Senghas, A., Brandt, F., & Ochsner, K. N., "The Effects of Botox Injections on Emotional Experience." *Emotion*, 10, no. 3 (2010): 433; Neal, D. T., & Chartrand, T. L., "Embodied Emotion Perception: Amplifying and Dampening Facial Feedback Modulates Emotion Perception Accuracy." *Social Psychological and Personality Science*, 2, no. 6 (2011): 673–678.

5. Michalak, J., Mischnat, J., & Teismann, T., "Sitting Posture Makes a Difference—Embodiment Effects on Depressive Memory Bias." *Clinical Psychology & Psychotherapy*, 21, no. 6 (2014): 519–524; Veenstra, L., Schneider, I. K., & Koole, S. L., "Embodied Mood Regulation: The Impact of Body Posture on Mood Recovery, Negative Thoughts, and Mood-congruent Recall." *Cognition and Emotion*, 31, no. 7 (2017): 1361–1376; Zaccaro, A., Piarulli, A., Laurino, M., Garbella, E., Menicucci, D., Neri, B., & Gemignani, A., "How Breath Control Can Change Your Life: A Systematic Review on Psychophysiological Correlates of Slow Breathing." *Frontiers in Human Neuroscience*, 12 (2018): 409421; Yang, K., Friedman-Wheeler, D. G., & Pronin, E., "Thought Acceleration Boosts Positive Mood Among Individuals with Minimal to Moderate Depressive Symptoms." *Cognitive Therapy and Research*, 38 (2014): 261–269.

6. Jospe, K., Genzer, S., Klein Selle, N., Ong, D., Zaki, J., & Perry, A., "The Contribution of Linguistic and Visual Cues to Physiological Synchrony and Empathic Accuracy." *Cortex*, 132 (2020): 296–308; Zaki, J., Weber, J., Bolger, N., & Ochsner, K., "The Neural Bases of Empathic Accuracy." *Proceedings of the National Academy of Sciences*, 106, no. 27 (2009): 11382–11387.

7. Hartung, F., Burke, M., Hagoort, P., & Willems, R. M., "Taking Perspective: Personal Pronouns Affect Experiential Aspects of Literary Reading." *PloS one*, 11, no. 5 (2016): e0154732.

8. E.g., Hunt, P. A., Denieffe, S., & Gooney, M., "Burnout and Its Relationship to Empathy in Nursing: A Review of the Literature." *Journal of Research in Nursing*, 22, nos. 1–2 (2017): 7–22; E.g., Duarte, J., & Pinto-Gouveia, J., "Empathy and Feelings of Guilt Experienced by Nurses: A Cross-Sectional Study of Their Role in Burnout and Compassion Fatigue Symptoms." *Applied Nursing Research*, 35 (2017): 42–47.

9. The phrase "walk a mile in his [shoes]" has been attributed to Mary T. Lathrap from a poem written in 1895 called "Judge Softly," and it may be older than that.

20: How to Get Along with People

1. Leach, M. J., "Rapport: A Key to Treatment Success." *Complementary Therapies in Clinical Practice*, 11, no. 4 (2005): 262–265.

2. Alison, L. J., Alison, E., Noone, G., Elntib, S., & Christiansen, P., "Why Tough Tactics Fail and Rapport Gets Results: Observing Rapport-Based Interpersonal Techniques (ORBIT) to Generate Useful Information from Terrorists." *Psychology, Public Policy, and Law*, 19, no. 4 (2013): 411.

3. Boyce, L. A., Jackson, R. J., & Neal, L. J., "Building Successful Leadership Coaching Relationships: Examining Impact of Matching Criteria in a Leadership Coaching Program." *Journal of Management Development*, 29, no. 10 (2010): 914–931.

4. E.g., Moore, D. A., Kurtzberg, T. R., Thompson, L. L., & Morris, M. W., "Long and Short Routes to Sucess in Electronically Mediated Negotiations: Group Affiliations and Good Vibrations." *Organizational Behavior and Human Decision Processes*, 77, no. 1 (1999): 22–43.

5. Miles, L. K., Nind, L. K., & Macrae, C. N., "The Rhythm of Rapport: Interpersonal Synchrony and Social Perception." *Journal of Experimental Social Psychology*, 45, no. 3 (2009): 585–589; Lakens, D., & Stel, M., "If They Move in Sync, They Must Feel in Sync: Movement Synchrony Leads to Attributions of Rapport and Entitativity." *Social Cognition*, 29, no. 1 (2011): 1–14; Muir, K., Joinson, A., Cotterill, R., & Dewdney, N., "Characterizing the Linguistic Chameleon: Personal and Social Correlates of Linguistic Style Accommodation." *Human Communication Research*, 42, no. 3 (2016): 462–484; Lubold, N., & Pon-Barry, H., "Acoustic-Prosodic Entrainment and Rapport in Collaborative Learning Dialogues." *Proceedings of the 2014 ACM Workshop on Multimodal Learning Analytics Workshop and Grand Challenge* (2014, November): 5–12.

6. One caveat regarding voice. Some research suggests that getting in sync on certain aspects of voice—like prosody—may not be directly relevant to rapport. It remains to be seen in the future whether getting in sync regarding different aspects of voice is as relevant to rapport as other behavioral ways of getting in sync. However, Reed (2020) also notes that mirroring still serves the purpose of supporting social bonds, even if not directly via rapport building. Reed, B. S., "Reconceptualizing Mirroring: Sound Imitation and Rapport in Naturally Occurring Interaction." *Journal of Pragmatics*, 167 (2020): 131–151.

7. Zaccaro, A., Piarulli, A., Laurino, M., Garbella, E., Menicucci, D., Neri, B., & Gemignani, A., "How Breath Control Can Change Your Life: A Systematic Review on Psychophysiological Correlates of Slow Breathing." *Frontiers in Human Neuroscience*, 12 (2018): 409421.

8. Note that we've used the words "feeling," "seeing," and "hearing" in most of this chapter, instead of "kinesthetic," "visual," and "auditory" to be more in sync with how people usually talk. But there is a little more nuance, especially to the word "kinesthetic." It encompasses various aspects of experience that have to do with the body, such as touch and movement. While touch and movement are things we can feel, the word "feeling" often connotes emotions, or mood, or feeling good or bad physically. So there is more richness to kinesthetic processing for interested students to explore. Also, in NLP people will reference VAK (visual, auditory, and kinesthetic) "predicates" to capture words or terms that reflect processing in

each of those modalities. It is a more precise way to refer to the target that we should listen for. These more precise labels can be useful for someone who would like to go deeper with NLP.

9. Herholz, S. C., Halpern, A. R., & Zatorre, R. J., "Neuronal Correlates of Perception, Imagery, and Memory for Familiar Tunes." *Journal of Cognitive Neuroscience*, 24, no. 6 (2012): 1382–1397.

10. Beeli, G., Esslen, M., & Jäncke, L., "Time Course of Neural Activity Correlated with Colored-hearing Synesthesia." *Cerebral Cortex*, 18, no. 2 (2008): 379–385.

11. Dijkstra, N., Bosch, S. E., & van Gerven, M. A., "Vividness of Visual Imagery Depends on the Neural Overlap with Perception in Visual Areas." *Journal of Neuroscience*, 37, no. 5 (2017): 1367–1373.

12. Zaki, J., Davis, J. I., & Ochsner, K. N., "Overlapping Activity in Anterior Insula during Interoception and Emotional Experience." *Neuroimage*, 62, no. 1 (2012): 493–499.

13. Pashler, H., McDaniel, M., Rohrer, D., & Bjork, R., "Learning Styles: Concepts and Evidence." *Psychological Science in the Public Interest*, 9, no. 3 (2008): 105–119.

14. Ibid.

21: Meet Them Where They Are Before Trying to Get Them to Follow

1. Roos, C. A., Postmes, T., & Koudenburg, N., "Feeling Heard: Operationalizing a Key Concept for Social Relations." *PLOS One*, 18, no. 11 (2023): e0292865.

2. Heslin, P. A., & VandeWalle, D., "Performance Appraisal Procedural Justice: The Role of a Manager's Implicit Person Theory." *Journal of Management*, 37, no. 6 (2011): 1694–1718.

3. Kerrissey, M. J., Hayirli, T. C., Bhanja, A., Stark, N., Hardy, J., & Peabody, C. R., "How Psychological Safety and Feeling Heard Relate to Burnout and Adaptation amid Uncertainty." *Health Care Management Review*, 47, no. 4 (2022): 308–316.

4. Ansems, L. F., Van den Bos, K., & Mak, E., "Speaking of Justice: A Qualitative Interview Study on Perceived Procedural Justice among Defendants in Dutch Criminal Cases." *Law & Society Review*, 54, no. 3 (2020): 643–679.

22: Are They Living It or Watching the Movie?

1. Ayduk, Ö., & Kross, E., "Analyzing Negative Experiences without Ruminating: The Role of Self-distancing in Enabling Adaptive Self-reflection." *Social and Personality Psychology Compass*, 4, no. 10 (2010): 841–854; Penner, L. A., Guevarra, D. A., Harper, F. W., Taub, J., Phipps, S., Albrecht, T. L., & Kross, E., "Self-distancing Buffers High Trait Anxious Pediatric Cancer Caregivers against Short- and Longer-term Distress." *Clinical Psychological Science*, 4, no. 4 (2016): 629–640.

2. Kross, E., Ayduk, O., & Mischel, W., "When Asking 'Why' Does Not Hurt: Distinguishing Rumination from Reflective Processing of Negative Emotions." *Psychological Science*, 16, no. 9 (2005): 709–715.

23: Use Your Time Machine

1. Trope, Y., Liberman, N., & Wakslak, C., "Construal Levels and Psychological Distance: Effects on Representation, Prediction, Evaluation, and Behavior." *Journal of Consumer Psychology*, 17, no. 2 (2007): 83–95; Odum, A. L., "Delay Discounting: I'm a K, You're a K." *Journal of the Experimental Analysis of Behavior*, 96, no. 3 (2011): 427–439.

2. Ibid; Rim, S., Uleman, J. S., & Trope, Y., "Spontaneous Trait Inference and Construal Level Theory: Psychological Distance Increases Nonconscious Trait Thinking." *Journal of Experimental Social Psychology*, 45, no. 5 (2009): 1088–1097.

3. The exercise we're referring to is based on an exercise Josh learned in his NLP training from Steven Leeds and Rachel Hott called the As If Frame Exercise—the original creator of the exercise is unknown to us.

4. D'Argembeau, A., & Van der Linden, M., "Individual Differences in the Phenomenology of Mental Time Travel: The Effect of Vivid Visual Imagery and Emotion Regulation Strategies." *Consciousness and Cognition*, 15, no. 2 (2006): 342–350.

24: Change Their Mental Image

1. Holmes, E. A., & Mathews, A. "Mental Imagery in Emotion and Emotional Disorders." *Clinical Psychology Review*, 30, no. 3 (2010): 349–362.

2. Ibid.

3. Ibid.

4. Davis, J. I., Gross, J. J., & Ochsner, K. N., "Psychological Distance and Emotional Experience: What You See Is What You Get." *Emotion*, 11, no. 2 (2011): 438.

5. Trope, Y., Liberman, N., & Wakslak, C., "Construal Levels and Psychological Distance: Effects on Representation, Prediction, Evaluation, and Behavior." *Journal of Consumer Psychology*, 17, no. 2 (2007): 83–95.

6. Van Boven, L., Kane, J., McGraw, A. P., & Dale, J., "Feeling Close: Emotional Intensity Reduces Perceived Psychological Distance." *Journal of Personality and Social Psychology*, 98, no. 6 (2010): 872.

7. Lee, W., & Gretzel, U., "Designing Persuasive Destination Websites: A Mental Imagery Processing Perspective." *Tourism Management*, 33, no. 5 (2012): 1270–1280.

8. Jia, Y., Huang, Y., Wyer Jr., R. S., & Shen, H., "Physical Proximity Increases Persuasive Effectiveness through Visual Imagery." *Journal of Consumer Psychology*, 27, no. 4(2017): 435–447.

25: Choose Your State and Help Others Choose Theirs

1. Barsade, S. G., & Gibson, D. E., "Why Does Affect Matter in Organizations?" *Academy of Management Perspectives*, 21, no. 1 (2007): 36–59.

2. Forgas, J. P., "Feeling and Doing: Affective Influences on Interpersonal Behavior." *Psychological Inquiry*, 13, no. 1 (2002): 1–28.

3. Forgas, J. P., "When Sad Is Better than Happy: Negative Affect Can Improve the Quality and Effectiveness of Persuasive Messages and Social Influence Strategies." *Journal of Experimental Social Psychology*, 43, no. 4 (2007): 513–528.

4. Forgas, J. P., Laham, S. M., & Vargas, P. T., "Mood Effects on Eye-witness Memory: Affective Influences on Susceptibility to Misinformation." *Journal of Experimental Social Psychology*, 41, no. 6 (2005): 574–588.

5. Davis, J. I., *Two Awesome Hours: Science-Based Strategies to Harness Your Best Time and Get Your Most Important Work Done* (HarperOne, 2015).

6. Marketers have been working hard to create such cues as long as there have been marketers. Their interests do not necessarily include our best interests. But the astonishing nature of their success, even despite that, suggests they are onto something. Some of our readers are old enough to remember these catchy doozies. In 1946, R. J. Reynolds started giving doctors a free carton of Camel cigarettes, and then surveyed them as to what brand they smoked. As a result, "More doctors smoke Camels than any other cigarette" became the motto that convinced scores of people to start smoking Camels. Asbestos was once hailed as a "magic mineral." Lead paint was marketed by the National Lead Company with ads showing the friendly and trusted "Dutch Boy" character. Crisco pitched trans fats as "It's digestible." These phrases and characters wormed their way into seemingly everyone's minds at the time and helped people remember the products they were associated with.

7. Herz, R. S., "Are Odors the Best Cues to Memory? A Cross-modal Comparison of Associative Memory Stimuli." *Annals of the New York Academy of Sciences*, 855, no. 1 (1998): 670–674.

8. Parkinson, B., "Interpersonal Emotion Transfer: Contagion and Social Appraisal." *Social and Personality Psychology Compass*, 5, no. 7 (2011): 428–439; Barsade, S. G., "The Ripple Effect: Emotional Contagion and Its Influence on Group Behavior." *Administrative Science Quarterly*, 47, no. 4 (2002): 644–675.

26: Don't Believe Everything You Believe

1. Norcross, J. C., Krebs, P. M., & Prochaska, J. O., "Stages of Change." *Journal of Clinical Psychology*, 67, no. 2 (2011): 143–154.

2. Hettema, J., Steele, J., & Miller, W. R., "Motivational Interviewing." *Annu. Rev. Clin. Psychol.*, 1 (2005): 91–111.

3. Zatloukal, L., "The Pie of Inspiration: Positioning the Therapist's and Client's Knowledge in Solution-Focused Brief Therapy." *Contemporary Family Therapy*, 46, no. 1 (2024): 87–99.

4. Beck, J. S.,Liese, B. S., & Najavits, L. M. Cognitive therapy. In Frances, R. J., Miller, S. I., & Mack, A. H. (eds.), *Clinical Textbook of Addictive Disorders*, 3rd ed. (Guilford Press, 2005); Burns, D. D., *The Feeling Good Handbook: The Groundbreaking Program with Powerful New Techniques and Step-by-Step Exercises to Overcome Depression, Conquer Anxiety, and Enjoy Greater Intimacy* (Plume, 1999).

5. Davis, D. I., *Alcoholism Treatment: An Integrative Family and Individual Approach* (Gardner Press, 1987).

27: Let Them Do the Work

1. Lynn, S. J., Kirsch, I., Terhune, D. B., & Green, J. P., "Myths and Misconceptions about Hypnosis and Suggestion: Separating Fact and Fiction." *Applied Cognitive Psychology*, 34, no. 6 (2020): 1253–1264. For a useful and quick description of what hypnotherapy is, see: https://www.psychologytoday.com/us/therapy-types/hypnotherapy.

2. Jensen, M. P., Jamieson, G. A., Lutz, A., Mazzoni, G., McGeown, W. J., Santarcangelo, E. L., et al., "New Directions in Hypnosis Research: Strategies for Advancing the Cognitive and Clinical Neuroscience of Hypnosis." *Neuroscience of Consciousness*, no. 1 (2017).

3. Jiang, H., White, M. P., Greicius, M. D., Waelde, L. C., & Spiegel, D., "Brain Activity and Functional Connectivity Associated with Hypnosis." *Cerebral Cortex*, 27, no. 8 (2017): 4083–4093.

4. Egner, T., Jamieson, G., & Gruzelier, J., "Hypnosis Decouples Cognitive Control from Conflict-monitoring Processes of the Frontal Lobe." *Neuroimage*, 27, no. 4 (2005): 969–978.

28: A Note on Combining the Tools from This Book

1. Astill Wright, L., Horstmann, L., Holmes, E. A., & Bisson, J. I., "Consolidation/reconsolidation Therapies for the Prevention and Treatment of PTSD and Re-experiencing: A Systematic Review and Meta-analysis." *Translational Psychiatry*, 11, no. 1 (2021): 453.

2. Sturt, J., Rogers, R., Armour, C., Cameron, D., De Rijk, L., Fiorentino, F., et al., "Reconsolidation of Traumatic Memories Protocol Compared to Trauma-focused Cognitive Behaviour Therapy for Post-traumatic Stress Disorder in UK Military Veterans: A Randomised Controlled Feasibility Trial." *Pilot and Feasibility Studies*, 9, no. 1 (2023): 175.

ABOUT THE AUTHORS

Josh Davis, PhD, is the international bestselling author of *Two Awesome Hours* and a certified Trainer and Master Practitioner of NLP. He earned his PhD from Columbia University, where he studied psychology and neuroscience. He is the founder and director of the Science-Based Leadership Institute. Previously, he was on the faculty at Barnard College of Columbia University, and has held senior positions at the NeuroLeadership and other leadership development institutes. He specializes in applying NLP and lessons from science to such topics as productivity, public speaking, communication, and behavior change. His past corporate clients include Goldman Sachs, Hasbro, IDEO, Lululemon, M&T Bank, and more. His writing has appeared in *Harvard Business Review, Fast Company*, and leading business and academic journals, and his contributions have been covered by various major news sources including *The Wall Street Journal, Financial Times*, and *The Times* (London).

Greg Prosmushkin was born in 1968 in Moscow, Russia. At the age of eleven, he immigrated to the United States with his parents, settling in Philadelphia, Pennsylvania. Growing up in a new country, Greg developed a passion for learning that has stayed with him throughout his life. He pursued his education with determination, earning degrees from Drexel University and Temple University School of Law. After practicing law for ten years, Greg embraced his entrepreneurial spirit and ventured into various industries beyond the legal field. His journey has led him to launch adult daycares, veterinary hospitals, and even a private tequila brand, reflecting his boundless curiosity and ambition to explore new opportunities. Greg's zest for learning remains a core part of his life, as he actively pursues new skills and insights on a near-daily basis.

At the heart of Greg's personal and professional philosophy are the core beliefs of NLP that possibility is limitless and that success can be modeled from those who have achieved it before. These beliefs have shaped the way he approaches challenges, always searching for solutions by studying and learning from the successes of others.

Put NLP and the science of positive change to work for you, your team, and your organization.

PROFESSIONALS

For exclusive content, tools, and more information about training and coaching options for professionals go to nlpdifference.com. Topics include:

- NLP for Lawyers
- NLP for Financial Advisors
- NLP for Managers
. . . and more

ORGANIZATIONAL LEADERS

For more information about having us speak at your organization, create and run training programs, consult, facilitate working sessions, or coach individuals within your organization, go to nlpdifference.com. Topics include:

- Accelerating learning
- Behavior and belief change
- Big-picture thinking
- Building trust
- Change management
- Changing values and culture
- Collaboration
- Commitment
- Communication
- Conflict resolution
- Decision-making
- Emotional intelligence
- Executive presence
- Goal attainment
- Influence
- Innovation and creativity
- Managing stress
- Modeling excellence
- Motivation
- NLP basics
- Operating as a high-functioning team
- Prioritizing and work-life balance
- Productivity, focus, and time management
- Public speaking
- Reducing bias
- Remote/virtual leadership and impact

. . . and more options that can be customized for your specific training and coaching needs

Topics offered for professionals are also available for organizations.